The
Principal's
Companion

Second Edition

To Pat and Loyd Wolfe
and
Rebecca Pearl Alvy,
a champion of all children

The
Principal's
Companion

Second Edition

Strategies
and
Hints
to Make
the Job
Easier

Pam Robbins
Harvey B. Alvy

Foreword by Kent D. Peterson

CORWIN PRESS, INC.
A Sage Publications Company
Thousand Oaks, California

For information address:

Corwin Press, Inc.
A Sage Publications Company
2455 Teller Road
Thousand Oaks, California 91320
www.corwinpress.com

SAGE Publications Ltd.
6 Bonhill Street
London EC2A 4PU
United Kingdom

SAGE Publications India Pvt. Ltd.
M-32 Market
Greater Kailash I
New Delhi 110 048 India

Printed in the United States of America

Library of Congress Cataloging-in-Publication Data

Robbins, Pamela.
   The principal's companion: strategies and hints to make the job easier / Pam Robbins, Harvey B. Alvy; foreword by Kent Peterson—2nd ed.
      p.   cm.
   Includes bibliographical references and index.
   ISBN 0-7619-4514-8 (cloth: alk. paper) — ISBN 0-7619-4515-6 (pbk: alk. paper.)
   1. School principals—United States—Handbooks, manuals, etc. 2. Educational leadership—United States—Handbooks, manuals, etc. 3. School management and organization—United States—Handbooks, manuals, etc. I. Alvy, Harvey B. II. Title.
LB2831.92.R63   2003
371.2' 012—dc21   2002031587

This book is printed on acid-free paper.

03   04   05   06   10 9 8 7 6 5 4 3 2

Acquisitions Editor:	Robert D. Clouse
Editorial Assistant:	Erin Clow
Typesetter:	Tina Hill
Production Editor:	Astrid Virding
Cover Designer:	Michael Dubowe
Production Designer:	Michelle Lee

Contents

Materials for Internal and External School Community
Members • Using Tips in Your Setting

Foreword

KENT D. PETERSON
University of Wisconsin–Madison

Many books, as with movies, come out in second editions or sequels but often are not as good as the original. *The Principal's Companion,* second edition, is even better than the first, and the first was very good. Some outstanding sections have been added on topics of key importance, such as strategies to address standards, data driven decision making, meaningful utilization of technology, effective professional development, brain-compatible teaching practices, and most importantly the notion of developing within students a "reverence for learning" to include those social and emotional skills that enable students to become productive citizens. These, and other new topics, enhance an already rich book for principals. Across the United States, policymakers, practitioners, and parents are concerned about supporting and building successful, high quality schools. Although there are many different approaches to reform, one factor seems to be part of everyone's framework—leadership from the school principal. This book continues to be one of the most important contributions to the literature designed to help principals enhance their leadership and management skills. It focuses on the critical work of school principals, with practical wisdom, conceptual ideas, and useful examples from many different settings. *The Principal's Companion* helps answer the questions, What skills and knowledge will help principals lead and manage better schools? and How can principals become successful leaders? This book adds extremely relevant knowledge and skills for innovative reformers and for more traditional leaders alike.

Let me make a few observations about the importance of school leaders, especially principals. To begin with, the daily work of school principals is extremely complex, demanding, intense, and, at times, surprising. Daily, principals must solve complex problems of practice, deal with demands and conflicts from parents and students, and maintain an intense work schedule filled with drama (will the new content standards fly with parents?), tragedy (a student is killed in a car accident), and, thankfully, comedy (a class accurately copies the principal's mannerisms for a school play). The days of principals are full of surprises; most days have a mix of totally unexpected happenings, from the birth of gerbils to the wonderful successes of students. It is within the flow of these days that leadership, decision making, school improvement, and change occur. This book provides a detailed, useful, and rigorous set of absorbing and shrewd suggestions for making the most of the panoply of these days—suggestions and approaches that can be used immediately by practicing principals.

The second key feature of principals and their complex work is the paradox that although they must gain certification through university training, much, if not most, of their learning occurs later, on the job. In the best cases, preservice training affords aspiring administrators concepts and models, as well as a modicum of practical knowledge that will get them started. But once on the job, these concepts and models get forged in the press of daily work. This handbook contributes significantly to both preservice and inservice realms, increasing the cache of available and easily readable information for this difficult but important role.

This book is the product of two educators who have worked with hundreds of schools, educators, and other organizations around the world. Their wide experience and insights permeate this book. The 23 chapters supply an excellent mix of the conceptual and the practical, the concrete and the abstract, the most current and the classic concepts. It should bridge the needs of preservice programs and inservice professional development, as well as be useful to the individuals who can learn on their own.

Books for principals should foster careful thinking and relevant new skills in an easily accessible format. *The Principal's Companion* accomplishes these things. The richness of ideas, breadth of examples, and thoughtful questioning make this book a unique tool for the development of more successful leaders. Effective principals should not be a luxury that schools only occasionally enjoy. Rather, effective leadership is needed and required in *all* schools. This second edition provides a rich array of ideas and suggestions for achieving this important end.

Preface

A principal interacts with hundreds of individuals on a daily basis, but the work life is ironically often one characterized by isolation, for there is no colleague on site with a similar role. Although constantly engaging in social interaction, the principal often recalls feeling isolated when reflecting on the merit of key decisions. Alone, the principal often wonders, "Am I doing the right thing? Is this the best and most ethical way to approach the task?" For example, alone in her office the high school principal wonders about the subtle and not so subtle remarks students are making about ethnicity. Having fifty-four nationalities represented in the school could make it a potential tinderbox, or an incredible context for teaching tolerance, valuing diversity, and building understanding. Her leadership actions will have a profound affect in determining which of these situations becomes reality.

Many principals reflect upon the nature of their work and describe it as characterized by paradox. For instance, *they feel like they are alone and in the spotlight at the same time.* Alone, in the privacy of his office, the middle school principal, having heard from teachers about students suffering from respiratory symptoms, contacts the central office about the need to have the air conditioning air filters replaced and the roof checked for mold. As the principal gets off the phone, the secretary lets him know that three reporters from local papers are waiting to interview him about environmental health hazards in the school. Now in the spotlight, the principal must quickly prepare to speak with reporters who were alerted to the potential environmental problem by a parent who had been volunteering in the school.

Principals feel alone when asked to lead an effort in an area in which he or she has no formal training. One district sent out a memorandum to all principals indicating that their evaluation will be based in part on their ability to lead efforts to improve test scores in their schools. Upon reading this message, an elementary principal reflects, "I value the notion of using student data to drive instructional decisions, but how do I get the training to do this? How do principals get data from various sources, interpret it, and make decisions for instruction? It is a big part of my job, yet I have never really had any help on how to do this"(A Principal's Voice).

Creating a learning environment that capitalizes on diversity to promote lessons on tolerance as well as academics, insuring school safety, adhering to environmental guidelines that protect the health and general welfare of staff and students, raising student test scores . . . never before has the principal's role as a public figure been so demanding. What's more, there is pressure to perform in a context where others frequently offer "expert" advice. After all, everyone's been to school! But, what is the best decision? How can the principal assure what is in the best interest of students and staff? Because of questions like these, *The Principal's Companion* has been written.

Why a Second Edition?

While some educational issues remain constant, practitioners, researchers, and the daily news remind us that much of the educational landscape has changed since the 1995 first edition of the *Principal's Companion*. In response to these changes, the second edition will examine the principal's role in relation to such topics as

- state and national standards
- data-driven decision making and high stakes accountability
- teacher supervision and evaluation that focuses on enhancing the quality of student work
- forms of professional development that build individual and school-wide capacity to address differentiated student needs in ways that leave their mark on policy and practice
- brain-compatible teaching practices
- social and emotional learning
- Individuals With Disabilities Education Act
- ethical leadership
- information technology for today's schools
- crisis management
- working with the media

While some of these issues have historically been part of the administrator's work life, many are new, or are being spotlighted more emphatically than in the past. As authors, we continue to feel compelled to explore both research and practice to support principals in their quest to effectively address important issues. However, we are quite cautious about "taking on topics" simply because they are in vogue. Our focus in the *Principal's Companion* is steered by a continuing commitment to promoting those actions that best serve all students, and a belief that human relations skills represent a critical leadership ability. For example, high test scores on challenging state and national performance measures are certainly important. But, equally important is developing within students a reverence for learning and those social and emotional skills that enable them to become contributing citizens in a democratic society. While these attitudes and skills often are not measured formally, research shows they are essential to leading a satisfying life and fostering a healthy society.

Enduring Features of the Book

The Principal's Companion seeks to explore both classical issues of leadership and current issues that are likely to impact student learning for many years to come. The primary purpose of this book remains the same—to provide ideas, approaches, strategies, resources, tools, techniques, and reflective opportunities for practicing and prospective principals and to facilitate educational improvement when and where it counts, in every classroom and school, each and every day.

There are countless theories and ideas about leadership, but there is no one secret formula for success. Effective leaders invent creative solutions as they face challenges associated with new demands on their role or new situations. As one principal put it, "I try to make thoughtful decisions. Operating by the seat of one's pants is not the best way 'to do' the principalship. Yet, the work demands that one address issues as they emerge. The bottom line is you try to do what is best for students and staff."Although principals cannot succeed without a fundamental understanding of theory, because of the immediacy of workplace demands, they often hunger for tried and true practices. Both theory and practice are essential for effective leadership.

Experience tells us that many principals have discovered strategies to tackle problems similar to those faced by their colleagues. However, because of the isolation that characterizes the principalship, there are seldom avenues to tap this tremendous potential resource. The *Principal's Companion* mines multiple sources to provide practical strategies for the principal who often operates alone. School principals need to know that they are part of a learning community of educational companions working together to help colleagues be the best they can be. This combined collegial effort will help principals create the kind of teaching and learning environment that supports teachers' efforts to bring about successful student performance. The interactive nature of the book, with reflective questions at the end of each chapter, is intended to help principals feel as if there is a colleague out there with whom to interact. The reader also will "hear" the voices of many practitioners who are quoted throughout the text. This will give aspiring principals a perspective of what it is like in the field and help them to connect with others. Ultimately, these newcomers will learn that all of us make mistakes, meet challenges, and succeed.

While this book is written primarily for current and aspiring principals, it will also be of interest to staff developers, university professors, school board members, directors of national and international principals' centers and associations, and leadership consultants. To assist programs using *The Principal's Companion* and the Interstate School Leaders Licensure Consortium Standards (ISLLC), a matrix aligning the chapters of *The Principal's Companion* with the Standards can be found at the end of this Preface.

Recognizing that principals are quite busy and have little time to waste, the chapters have been kept short and to the point. Each chapter reflects a topic that principals have indicated is important. The ideas, experiences, strategies, and techniques described in each chapter are grounded in research and practice. Each chapter concludes with a set of questions. There is also space following the last question of each chapter for the reader to write reflections inspired by the chapter or note strategies he or she wants to try. This is an invitation to write between the lines, to add to one's collective knowledge base, thus enhancing the value of the book for the reader. Each chapter is designed to stand on its own and can be read in one sitting. Because of this feature, some ideas will appear in several chapters but may be addressed with a different perspective.

Success in the principalship depends on many factors. The book addresses these factors in seven parts, with chapters included under umbrella themes. These parts are as follows:

Part I: *The Principal's Role* is that of learner, manager, communicator and leader during a crisis, creator of the learning organization, and shaper of school culture. In this section, a strong case is made for recognizing that effective principals play a variety of roles—all of which are necessary for success. Fulfilling the roles that create a climate for growth, making sure schedules work, and setting a personal example of learning from successes and mistakes are some of the issues addressed in this section.

Part II: *Critical Skills for Effective Leadership* examines and makes many suggestions regarding effective human relations strategies characterized by Emotional Intelligence and the vitally important function of time management and working effectively with the central office. We emphasize that these are critical areas because one cannot get the job done without succeeding in cultivating, practicing, and maintaining collegial relationships at the school site and central office, and without taking control of one's time.

Part III: *Honoring the School's Mission* concentrates on the importance and process of mission building as a guiding force in the organization. We also examine implementing change in a way that provides meaning and constant renewal of the school's mission.

Part IV: *Working Together to Build a Learning Organization* links a variety of components that must interact synergistically if a school is to truly be a learning community. These components include building a collaborative environment; addressing critical issues in instruction, curriculum, and assessment that relate to classroom decisions that enhance student work; effective use of technology; and meeting a variety of professional growth needs focused on building teachers' collective capacity to promote student learning. Additional components include supervision and evaluation of teachers to promote quality teacher decision making based on student learning and strategies to maximize feedback to teachers regarding their performance in meeting professional goals and student needs.

Part V: *Keeping the Pipes From Leaking: Adding Meaning to Traditional Practice* looks at the importance of providing meaning to such traditional events as faculty meetings and the first days of school. Often principals miss opportunities to see how these events can serve as key tools for shaping the school's culture and providing a foundation for continuous growth. Practical tips to enhance a principal's effectiveness also are described within this section.

Part VI: *Understanding Your Constituencies* provides strategies to enhance one's interactions with students, parents, and the greater community, including businesses, emergency service personnel, social services, senior citizens, politicians, and the media. This section takes a holistic approach, viewing parents and the greater community as an integral part of the school.

Part VII: *Professional and Personal Issues* looks at the individual principal. The focus here is to examine ways for the principal to grow, personally and professionally, and to remain vibrant, healthy, and continuously engaged in the pursuit of best practice regarding teaching, learning, and ethical school leadership.

The individual chapters serve as a menu of options from which the reader can select to meet pressing needs, assist in planning, or use as a resource. Many readers of the first edition commented that *The Principal's Companion* validated their existing practices, foreshadowed situations that needed to be addressed, and served to raise the bar for professional practice. In lonely moments of reflection, it also served as a "companion." Collectively the chapters offer a concise library of both research-based and tried-and-true practices. Finally, we invite you to join in a continuing conversation about the principalship.

PAM ROBBINS
Napa, CA, and Mt. Crawford, VA

HARVEY B. ALVY
Cheney, WA

**Matrix aligning the twenty-three chapters of
The Principal's Companion with the
Interstate School Leaders Licensure Consortium Standards (ISLLC).
This matrix is intended to serve the needs of state,
district, professional development, and university programs
that are using the ISLLC Standards. (Green, 2001)**

Interstate School Leaders Licensure Consortium Standards	Aligned chapters of *The Principal's Companion*
A school administrator is an educational leader who promotes the success of all students by:	(Several chapters are aligned with more than one standard.)
Standard 1—facilitating the development, articulation, implementation, and stewardship of a vision of learning that is shared and supported by the school community.	Chapters 1, 8, 11, 15
Standard 2—advocating, nurturing, and sustaining a school culture and instructional program conducive to student learning and staff professional growth.	Chapters 3, 7, 8, 9, 10, 11, 12, 14,15, 19, 20, 21, 22
Standard 3—ensuring management of the organization, operations, and resources for a safe, efficient, and effective learning environment.	Chapters 2, 5, 6, 12, 13, 16, 17, 18
Standard 4—collaborating with families and community members, responding to diverse community interests and needs, and mobilizing community resources.	Chapters 4, 16, 18, 19
Standard 5—acting with integrity, fairness, and in an ethical manner.	Chapters 1, 4, 18, 19, 22, 23
Standard 6—understanding, responding to, and influencing the larger political, social, economic, legal, and cultural context.	Chapters 2, 3, 6, 12, 18, 23

Acknowledgments

W e are indebted to many professional educators and family members who by their example have helped to steer the direction of this book. First and foremost, we would like to acknowledge Pat Wolfe, who brought us together to write this book and greatly influenced our thinking.

Harvey Alvy's first principal while teaching in the Harlem section of New York City, Lionel McMurren, will always remain as an example of an ethical leader whose support for new teachers inspired them to reach great heights in the classroom. Harvey is especially indebted to other administrators, teachers, school secretaries, and friends who have shared ideas, provided constructive criticism, and supported him while he served as an elementary, middle and high school teacher, as an elementary and secondary principal, and currently as a college professor. These include Bob Gibson, Richard Shustrin, Alan Siegel, David Chojnacki, Steve Kapner, Forrest Broman, Elaine Levy, Don Bergman, Roger and Betty Bicksler, Rob Beck, Nelson and Lisa File, Bob Connor, Drew Alexander, Bob Stockton, Paul Schmidt, Ted Coladarci, Claire Brusseau, Uma Maholtra, Sandy Bensky, Christina Campbell, Sandy Domitrovich, Les Portner, Billie Gehres, Sharon Jane Boni, Aziza, Siti, Rozi and Leonie Brickman in addition to other wonderful administrators, teachers and support staff of the American Embassy School in New Delhi, India, the American International School in Israel, the Singapore American School, and Eastern Washington University. To Norman Alvy and Vicki Alvy, "you're the best." Harvey's wife, Bonnie, and daughter Rebecca, as always, deserve a degree of recognition that cannot be measured.

Pam Robbins would like to acknowledge Percy Haugen and Ernie Moretti, educators who provided inspiring induction experiences for her and created a strong sense of meaning and enthusiasm for her work. Special thanks are due to Margaret Arbuckle, Terry Deal, Karen Dyer, Linda Gaidimas, Carl Glickman, Tony Gregorc, Gene Mateff, Lynn Seay, Allen Haymon, Kent Peterson, Jane Scott, Dennis Sparks, Karen Steinbrink Koch, Leslie and Mike Rowland, Judy Mullins, Pat Montgomery, Helene Paroff, Kathleen McElroy, Lou Martin, Ann Cunningham-Morris, Gayle Gregory, Stephanie Hirsh, Tom Guskey, Jane Bailey, Betsy Dunnenberger, Doug Guynn, and the late Susan Loucks-Horsley for their professional collegueship, insights, wisdom, thoughtful feedback, and willingness to collaborate. The late Judy Arin Krupp deserves special mention for her expertise regarding adult learning and for the inspiration she provided as a friend and professional colleague.

Heartfelt thanks are due to Ray Cubbage for his sage advice, companionship, love, patience, support, and inspiration. D.D. Dawson deserves special acknowledgment for her expertise in technology, and for her good humor, reflections, insights, and friendship. Alexandria Cubbage deserves special mention for her assistance in thoughtfully and carefully reviewing the original manuscript. Lydia Cubbage is also to be thanked for all her support in assuring the original manuscript met its deadline.

Gracia Alkema, founding president of Corwin Press, deserves sincere thanks for her friendship and recommendations regarding the book's content and organization, as well as that little "push"she provided when we needed it! Robert Clouse deserves special thanks for his advice, guidance, and patience with the development of this second edition. We appreciate the support of Douglas Rife, president of Corwin Press.

Finally, to our parents David and Muriel Robbins and Daniel and Rebecca Pearl Alvy, thanks for the good humor, encouragement, support, and modeling.

The contributions of the following reviewers are gratefully acknowledged:

Kent D. Peterson
Professor
Educational Administration
University of Wisconsin–Madison, Madison, WI
Co-author of *The Leadership Paradox: Balancing Logic and Artistry in Schools*

Margaret McLaughlin
Assistant Director
Institute for the Study of Exceptional Children
University of Maryland, College Park, MD
Author of *Accessing the General Curriculum*

Allan A. Glatthorn
Professor Emeritus
School of Education
East Carolina University, Greenville, NC
Author of *The Principal as Curriculum Leader*

John C. Daresh
Professor
Educational Leadership
University of Texas, El Paso
Author of *Beginning the Principalship*

Robert D. Ramsey
Educational Consultant
Author of *Lead, Follow, or Get Out of the Way*

About the Authors

Pam Robbins earned her doctorate in educational administration from the University of California, Berkeley. Her professional interests include leadership development, supervision, developing learning communities, brain research and brain-compatible instruction, teaching in the block schedule, peer coaching, mentoring, promoting quality teaching, and presentation skills.

Her teaching career began in 1971 in special education. She later taught intermediate grades, and coached high school basketball. As an administrator, she served as Director of Special Projects and Research for the Napa County (CA) Office of Education and Director of Training for the North Bay California Leadership Academy. She has lectured at several universities, authored and co-authored books, developed videotapes, and consulted with principals' academies in Alaska, California, Kentucky, Tennessee, Massachusetts, Utah, Pennsylvania, Europe, Great Britain, the Far East, and South America.

In addition, she has provided national and international training sessions for the Department of Defense Education Equity Division, the Ford Motor Company, the Association for Supervision and Curriculum Development (ASCD), the American Society for Training and Development (ASTD), the Wisconsin Academy Staff Development Initiative (WASDI), the National Staff Development Council (NSDC), Phi Delta Kappa (PDK), the National Association of Elementary School Principals (NAESP), and the National Association of Secondary School Principals (NASSP).

Currently, she is consulting with school districts, state departments of education, educational service centers, and corporations throughout the United States,

Canada, Europe, Great Britain, and the Far East. She may be contacted at 1251 Windsor Lane, Mt. Crawford, VA 22841 or by e-mail: probbins@shentel.net. For additional information, visit Pam's Web page at user.shentel.net/probbins.

Harvey B. Alvy served as a practicing principal for fourteen years. His experience in multi-cultural international schools is extensive. Harvey held positions at the American School in Kinshasa, Zaire, the American International School in Israel, the American Embassy School in New Delhi, India, and most recently, the Singapore American School. Before serving as an international educator, Harvey worked as an elementary and high school teacher in U. S. public and private schools. In 1991, the National Association of Elementary School Principals selected him as a National Distinguished Principal for American Overseas Schools. He is also a founding member of the Principal's Training Center for International Schools. Harvey earned his doctorate at the University of Montana concentrating on the "Newcomer to the Principalship." He has conducted seminars, workshops, and presentations both nationally and internationally on the principalship, ethical leadership, characteristics of great teachers, supervision and evaluation, assisting new teachers, and enhancing teacher growth. Currently on the faculty of Eastern Washington University, Harvey specializes in educational leadership and foundations. He can be reached via e-mail at harvey.alvy@mail.ewu.edu or on his Web page at cehd.ewu.edu/faculty/halvy/home.html.

PART I

THE PRINCIPAL'S ROLE

1

Leader as Learner

Just when I'm ready to retire, I'm beginning to learn what this job is all about.

A PRINCIPAL AFTER 33 YEARS OF SERVICE

Principal as Lifelong Learner

There is no setting in which the concept of the lifelong learner is more important than a school. In fact, many professionals now conceptualize the school as a learning community or a learning organization, not only for students but for administrators and teachers. This is a powerful notion that can impact student success. Barth (2001) notes, ". . . More than anything else, it is the culture of the school that determines the achievement of teacher and student alike" (p. 33). Bennis and Nanus (1985) remind us that successful leaders are "perpetual learners." Schlechty (2001) stresses, "If the principal is to help teachers improve what they do, the principal must continuously be learning to improve what he or she is doing" (p. 145). Senge (1990) suggests that a characteristic of the successful leader is the ability to instill in others the desire to learn what is necessary to help the organization reach its mission. Applying this notion to the principal of a school, the leader can model for all within the workplace what lifelong learning means. For modeling to be effective, it should be sincere, consistent, and purposeful. There are several ways that this can be done.

Learning in Many Contexts

One way the principal can model lifelong learning is by continuing to participate in the development and demonstration of effective teaching practices. For example, a principal collaborating with teachers can help to create faculty meetings in which conversations about teaching become institutionalized through various activities. During these conversations, principals should purposefully support the remarks of both new and veteran teachers to model a high regard for the contributions of all faculty. Another context in which the principal can function as learner is

3

during the supervision process. The following scenario will demonstrate how the leader-as-learner theme is played out in two ways: learning about behaviors and activities that facilitate student and teacher learning and those behaviors and strategies that enhance the principal's effectiveness in the supervisory process. An effective and common supervisory technique includes a preconference in which the principal and teacher, through a questioning process, together "unpack" the teacher's thinking about the lesson to be taught. Together they discuss planned teaching behaviors and the expected student outcomes. They problem-solve potential obstacles and fine-tune the lesson plan. The teacher identifies the focus for the observation, and collaboratively the teacher and principal decide on the best method for data collection. During the observation, the principal, steered primarily by the teacher's request for information, collects data, learning both about curricular and instructional practices that work to produce desired student outcomes and about what types of data collection work to capture the essence of the desired supervisory focus.

In the postconference, the principal and teacher ask questions that foster reflection and analysis of the lesson. Together they discuss what worked to facilitate student learning. At the conclusion of these reflections, they analyze what would be done the same and what would be done differently if the lesson were to be taught again.

Additionally, the principal asks, "Thinking about this conferencing process, what strategies and techniques did I use that facilitated your thinking as a teacher?" Furthermore, the principal might ask, "What might I have done differently?" Thus the principal and teacher collaboratively analyze the conferencing practices that enhance or hinder teacher thinking and learning about curriculum and instruction. Together they find ways to make the conferencing experience worthwhile for both.

"Principal as student" experiences can be an innovative way to provide a new perspective and important insights about a school. The principal can spend time in classrooms taking on the role of a student as a participant in a discussion, as a team member in a cooperative group, or as a reader or teacher. A particularly successful "principal as student" strategy is "Principal for the Day." One high school principal holds an essay contest each year that results in a student exchanging roles with the principal for one day. The principal takes on the class schedule of the student selected as principal and completes the student's homework assignments, attends classes, and takes examinations. This activity is a wonderful way to remain visible, attend classes, and shadow other students.

What can be a better learning experience for students than to see the principal struggling with these roles? These experiences can be shared on a schoolwide basis, in faculty meetings, or with the parent-teacher organization for the school. Students and teachers appreciate the interest in them and will enjoy the novelty of the situation. If a principal has not functioned in these roles before, it is useful to let teachers know ahead of time "what you're up to."

Principals can teach demonstration lessons, possibly on technology, and might videotape these to use at a faculty meeting. This provides an opportunity to apply new ideas and practices. Then a principal can talk with staff about experiences in teaching and learning associated with presenting lessons. If the principal's lesson is only fair, and the principal's "rough edges are showing," this can be comforting to staff. It is nice to know that leaders are not flawless. This also builds trust as teachers realize the principal has walked in their shoes, is willing to accept feedback from the faculty, and has an understanding of classroom conditions.

Also, the principal functions as a learner by reading and sharing research with teachers and parents. By writing or speaking about new learnings, the principal can pass on knowledge of recent research while modeling a love of learning.

Still another way the principal functions in the learner role is by participating in staff development sessions. Too often principals introduce the speakers and then have to run off to another meeting. Principal participation also points out the importance of these staff development opportunities and validates the teachers' time spent at these same sessions.

When the principal attends a conference, there are frequently opportunities to purchase audio- or videocassettes of sessions. Teachers should be encouraged to do the same. Try picking out the best sessions, purchasing audio- or videocassettes, and starting a cassette collection in the staff room, teachers' center, or library. These can be borrowed by staff or parents. A follow-up report on the conference e-mailed or hard-copied, or a volunteer brown-bag lunch on key conference ideas, can be presented to the staff.

Principals can help encourage action research projects by individual or groups of teachers on particular educational ideas of interest to the staff. To illustrate, in one particular school, several elementary and high school teachers engaged in a project exploring the use of student portfolios. Teachers met periodically to discuss their experiences and student reactions. The principal facilitated the process by helping to gather articles on portfolios, keeping a record of the project, and helping to develop an action research report with the staff. Several recommendations from the report were used by the staff to pursue the project during the following school year. The portfolio recommendations included

- Continuing the project on a voluntary basis
- Developing portfolio partners among the faculty to compare notes every couple of weeks during the year
- Having students in one class share portfolios with other classes
- Collecting more nuts-and-bolts ideas on portfolios
- Finding a quiet area to record or videotape student work
- Refining ways to help students reflect and evaluate their progress through self-assessment and use of rubrics
- Assisting teachers to fine-tune their conferencing skills with students

- Providing information for teachers on the "teacher as facilitator" notion for those who desire strategies to organize their classes in order to engage in frequent conversations with individual students

These suggestions by teachers assisted both the principal and teachers in their quest to continually learn. By using the resources of a principal's office, including the use of secretarial services, and maintaining a database on portfolio progress, principals send a clear message of support for staff development and can be a great help to teachers engaged in learning activities designed to enhance classroom experiences for students.

Another strategy to support learning includes organizing "book study" groups or clubs among teachers and parents. When principals are involved in these groups as a facilitator or participant, the leader as learner role is strengthened and modeled. In one high school a successful book study group read *A Tribe Apart* by Patricia Hersch and *Reviving Ophelia* by Mary Pipher. (See Chapter 18 for a detailed explanation of a book study group.)

Principals who solicit comments from the staff members on their job performance at the end of the year send a strong message to the teachers that they seek and appreciate their input as another resource to promote learning. Furthermore, asking for staff feedback models a stance of openness and a commitment to ongoing learning. The following form has been used for several years by one of the authors to gain faculty input on a principal's performance.

Dear Faculty,

Over the years I have asked each faculty [member] that I have worked for to give me helpful hints to improve my job performance. I know that you are all very busy, but I would appreciate it if you could take a few minutes to answer the questions below and help me evaluate my performance so I can do a better job next year. Obviously, your comments will remain confidential. If you would like to remain anonymous, please word process your comments. Please put your comments in the "Harvey" envelope on Prema's desk. I would appreciate your comments by the last faculty day, May 27.

Thanks,
Harvey

1. What are some of the things that I am currently doing that you would like to see me continue?
2. What am I currently doing that you would like to see me discontinue next year?

3. What suggestions do you have to help me *improve* my job performance (e.g., Is there a particular area that I should pursue for additional training? Is there a book or article that you suggest I read?)?

4. Additional comments?

This procedure is simple to execute and often yields constructive feedback and helpful ideas. In addition, it provides an opportunity for the principal to assess the perceptions of staff in relation to one's own perception of self. Feedback can be enhanced when perspectives of students, classified staff, parents, assistant principals, and community members are solicited. This type of feedback, often referred to as 360° feedback, can offer multiple perspectives for consideration.

Principals who have kept reflective journals often share insights derived from this activity with staff. Sometimes this encourages staff members to become reflective about their craft experiences and practices. Barth (1990, pp. 63-73), supporting the notion of leader as learner, emphasizes the tremendous capacity that principals have to release energy in a school by becoming sustained, visible learners themselves. He also describes the phenomenon of an "at-risk" principal as any educator who leaves school at the end of the day with little possibility of continuing learning about the work they do (cited in Sparks, 1993, p. 19). Rolf P. Lynton of the World Health Organization offered some powerful insights about reflection when he noted that we all go through events on a daily basis. What distinguishes an event from an experience is that an event only becomes an experience after you have time to reflect.[1] Each experience offers an opportunity to learn. When teachers, students, and parents see a principal's desire to learn and share ideas, norms and expectations that celebrate learning can develop within a school. Moreover, the leader-as-learner model transfers to the classroom where teachers demonstrate for students that they too are both leaders and learners.

Schoolhouse as a Powerful Context for Learning

Finding time for such reflective endeavors is a challenge and yet critical. "We must also find imaginative ways of separating adults from youngsters at times during the school day for conversation, brainstorming, reflection and replenishment" (Sparks, 1993, p. 20) so that the learning and the growth process continues. Barth (1990) notes, "I believe the schoolhouse itself is the most powerful context for the continuing education of educators" (p. 20). Creating a learning community in some cultures is so valued that a considerable amount of time within the duty day is allocated to this endeavor. For instance, in some Japanese schools, 40% of the duty day is devoted to teacher planning, often in a collaborative context.

Reflecting on our conceptualization of leader as learner, we can see that there are numerous ways to learn while on the job. Once time is identified, learning experiences can come from workshops, class visitations, demonstration lessons, Action

Research projects, analyses of student data, reflective journal writing, books, educational journals, conferences, and discussions with and visitations to other principals.

When Old and New Ideas Converge:
The Value of Repertoire

A final but important note: As the principal's knowledge and experience increase, he or she is often faced with new ideas that appear to conflict with previous learning. Educators are expected to make either/or decisions regarding innovations that affect instructional practices and consequently students. To illustrate, suppose a district commits to a staff development focus on brain-based learning. Does this mean that the previous insights and learnings from Madeline Hunter's direct instruction model are no longer valid? Rather, the strengths from both instructional approaches should be celebrated. Too often we are encouraged to discard one idea for another. However, leaders as learners should develop the ability to take the best out of each new idea and synthesize information into an eclectic model. This enables the principal to diagnose a situation and draw from a repertoire of strategies to meet a particular need.

A critical learning for leadership is acknowledging that there will always be a need to learn more. One of the most essential behaviors a principal can model is a devotion to lifelong learning, and a willingness to dialogue with members of the learning organization about how new learnings reshape existing knowledge. To demonstrate this ongoing pursuit of knowledge, one principal regularly hangs a sign on the doorknob of her office that reads "Out Learning." This reminds all the members of the learning organization of the importance and power of learning about learning.

Note

1. The authors thank Dr. Steve Atwood of UNICEF for introducing us to Dr. Lynton's ideas.

Reflections

This space is intended to provide an opportunity for you to write in ideas that have been generated by this chapter, things you want to try, or adaptations of ideas presented herein.

1. What are some things you might do to model "leader as learner"?

2. What might be some observable indicators or artifacts of a school that is functioning as a learning organization?

3. How can principals facilitate a learning environment for adults within a school?

4. What strategies should principals or assistant principals use to gain helpful feedback on their performance?

5. Why did you become a school principal, or why would you like to become a principal?

6. What insights or new questions do you have as a result of reflecting on the ideas presented in this chapter?

2

Leader as Manager

To facilitate learning, the instructional leader also makes sure that the class-room lights are working.

A PRINCIPAL'S VOICE[1]

Although the concept of the principal has shifted from "gatekeeper" (Deal & Peterson, 1994; Goldring & Rallis, 1993) to "instructional leader," "collabo-rative decision maker," "leader of leaders," and "results-oriented instructional leader," any discussion on leadership can become a romantic concept if leadership is not discussed hand-in-hand with management (Fullan & Stiegelbauer, 1991). One has to manage leadership. Part of management is paying attention to a school's physical environment. It is difficult to focus on learning if the physical en-vironment does not promote it. For example, simply changing the contents of a dis-play case outside of a high school office each month can send a strong message about student learning. If the display case includes work from various subjects and extracurricular activities, the school is honoring each discipline.

As practitioners, we need to make sure that schedules work, the chalk is in the classroom, and transition times run smoothly. However, one should not be fooled into thinking that success as an educational leader ends with neat bookshelves, quiet hallways, or the latest software for student records. We must not forget that students should be the ultimate beneficiaries of all management actions. Yet much of the leadership literature contains a subtle disdain for management.

Good Leadership
Requires Effective Management

Effective principals are effective managers. They must communicate and de-velop relationships with teachers, assistant principals, custodians, secretaries, counselors, librarians, students, cafeteria workers, parents, transportation work-ers, and central office and security personnel. As managers, it is critical to display respect for every individual who contributes to the success of the school. Principals should remember, always, that although some employees may appear to be on the periphery when considering the primary purpose of schooling, everyone contributes in his or her own way to a school's success. Principals must model in all their relationships the behavior that they expect throughout the school and the community. To illustrate, a principal or assistant principal should work closely with classified staff, such as bus drivers, who appear on the "fringe" of the classroom experience, because they can offer a valuable perspective. Principals, assistant principals, or district personnel should share school goals and advocate important programs (e.g., decreasing harassment) with classified staff. Bus drivers, because of their unusual schedule, are in the community, the diners, and the barbershops during part of the school day. What individuals say about the school in these venues can go a long way in influencing how the school is perceived in the community. Honoring these workers can have a very positive affect on them. To illustrate, Ramon Curiel, who recruits and hires the 6,000 bus drivers, teacher aides, custodians, and other classified staff in Long Beach, California, gave credit to and celebrated their contribution to the overall improved grades of the students in the district because of the role they played in developing school climate. To the classified staff he said, "Look, you had something to do with this" (Johnson, 2001).

Moreover, a principal's work produces many additional management challenges. This work involves policies, resources, behaviors, procedures, and data. These challenges can be classified into four categories: classroom, school site, community, and support services. (An additional category, working with central office, is discussed in Chapter 6.) These four categories reflect the various arenas in which the leader must function as manager.

Management Responsibilities and Strategies
Including Crisis Management Planning

Classroom

Principals must help to maximize the availability of sufficient and high-quality classroom supplies (e.g., erasers, pencils) and instructional resources (e.g., math manipulatives, globes, laptops) to enable teachers to focus their attention on instructional and curricular issues. Thus principals need to be on top of the classroom supply inventory so that key items are available during the year for teachers and students.

This can be accomplished in a variety of ways. Some principals delegate this job to a responsible supply clerk or secretary. In small schools, principals retain this function for themselves. Although it is important to know how to delegate, one can never give up the responsibility for the task. When you delegate, you need to check for clear understanding, provide support, and follow up regularly. If the person to whom you have delegated comes up with an innovation, assure the person that you have confidence in him or her and encourage the resourcefulness, yet make sure you are not the last one to find out about the innovation.

The availability of classroom supplies and instructional resources for staff is heavily reliant on data relating to curricular needs and the quality of the material. One must ask teachers whether the resources are serving their purposes. Does the particular instructional resource improve the quality of the educational program? Are the resources helpful for gathering assessment data to measure student progress? Is there enough money in the budget for a year's supply of computer diskettes? What classroom supplies were consumed completely last year? What instructional resources are in great demand at the start of the school year? What are some of the new resources available to make life easier for the staff? How can the resources be distributed more efficiently? Is waste taking place and why? A variety of people as well as observations can provide this information. System checks are crucial. Ultimately, feedback should provide data about whether supplies are meeting the instructional needs of the students in a quality way. Such feedback could be facilitated by developing a form to solicit input from the staff as to the adequacy and appropriateness of supplies.

Staff members' perceptions of resource availability are another important consideration. The policies for allocating classroom supplies and instructional resources reveal much about the values and beliefs in the organization. For example, is the supply room locked and materials strictly allocated, or is it open with a sign-out sheet? Are the veteran teachers in possession of the best resources? With your own school in mind, reflect on how "the system" works. Does it match the mission of the school?

Thinking about the allocation of resources in relation to the school's mission, if your school promotes enrichment for all students, then you must have enrichment material and classroom options available for various instructional disciplines (e.g., novels, technology resources, independent science projects, challenging math manipulatives) that can be used by all classroom teachers. A teachers' resource center in a school or district office can serve as a central area for instructional material to be used by all teachers. This can diminish greatly the desire to hoard the best instructional material.

With regard to the environment, is your school ecologically conscientious? Are you recycling paper? Does each classroom and the school office collect paper to be reused or sent to a recycling plant? Are plastic containers, cans, and bottles collected for recycling? One high school ecology club convinced the superintendent to purchase copier paper for the district that was ecologically superior to paper purchased previously.

Some principals have encouraged staff input on the creation of policies and procedures related to resource requisition and allocation. This is expanding the leadership function of many staff members. These new roles build ownership in school-level practices and policies. Principals have provided site-based teams and individual teachers with school and classroom budgets to be used according to their discretion. If greater teacher involvement in resource allocation follows expanded teacher involvement in curricular and instructional decisions, then the resources will surely be used more efficiently and with greater meaning.

Other managerial responsibilities include such tasks as record keeping for attendance and tardiness, lunch count, federal aid to dependent children, and completing cumulative record cards. In general, teachers disdain these responsibilities (as they should!) because these responsibilities keep them away from their primary responsibility—teaching. The principal must carefully review these chores to see what can be removed from the teacher. How can the secretary assist? What responsibilities can be picked up by students, teacher aides, or parent volunteers? For example, students in elementary, middle, and high school can help with lunch count chores for service credit. Consider how technology might be used to free up the teacher. For instance, how can I.D. scan cards be used for attendance? Computerized programs are used in more and more schools to complete various student data records. Each school has a unique set of routines and chores. Important questions to ask are, How do the current routines and tasks serve to enhance the educational program? What routines and tasks can be eliminated or trimmed in your school to increase instructional time?

School Site

A safe environment contributes to an effective school. Furthermore, the physical appearance of a school can contribute to positive or negative school climate or morale. Conversely, the physical appearance of a school reflects the climate. Graffiti and vandalism affect the school and its administration, teachers, students, and community. Thus principals should inform school custodians to remove graffiti immediately and quickly repair broken lights and windows, loose banisters, or damaged lockers to maintain pride in the appearance of the school. Recently, a principal, bothered by the school's drab brown entrance doors, had the art department work with talented students to paint the doors as bright-colored murals. Other schools invite classes to adopt and care for a certain portion of buildings or grounds. Classes at some schools have donated benches, trees, and flower gardens as an indication of their commitment to the school. This has served to significantly decrease vandalism. Principals and teachers encourage classes or school clubs to garden or plant in particular areas.

Principals and teachers also need to recognize that a school's physical environment or air quality may be a contributing factor if students appear to be lethargic, or are experiencing frequent nasal, throat, eye, skin, or lung problems. Environmental Protection Agency officials have noted that, "the air quality in many schools could be improved dramatically simply by replacing filters on heating and air conditioning units on a regular basis" (Sack, 2002). According to Michelle Guarneiri, an EPA official, "The worst problem is mold, and most schools have mold everywhere from Alaska to Florida" (Sack, p. 12). A school principal, working with local department of health officials, can identify issues relating to the air quality and environment by developing a questionnaire for teachers and students that addresses topics relating to noise, ventilation, lighting, wall or ceiling leakage, and various odors including gas, propane, sewage, mold, glue, smoke, dust, and ammonia. The EPA has published voluntary guidelines to help schools with environmental concerns on its Web site (www.epa.gov/iaq/schools).

Management by Wandering Around

In addition to physical appearance and air-quality issues, plant maintenance and safety is another critical management dimension. One way to assure safety is through managment by wandering around (MBWA). MBWA involves the principal purposefully getting out from behind the desk and walking around the school. In this chapter, the strategy of MBWA refers primarily to maintenance types of concerns. However, MBWA has an additional, powerful application: promoting instructional excellence. This will be discussed later. A key attribute of this technique is that the principal must have a clear plan for where the "wandering" will occur. Some principals have identified on a checklist key areas from classrooms to storage sheds, keeping a record of visits to each place. The goal is to visit classrooms frequently and other areas once a month. Make classrooms your top priority. Figure 2.1 is an example of what a list for an elementary principal might look like.

Many principals keep a clipboard by their desk and post this checklist on it. Others keep the list on an index card or on a personal digital assistant in their pocket. Then, whenever they have a few minutes here or there, they look down the checklist, determine where they have not visited during the month, and purposefully wander to one of those locations. In doing this, one principal discovered an electrical outlet was located next to a sink in the boys' restroom. A call to the maintenance department quickly corrected this hazardous condition. A great way to visit classrooms and the rest of the school is with the school custodian. Often a principal meets with the custodian once a month, and they walk around the school (the custodian with a notepad in hand). This enables them to see maintenance needs and communicate about school programs and activities as well as get input from teachers. On these walking tours the building "talks." A strong message is conveyed to students, teachers, parents, and visitors by what is on the hallway walls, on the walls of the cafeteria, in the display cases, or on the floor. A walk in one school revealed that the lawn was being watered 5 minutes before physical education classes were going to play on the field. Usually, there are 5 or 10 maintenance requests that result from the walks. Also, these walks let the staff know that the principal is interested in the day-to-day running of the school.

Spending time in corridors, classrooms, stairwells, and throughout the building gives the principal a chance to spread good news and caring words to the staff, students, community members, and parents as well as oversee plant safety. Using this approach, the principal is able to manage more than just plant safety. Communication occurs, and disruptions are minimized.

Another proactive management technique is to visit classrooms before or after school to see bulletin boards, special displays, learning centers, and student work.

Figure 2.1. Example of Management by Wandering Around (MBWA) Record

	September	*October*	*November*
Kitchen			
Cafeteria			
Custodian's office			
Boiler room			
Girls' restroom			
Boys' restroom			
Library			
Storage shed			
Bike rack			
Kindergarten playground			
Regular playground			
Baseball diamond			
Classrooms—Wing A			
Room 1			
Room 2			
Room 3			
Room 4			
Room 5			
Room 6			
Classrooms—Wing B			
Room 7			
Room 8			
Room 9			
Room 10			
Room 11			
Room 12			
Kindergarten room			
Computer lab			

A principal can note whether a computer lab or journalism classroom is used actively during these times. When staff members receive a complimentary note from the principal about their rooms, it is a great way to start the day and reinforces the notion that the classroom is the center of the school. This minimizes classroom intrusions and disruptions. These visits also increase a principal's awareness of each classroom's current activities. This allows for channeling of resources in particular areas. When fliers, pictures, or book samples come across the principal's desk, they can be forwarded to the appropriate classrooms.

MBWA is an excellent example of time management as well. The principal uses precious minutes in a time-efficient way to manage what is important. One principal talked of conducting "one-legged conferences" during her walks about campus. As an example, she cited talking with a custodian about his excellent care of the front lawn and simultaneously requesting that he mow the lawn by the primary wing at a time other than 12:45 when students were doing sustained silent reading. She invited him to participate in the reading program at that time so that students could see him modeling reading as a lifelong skill. Another idea might be to invite the custodian in to talk about how he uses math in his daily work. Cafeteria staff, the nurse, librarians, teachers, parents, and community members could be asked to share how they have applied learnings from schooling.

One of the most troubling and sensitive problems is managing individuals who are not succeeding, whether they are teachers or other school personnel. MBWA increases the principal's awareness of these situations. Unless there is an immediate act that necessitates dismissal, long-term documentation is usually necessary. The principal should take notes as the MBWA visits are made. When this is the case, careful documentation, following legal standards, is essential to collect data that is defensible in court hearings.

Additionally, MBWA can help principals determine whether an employee's poor performance is due to systemic failure or professional inadequacy. One should consider the view of W. Edwards Deming, the management expert, who maintained that systemic failure accounted for up to 85% of employee problems, whereas workers were responsible for only 15% of the problems (Walton, 1986).

Another area of school management is maintaining a litter-free environment. Principals have organized "trash patrols" and other activities to assure an attractive campus. One principal developed a program called "the eagle's eyes." The eagle was the school's mascot. Anytime someone was observed doing something to enhance the campus, from picking up litter to planting a tree, they would be acknowledged with a note written on stationery headed with "The eagle's eyes saw . . ." These individuals could be celebrated during assemblies.

Another area of management responsibility is transportation. To end teacher and office confusion about which bus a new student should ride, a Georgia principal makes an alphabetical listing of all streets, subdivisions, and day care centers with the appropriate bus number listed by each entry. The route times might also be listed. A teacher can just look up the student's address by street name on the list and assign the proper bus quickly and accurately.

Often overlooked as a management responsibility is the need to keep support personnel informed about student behavior and expectations. Principals find student behavior to be an essential topic, not only for teachers but for parent volunteers, paraprofessionals, and support personnel such as school bus drivers, cafeteria workers, classroom aides, or library personnel. To address this topic, seminars can be planned at which issues related to student behavior are discussed. These seminars might also include motivation and reinforcement theory. When the emphasis is on organizing, teaching, and reinforcing students during the first 3 weeks of school, the staff and support personnel generally report fewer discipline referrals and headaches. Thereafter, attention to behavior should continue with a focus on "catching students being good!" Thus making sure the school is a safe place for students is another essential management responsibility.

Proactive Crisis Management Planning

Each school faces the possibility of an emergency at any time. Weather emergencies may include excessive rain, windstorms, fires, floods, earthquakes, tornadoes, or hurricanes. School, medical, or drug emergencies may include kidnapping, shootings, overdose of drugs, traffic accidents, or a tragedy in the community.

Tragic school shootings in the United States and abroad, and the horrific events of September 11, 2001, have been wake-up calls for everyone associated with schools to proactively develop crisis management plans. We know that an effective plan is our best opportunity to reduce the chance of a tragedy, and to minimize injuries and save lives when a tragedy does occur.

Shortly after the tragedy of September 11 some of the nation's chief executives were asked to "offer a vision for tackling an overwhelming disaster. Their wisdom, distilled, came down to four basic truisms: be calm, tell the truth, put people before business, then get back to business as soon as possible" (Wayne & Kaufman, 2001). Following this wisdom also entails preparation. If crisis management tactics and practices are well planned and in place, they provide the scaffolding for leadership action when an unexpected crisis occurs.

Every school should have a crisis management planning manual that includes appropriate steps for each type of emergency. Procedures should be developed through collaboration of staff, students, administration, and classified and support staff as well as local safety officers. Such collaboration increases the knowledge base and number of personnel able to cope with emergencies. Developmental work of this type also increases ownership for the manual and its contents.

Developing A Crisis Management Planning Manual

The following guidelines for a crisis management planning manual were adapted from several excellent sources (Dwyer, Osher, & Warger, 1998; Warner,

2000; Bagin & Gallagher, 2002; Lawton, 2002; National Mental Health Association, 2001; and the National School Public Relations Association).

An effective plan should include the following parts:

- Rationale for the plan, noting that prevention is the first step to avoiding a crisis (e.g., zero tolerance for bullying, monitoring of hallways)

- Listing of crisis team members. Although the school will have a core team on campus for the initial crisis period, an expanded team should be included in all planning and used during the crisis (e.g., principal, assistant principals, counselors, school psychologists, classified representatives, central office personnel, school nurse, school security officers, appropriate safe and drug-free program coordinators, law enforcement, fire and emergency service personnel, community social service and health service agency representatives, clergy, media representatives, parent and student representatives)

- Generic form to define and assess a crisis situation

- Generic procedures that go into effect for all crisis

- Emergency phone tree with chain of command information

- Description of types of crises covered and procedures for each crisis, with clearly coded or separate colored pages for each type of crisis

- Listing of crisis code signals for faculty, students, and fire, police, and emergency service personnel

- Maps of facilities with areas for crisis control center, distributed to faculty and fire and police personnel

- Maps clearly delineating evacuation procedures, distributed to faculty and fire and police personnel

- Designated crisis spokesperson for faculty, media, and parent communication

- Description of communication procedures with emergency service personnel for immediate contact

- Information on faculty and community training procedures and school drill schedules (e.g., lockdown, earthquake, and fire drill)

- Plan to ensure that all critical parties have received the Crisis Management Planning Manual

- Copies of brochures distributed to parents relating to school crisis planning

- Copies of "backpack" letters

- Procedures to ensure that students, staff, parents, and community are kept informed and comforted during the aftermath of the crisis

- Evaluation process to update plans each year, or following a crisis

National School Public Relations Association (NSPRA) Guidelines for the First 30 Minutes of a Crisis

NSPRA suggests the following for the first 30 minutes of a crisis:

- A member of the administration must take charge of the situation.
- The exact nature of the crisis situation must be defined.
- Initially, take all necessary action to ensure the safety of students and staff. Additionally, take appropriate action to protect district property.
- Inform staff, students, parents, and the media of key events.
- If possible, avoid large student meetings—keep them informed in the classrooms.
- Implement a *Crisis Assessment and Information Sheet.* The sheet should include the following: description of crisis, action initially taken, description of harm or injuries, property damage, assessing the necessity of evacuation, students or facilities at risk, media to contact, list of human and material resources needed (e.g., counselors, medical personnel, food service, transportation), likely events for the next few hours.

—National School Public Relations Association (1996, pp. 143-145)

Developing a Plan for the Prevention of Serious Violence

To be truly proactive, *preventive measures* relating to the possibility of serious violence should also be part of crisis management planning. The U.S. Department of Education report *Early Warning, Timely Response: A Guide to Safe Schools* (Dwyer, Osher, & Warger, 1998), includes many excellent strategies to help schools prevent and deal with violent incidents. As former Secretary of Education Richard Riley noted in the introductory section of the report, ". . . every school in the nation [should have] a comprehensive violence prevention plan in place" (p. 2). In addition, that all members of the community, administrators, teachers, families, students, classified staff, and community members must collaborate to develop positive relations with students. The difference that one individual can make, connecting with a potentially violent student, is a primary theme of the report. The following essential points are made in the report:

- Safe and responsive schools are characterized by a focus on academic achievement; welcoming and involving families into the school; links to important community agencies including the police, emergency and health services and the faith-based community; an emphasis on positive relations among students and staff; an open school discussion concerning safety issues; fair and equal treatment by faculty and students related to racial groups, ethnic backgrounds, religious preferences, and sexual orientations in a school; eliminating targeting or bullying of students; creating safe and nonintimidating ways for students to share concerns with administration, faculty, counselors, or parents about potential violent acts; disciplinary policies that include a code of conduct with specific consequences and clear policies concerning antiharassment, antiviolence, and due process rights.

- Early warning signs of possible violence include feelings of rejection, persecution, social withdrawal and isolation; having been a victim of violence at home or in school; low interest in school and academics; expressions of violence in drawing, writings, or speech; impulsive, threatening, and bullying behavior; disciplinary and violent history; intolerance and prejudicial attitude; drug or alcohol abuse; gang affiliation; and access to firearms.

- Imminent warning signs of serious violence include severe physical fighting at home or school, vandalism of property, rage for minor reasons, detailed threats and plans to harm or kill others, possession and use of firearms, and self-injurious behaviors or threats of suicide.

- Intervention practices, depending on severity of threat, include contacting the principal, guidance counselor, school psychologist, family, health service, or law enforcement agency; a persistent effort to help a student and cut through the bureaucracy even when threat is diminished; avoiding inappropriate labeling of a student because of profiling; enforcement of the *Gun Free School Act* requiring expulsion of students for a minimum of one year for bringing a firearm to school.

- Intervention practices to improve the behavior of violent children include access to a team of education specialists to assist students; parents and teachers sharing responsibility with child and family service agencies, law enforcement, the juvenile justice system, and other agencies; working closely with parents of troubled children; maintaining confidentiality when appropriate; developing the capacity of staff, students, and families to help; simplifying staff requests for assistance; implementing early intervention procedures; developing social-skills programs; and referring children for special education evaluation.

- Action steps for students to create safe schools include participating in peer mediation and conflict resolution programs; listening to friends and encouraging them to seek out a trusted adult; joining organizations that oppose violence in schools; joining community youth-oriented activities; working with teachers and the administration to create a safe and nonbureaucratic process for reporting violence-related activities; knowing the school code of conduct; working with law enforcement officials in the school on safety audits and safety tips; role modeling appropriate behavior when intensive feelings of anger arise; and seeking help from a trusted adult

- Suggestions by experts to maintain a safe physical environment include supervised access to building and grounds; reducing class and school size; adjusting schedules to minimize time in hallways or other potentially dangerous locations; modifying traffic flow patterns to limit conflicts; conducting a safety audit; closing campuses during lunch; supervising key areas at critical times; prohibiting congregating students in at-risk areas; having adults, including parents, visible in the school; staggering dismissal and lunch periods; monitoring areas around the school; coordinating with law enforcement officials safe routes to and from school.

- Critical and immediate intervention procedures during a violent crisis include using well-planned lockdown or evacuation procedures to protect students and staff; immediately identifying safe areas during the crisis; a fool-proof communication system with designated roles for members of the crisis management team; a process for securing immediate support from law enforcement officers and appropriate medical and emergency service personnel.

The following example of a crisis procedure checklist from the Department of Education report can serve as an action guide during a violent emergency:

___Assess life/safety issues immediately

___Provide immediate emergency medical care

___Call 911 and notify police/rescue first. Call the superintendent second

___Convene the crisis team to assess the situation and implement the crisis response procedures

___Evaluate available and needed resources

___Alert school staff to the situation

___Activate the crisis communication procedure and system of verification

___Secure all areas

___Implement evacuation and other procedures to protect students and staff from harm

___Avoid dismissing students to unknown care

___Adjust the bell schedule to ensure safety during the crisis

___Alert persons in charge of various information systems to prevent confusion and misinformation. Notify parents

___Contact appropriate community agencies and the school district's public information office, if appropriate

___Implement postcrisis procedures

—(Dwyer, Osher, & Warger, 1998; pp. 4-11)

Final Thoughts on Crisis Management

Douglas Huston (*The Oregonian,* April, 2002), a nuclear safety specialist, noted during a crisis communication conference that, "You have a moral and ethical obligation to be truthful. People are more afraid of what they don't understand than what they do understand. This [providing accurate information during a crisis] is about reducing uncertainty" (p. C5). Providing honest information during a crisis helps individuals gain a sense of control. Individuals can also feel control when they contribute to minimizing the effect of a tragedy. Promoting and participating in a blood drive, for example, can help one cope with the disaster.

If a school leader is asked for information during a crisis, a "no comment" remark will likely lead to speculation about what is being concealed. Rudolph Giuliani's honesty during the moments and days following September 11 helped New Yorkers and the nation gain strength to deal with the aftermath of the horrific tragedy.

Once developed, the procedures should be taught, modeled, and practiced. Although drills interrupt instructional time, if the school principal is serious about the importance of these drills with staff and students, then these emergency preparation procedures can be a useful educational experience. In some schools, teachers have integrated teaching about AIDS and disaster or emergency preparedness into reading, writing, science, and history classes. Some schools have students write letters home explaining the disaster preparedness procedures to their parents. Crisis planning teaches a great deal about decision making as well.

Bringing in key community members involved in emergency work, such as, firefighters, protective service workers, and trauma unit personnel to speak with students helps to develop a respect for and awareness of emergency procedures. Furthermore, a strong public relations program with the local police department, including officers speaking in the schools about proactive crime prevention or automobile safety, could later prove very valuable if the police need to be called into the school's vicinity because of an emergency.

It is helpful, also, to provide time for school pupil service teams (e.g., nurses and school counselors) to have regular contact with related community health professionals. Communication between school personnel and community professionals can increase knowledge and significantly inform actions. In the most serious cases, this can lead to valuable coordination regarding potential teenage suicides or gang violence. The contact also keeps school personnel informed about current research to help students who are bulimic or anorexic. Child protective service personnel can offer useful information about child abuse—how to recognize it, how to raise teacher and student awareness, and how to work with abused students. Moreover, administrators and teachers are legally required by federal law to report suspected cases of child abuse. Indicators of abuse related to physical abuse, physical neglect, sexual abuse, emotional abuse, and neglect must be followed up by school personnel (Morrison, 2000).

Although very rare, students have died from eating foods with ingredients to which they are extremely allergic. The ultimate tragedy for a family, school, and community is, of course, a child's death. Schools must ensure that they have updated information regarding health, medication, and psychological needs. Those who need to know should be informed. Health and emergency procedure cards should be updated regularly. Computer disks with student emergency information and yearbook photos are vital during a crisis. Key facts such as food allergies or medical/health problems, custody issues, and other important information should be highlighted and communicated to appropriate personnel. This might include the school secretary, nurse, cafeteria workers, and teachers. Many schools offer workshops for teachers, support staff, and administrators to prepare for emergencies. Medical preparedness can include training to cope with shock victims, people having epileptic seizures or who are choking, severe bleeding, and those who need CPR. Areas where accidents might occur should be identified and procedures developed to address each possible accident. Obvious locations are playgrounds, hallways, locker rooms, cafeterias, or bus stops. An emergency crisis kit might include a computer disk with student data, a crisis management manual, a bull horn, phone tree, permanent markers, wrist bands, legal pads, pens, an active cell phone, and a current yearbook, in addition to the typical first-aid resources.

Finally, to be sure all possibilities have been considered, the staff might brainstorm potential emergency situations and design related precautions to be included in the crisis management manual. An example might look like this:

Possible Situation	Plan
Evacuation of building	Evacuation plans taught and practiced, as well as posted on each classroom, library, office, and gym door Busing plans posted
Shooting on the playground or in the classroom	Locations of phones to dial 911 specified Contact school nurse Lockdown plan implemented Provide counseling for those impacted by the event

Planning ahead can pay off dramatically in speeding up effective response and reaction time. When every second counts, it may spell the difference between life and death.

Community

Principals manage the image of the school in the community and the communication flow between school and community by adopting a proactive stance. This can affect greatly the community perception of the school and support for school activities and funding, as well as students' perceptions of parental support for the school. Several examples that follow were shared at a job-alike session held in Washington, DC, for nationally distinguished principals.

For example, principals can conduct a regular "neighborhood walk and watch." This activity is designed to take the principal into the neighborhood that surrounds the school to talk with community members, spread good news about the school and students, find out about community developments, and lend an interested ear.

One principal organizes a late spring "Dinner on the Grounds." Each class prepares for this event by writing letters of invitation home and to key civic leaders. (Reservations are made to attend this function.) A special assembly is held during the evening in which the school takes the opportunity to highlight its mission and important values by conducting a ceremony in which awards are given for the most improved student, student leadership, good citizenship, and academic excellence. Following the assembly, quilts and blankets are spread out, sack dinners are handed out, and the school band plays.

Many principals enhance the image of the school in the community by joining civic service clubs and regularly reporting on school affairs. In addition, they have met with education reporters and editors from the local newspaper and cultivated positive relationships with them.

One principal challenged the president of a large international seed company to trade places with him for a day. This joint get-acquainted venture resulted in a delightful school-business partnership. Scientists and other personnel from the company worked with the teachers to develop a project in which students formed greenhouse "companies" in their classrooms and produced plants for a Mother's Day plant sale.

Another principal initiated an e-mail "pen-pal" program between students of the school and a local Navy submarine unit. In one high school, students corresponded with scientists at the South Pole.

Recognizing the rising costs of feeding families, one school extended a hand to community members by organizing a bulk food purchase. This involved placing large orders for frozen foods to secure a substantial discount for community members.

Still another example of managing the school in the community occurred when the principal and staff of a school in Hawaii realized that many parents of preschoolers had negative school experiences themselves and were therefore reluctant to come to school. So the school decided to go to the community. They set up blankets in a local park and invited the parents to visit. On each blanket was a learning station for parents. Refreshments were provided. This activity demonstrated to the community that the school was approachable and could offer much to them.

In Rockingham County, Virginia, a school's staff volunteered to conduct parent conferences at a local chicken-processing plant where a large number of parents worked. This increased parents' access to the school and greatly enhanced school-community relationships.

Support Services

Societal conditions and increased social service agency cooperation have made support services in the community still another facet of management responsibility for the principal. That is, to serve students, staff, and parents, principals need to know about the community resources available to support the local school. Many principals, especially in full-service schools, work with agencies that could provide support. Examples of these might include Big Brothers and Big Sisters organizations, the community clothes closet, the county health department, mental health services, child protective services, crisis lines, the community library, and services for the homeless. Resource files have been established in the school office with the name, address, and phone number of each agency. Inside the files might be literature collected during "get acquainted" visits to these organizations. Having well-organized files enables easy access to this information for parents and students in need. During Open House or Back-to-School Night, a directory of information regarding support services can be distributed to parents. This same information can also be provided to students. (For an additional discussion on community-based organizations that assist the school, see chapter 18, "Working With Parents and Partnering With the Greater Community.")

A Final Observation Regarding School Management

When considering the classroom, school-site, community, and support service management responsibilities of the principal, it is interesting to note that the responsibilities seem to move from the inside of the school (the classroom) to the outside world (support services). Clearly, the classroom, school site, community, and support services are linked, and the principal's ability to successfully take advantage of this linkage will rest to some extent on his or her ability to see the linkage as based on relationships among people, not simply as structural entities that need to remain in communication with one another. Certainly, leadership and management go hand in hand as the principal manages this responsibility.

Note

1. Authentic principal voices from interviews, workshops, writings, and informal conversations will be heard throughout the book.

Reflections

This space provides for you a place to write in ideas that have been generated by this chapter, things you want to try, or adaptations of ideas presented herein.

1. Separately, consider several characteristics of effective leaders and several characteristics of effective managers. What conclusions can you draw about management or leadership from your selected characteristics?

2. Brainstorm a list of leadership responsibilities and another list of management responsibilities. Which list is longer? Why? Are there ways of integrating the two lists?

3. Develop a key area checklist for MBWA at your school.

4. Make a list of various types of crises that should be addressed in a crisis management plan. Are there some generic planning elements that would apply to most crises on your list? What are these elements?

5. What insights or new questions do you have as a result of reflecting on the ideas presented in this chapter?

3

Leader as Shaper of School Culture

There is a subtle spirit that can be sensed the moment one walks into a school . . . that subtle spirit is the school culture.

CALIFORNIA SCHOOL LEADERSHIP ACADEMY

Within any organization, there is an "inner reality" (Deal & Peterson, 1993) or culture that influences the way people interact, what they will and will not do, and what they value as "right and rude" (Little, 1982). This inner reality reflects what organizational members care about, what they are willing to spend time doing, what and how they celebrate, and what they talk about. It is evident in daily routines. The inner reality or culture of a school influences its productivity, professional development, leadership practices, and traditions. The same stable culture that brings meaning to a school can also frustrate efforts to implement new, innovative ideas, especially if they are contradictory to the existing culture. Consider, if you will, the open classroom of the 1960s. It soon became walled up because the culture of the one-room schoolhouse was so strong. Hence one understands Fullan and Stiegelbauer's (1991) words "to restructure is not to reculture."

Despite its pervasive nature, culture or inner reality is often overlooked as a critical force. Instruction, curriculum, quality assessment, and leadership surely all contribute to a quality school. But "the inner, unspoken set of values and purposes that weave quality into the daily routine and motivate everyone to do his or her best" (Deal & Peterson, 1993) is equally if not more powerful in moving a school toward achieving a vision of quality. A school's culture is reflective of its organizational members. The culture is the "meaning" individuals create in their world of work. Bennis (1991) has written, "Each employee is, to a remarkable extent, the organization in miniature" (p. 156). This explains both why culture is such a critical force and how individual interactions influence the culture. Because the way people interact daily or "do business" at a site dramatically influences its ultimate productivity for all members, culture is a powerful school improvement tool. It is not surprising, however, that if a culture is a negative one, it can serve as a hindering force to school improvement efforts. In such cases, the culture must first be studied and then transformed if school improvement efforts are to thrive. This will be

Figure 3.1. Elements of School Culture

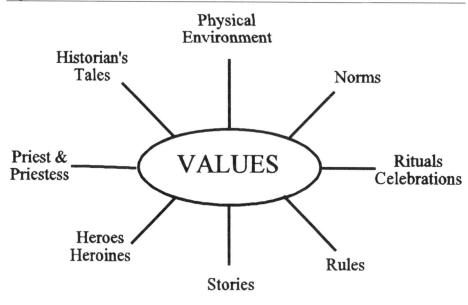

discussed later in the chapter. Figure 3.1 illustrates the elements of school culture. All of the elements should reflect the core values and beliefs if the culture is cohesive. In the stories from a variety of schools that follow, you will see how these elements function.

These accounts, which combine practices used successfully in several schools, will demonstrate some of the ways that principals and staff can use culture as a quality tool for school improvement.

Core Beliefs and Values Are the Heart of Culture

The principal at Lincoln School endeavors to facilitate a learning culture. He believes the leader's role is to provide a facilitating environment that contributes to teacher self-empowerment. In a recent interview, the principal explained that to construct a context within which this can occur, principals should help create a culture that celebrates growth and shared decision making. Teachers need to feel confident and safe. It is very important that regardless of what is taking place outside of the school, the school culture must remain positive and clearly aimed at making the school a better place for students. The culture should emphasize that the school is a community of learners and that all can learn from one another. As one teacher stated, "The belief in teaching [as] a learning experience has enabled me to deal with problems as opportunities for problem solving."

In this setting, risk taking and experimentation, if they are directed toward goals of enhanced learning, are recognized and rewarded. According to Barth (quoted in Sparks, 1993), "to unlock energy and inventiveness, people have to take risks" (p. 18). Teachers, students, and parents are far more likely to take risks when principals frequently and visibly take risks themselves. The willingness of people who inhabit a school to take risks directly influences their capacity to learn. Learning from one's "mistakes"—risk taking—and exploring heretofore undiscovered dimensions of one's competencies can contribute to an environment characterized by teaching and staff collaboration committed to continuous improvement. Moreover, every aspect of the program should emphasize quality, and all personnel should feel professional and personal pride as individuals and as part of the group, from teachers, principals, and aides to lunchroom personnel, custodians, and security guards. Quality should be emphasized in interpersonal relationships, resources, teacher meetings, playground equipment, and the physical condition of the school.

The Physical Environment Reflects Core Values

In a culture where learning, collaboration, and quality are valued, there are visible places where this occurs. The teachers' center provides one such example. A key aspect of the center at the Lincoln School is a professional library that includes current journals and professional videos. It is a setting where ideas are exchanged, and books, articles, and lessons are discussed. Teachers find resources there to develop curriculum materials, plan instruction, or assess the impact of curriculum and instruction on students.

Activities are also in place within the physical environment to remind organizational members of the importance of learning, collaboration, and quality and to provide avenues for such ends. Examples of this might be a schedule for peer coaching or a time when, on a schoolwide basis, everyone reflects through journal writing.

A celebration of student work also reflects core values. This can occur with an "On Showcase" bulletin board. This board highlights the work of different classes every 2 weeks. It is generally in a prominent area of the school, such as on the wall outside of the principal's office. Items for display may include work from a recent unit, a special project emphasizing the value of diversity, or an idea such as respect being promoted on a schoolwide basis as a result of an emphasis on social and emotional learning. What is most important is that the display calls attention to student work, and core values of the school culture.

One school in Israel displayed a bulletin board in the entry hall with a vineyard. Interspersed with the vines was every student's name. This symbolically communicated the importance of each student, as well as their connection to each other and the learning community. On a similar note, a principal commented, "You can tell what's important in a school by what you see when you walk in the front

door. What's on the walls, what's in the trophy case, sends a strong message to all
who enter the building."

Rituals Display Core Values
and Call Attention to What Is Important

There are many rituals in a school. A familiar one is the faculty meeting. In a
culture that values learning from one another, the faculty meeting can become a forum for learning. Meetings can be organized to have teachers share ideas that are
working in their classrooms. For example, elementary school teachers who are experiencing success with differentiating instruction or publishing student work can
show samples and lead a discussion on their experiences. If an atmosphere of trust
exists, ideas that were not successful can also be shared. The principal can also
share successes and failures. Remember, you are promoting the idea of leader as
learner. How can one learn without making some mistakes and taking some risks?
As a member of one large corporation once stated, "Failure is the opportunity to begin again more intelligently." This also encourages teachers to try lessons that are
experimental and demonstrates principal support.

Another activity that can be used to foster learning and model a classroom instructional strategy is the "jigsaw." For example, if staff members are learning
about and using cooperative learning in their classrooms, the principal could use
the jigsaw cooperative learning activity as part of the format for a faculty meeting.
Suppose there are four articles about cooperative learning or approaches to integrating the curriculum that members of a leadership team would like to share as a
cooperative activity with the faculty. Staff members could be asked to form "home
groups." Within each group, individuals would count off one through four. "Ones"
would read article 1, "twos" article 2, and so on (see Figure 3.2a). Following this,
staff members sharing the same number would meet to become "expert" in the
content of the article they read. This would involve discussing key points, identifying helpful examples, and deciding how they would share with others what they
read (see Figure 3.2b). Finally, home groups would reconvene, and each member
would explain to the others what he or she read (see Figure 3.2c).

At the conclusion of the teaching episodes, groups would synthesize their collective learnings and report to the total group. The principal would function as a
group member during the entire jigsaw process.

Many principals have used the jigsaw technique with different types of content. For instance, at the beginning of the year, some have used it to review information contained in the faculty or school handbook. Others have used it to share
articles about working with special education students, at-risk students, effective
teaching practices, or strategies to close the achievement gap. This strategy celebrates individual accountability and fosters collaboration and interdependence
among faculty members. These attributes reflect the values that are being developed and reinforced in the culture.

Figure 3.2. Jigsaw Activity

"Home Group"

a. Each reads his or her assigned article, highlighting key points.

"Expert Group"

b. Number-alike groups meet to discuss key points and to decide how to share the article's content with fellow members.

"Home Group"

c. Each group member summarizes what they read.

Another technique that calls attention to learning together is the "listening posts" activity. The faculty meeting facilitator asks the group members to generate possible topics for discussion. These may include such items as working with at-risk youths, integrating the curriculum, or portfolio assessment. Topics for discussion are then posted in different locations of the room. Individuals gather around topics of interest and have a 15- to 20-minute discussion. Each group's ideas are recorded on butcher paper posted around the room. These ideas are often typed and later distributed to the faculty. Following the discussion, each group prepares a 2-minute summary of its conversation and reports. Many times the "reporting out" phase plants seeds of interest among other faculty members. A variation of this activity is the use of classrooms instead of areas of the room as listening posts. This has the added value of getting faculty members into classrooms other than their own.

Another learning ritual is the brown-bag lunch. One staff member at the Lincoln School who attended several cooperative learning workshops shared her experiences with interested staff during lunch. Teachers followed up these sessions by experimenting with cooperative learning techniques in their classrooms. At the final session, teachers decided they wanted to support one another in their cooperative learning activities. As a consequence, they decided to continue meeting once a month at lunch to exchange ideas. The principal supported this activity by publicizing the meetings and by providing logistical support and refreshments.

Celebrations Call Attention to What Is Important

In a community of learners, learning is valued and celebrated publicly. Student recognition assemblies are held every 6 to 8 weeks to celebrate student successes. Students are cited for helping out a new colleague in class, improving attendance, making significant academic improvement, or teaching another student. Groups of students are complimented for excellent behavior in the cafeteria or keeping the campus clean. Whatever is celebrated reflects what is being emphasized in the school. Following the assembly, notes are sent home to parents from the principal, informing parents of their child's accomplishments. It is important that the celebrations and recognition program reflect the culture's values. For example, if the school culture places value on teamwork, it would be important to recognize teams or groups of students rather than a "student of the month."

Celebrations put the school's values on display. At one school, Martin Luther King Day was celebrated by faculty, parents, and students. First, the principal gave a presentation about what Martin Luther King Jr. stood for. He emphasized values such as the love of fellow human beings, nonviolence, and equal opportunity. Next, he pointed out how these same values were shared by the school and cited specific examples that students could relate to. As an example, the principal asked the students how they would feel if because of their hair color, they had to use separate drinking fountains, restrooms, and cafeterias. Finally, students and faculty sang songs such as "Lift Every Voice and Sing" and "We Shall Overcome," followed by a video clip of Martin Luther King Jr.'s speech "I Have a Dream." The assembly provided some insight into what it was like to live through the 1960s. When the ceremony was over, many participants had tears in their eyes. One teacher remarked, "As a school, we're closer now, and have a feeling of what we're all about." In the wake of September 11, one high school had an assembly around the themes of developing tolerance and acceptance, and valuing diversity.

It is important to make sure that all programs—even holiday programs—have meaning, relative to what the school is about.

How People Spend Time Reflects Core Values

A middle school's staff saw the value of providing an integrated course of study for its students. As a result, they reorganized the schedule so teachers had 74 minutes of common planning time to develop rich learning experiences for students.

Charity drives in schools or sending middle or high school students out to volunteer in the community for service credit sends a clear message that the school is concerned about others. Such activities also teach about empathy and community service. The December holiday season is an excellent time to have a food, clothing, or toy drive for those in need. The student government can help organize these events, assisted by faculty advisors, so that it becomes a collaborative enterprise.

History reminds people about what an organization has stood for over time. On the 40th anniversary of the American Embassy School in New Delhi, India, a teacher received a stipend to write a history of the school. This has gone a long way to build the idea of tradition. The middle school, on its 40th anniversary, buried a time capsule with a video of the school and samples of schoolwork. The elementary school student council took the lead in renaming two school buildings after famous people who exemplified the values for which the school stood.

A school song to reflect the core values was written by one of the teachers, and there was a student contest to select the title.

The World of AES

To the city of New Delhi
We come from far and wide
Boys and girls of every nation
Standing side by side
In the beauty of the gardens
We learn to take good care
Of ourselves and of each other
And this world that we all share
At AES, AES the finest school we know
Where the boys and girls and grown-ups
All really like to show
That we're smart and clean and friendly
And we lend a helping hand
In this very special school
In a very special land

Each day we try our very best
In everything we do
The school is like a sailing ship
And we are all the crew
We work and play together
As we sail upon the sea
There's no other place in India
That we would rather be than . . .
AES, AES the finest school we know
Where the boys and girls and grown-ups

All really like to show
That we're smart and clean and friendly
And we lend a helping hand
In this very special school
In a very special land

Marilyn Ferguson

Norms Are the Unwritten Rules of Culture

Generally, individuals within an organization behave toward one another according to the expectations they perceive to exist within the culture. These group expectations are usually a function of an unwritten code for behavior called *norms*—or, more simply stated, "The way we do things around here" (Terry Deal, personal communication, San Francisco, 1989).

In some schools, for example, there are norms that encourage people to voice their opinions, even if those opinions go against the grain of the majority voice. As one teacher from Maine explained, "At our school, everyone has a right to disagree. No one must voice their opinion. But, if you don't take responsibility for voicing your opinion, and a decision is made by the rest of the staff, you must agree not to stand in the way of the wheels of progress." In schools where this type of norm is strong, individuals who risk offering an opposing viewpoint have often become celebrated as heroes because they make others think about their attitudes and actions. One teacher noted, as an example, "At our school, we can always count on Andy. He has his feet planted firmly in concrete . . . but he reminds us, who often have our heads in the clouds, of brass tacks reality!"

These norms often govern learning opportunities within the culture in addition to traditional activities such as workshops or guest speakers. When norms at a school encourage prospecting for internal resources, the activities reflect that stance. Peer-coaching programs are one such example. At one school, a peer-coaching program has been operating successfully for 3 years. To keep the project ongoing, teachers divide into newcomer and veteran groups. There are strong norms within this culture that emphasize the importance of teaching and learning from one another. When practices such as peer coaching support collegiality and cooperation in this way, they become embedded in the fabric of school life.

When new information or learning opportunities are needed in collegial cultures, the norm has often become "Let's look within our own rich reservoir of talent to see what we might tap." When one school's staff development committee surveyed the teachers about what they were most interested in, it came to light that improving questioning techniques was a major area of interest. The teachers organized some of the homegrown talent to put on a staff workshop. Topics such as Bloom's taxonomy, Socratic seminars, developing questions and activities that require higher level questions, and using wait time became schoolwide objectives as a result of the workshop.

Stories Communicate and Reinforce Cultural Values

The use of story is one avenue through which new and existing members of a culture are informed about and reminded of its values. Every school has stories that, as a matter of tradition, are passed on to new staff members. Generally, these stories signal important values or beliefs. For example, at one school, new teachers are told about a former teacher who always had special techniques for helping at-risk youth. Through the story, they learn that because the school did not at that time have a forum for staff sharing, when that teacher retired, a library of knowledge "burned." Hence that teacher left her mark on students, but not on the teaching profession. Because of this great loss, teachers at the school now take special care to make sure quality time is set aside for professional dialogue and the sharing of ideas and practices. A ritual called "See Them Teach Before They Leave" is instituted each spring in which returning faculty members are encouraged to visit classrooms of departing teachers. Following this ritual, an assembly is held wherein the bronzed classroom doorknob of the departing teacher, affixed to a wooden plaque and inscribed, is presented to the departing teacher. The plague inscription reads, "Thank you for opening your door and sharing your classroom secrets. You kept a library of knowledge from burning."

In addition to reminding organizational members about important values, stories can also provide a way of talking about issues that hit close to home or are sensitive, with a more comfortable distance. One principal used the following story during the first faculty meeting to remind teachers of the tremendous influence they have on students' lives, beyond the academic arena.

The story is taken from a speech by Sir Winston Churchill before the House of Commons on June 4, 1940.[1]

The Honorable Profession of Teaching

Teddy Stallard certainly qualified as "one of the least." Disinterested in school, he wore musty, wrinkled clothes; his hair was never combed. He was one of those kids in school with a deadpan face, expressionless—sort of a glassy, unfocused stare. When Miss Thompson spoke to Teddy, he would always answer with a "yes" or a "no." Unattractive, unmotivated, and distant, he was just plain hard to like. Even though Miss Thompson said she loved all of the students in her class the same, deep down inside she wasn't being completely truthful.

Whenever she marked Teddy's papers, she got a certain perverse pleasure out of putting Xs next to the wrong answers, and when she put Fs at the top of the papers, she always did it with a flair. She should have known better; she had Teddy's records and she knew more about him than she wanted to admit. The records read

- First grade: Teddy shows promise with his work and attitude but has a poor home situation.

- Second grade: Teddy could do better. His mother is seriously ill. He receives little help at home.
- Third grade: Teddy is a good boy, but much too serious. His mother died this year.
- Fourth grade: Teddy is very slow, but well behaved. His father shows no interest.

Christmas came and the boys and girls in Miss Thompson's class brought her Christmas presents. They piled their presents on her desk and crowded around to watch her open them. Among the presents was one from Teddy Stallard. She was surprised that he had brought her one, but he had. Teddy's gift was wrapped in brown paper and was held together with Scotch™ tape. On the paper were written the simple words, "For Miss Thompson, from Teddy." When she opened Teddy's present, out fell a gaudy rhinestone bracelet, with half of the stones missing, and a bottle of cheap perfume.

The other boys and girls began to giggle and smirk at Teddy's gifts, but Miss Thompson at least had enough sense to silence them by immediately putting on the bracelet and putting some of the perfume on her wrist. Holding her wrist up for the other boys and girls to sniff, she said, "Doesn't it smell lovely?" And the children, taking their cue from their teacher, readily agreed.

At the end of the day, when school was over and the other students had left, Teddy lingered behind. He slowly came over to her desk and said softly, "Miss Thompson . . . Miss Thompson, you smell just like my mother, . . . and her bracelet looks real pretty on you too. I'm glad you liked my presents." When Teddy left, Miss Thompson sobbed.

The next day when the children came to school, they were welcomed by a new Miss Thompson. She had become a different person, a person committed to loving all of her students, especially the slow ones. Especially Teddy Stallard. By the end of that school year, Teddy showed dramatic progress. He had caught up with most of the students and was even ahead of some.

The school year quickly came to an end, and Teddy went on to another school. She didn't hear from Teddy for a long time. Then one day, she received a note that read

Dear Miss Thompson,

I wanted you to be the first to know. I will be graduating second in my class.

Love,
Teddy Stallard

Four years later, another note came:

Dear Miss Thompson,

They just told me I will be graduating first in my class. I wanted you to be the first to know. The university has not been easy, but I liked it.

Love,
Teddy Stallard

And four years later:

Dear Miss Thompson,

As of today, I am Theodore Stallard, MD. How about that? I wanted you to be the first to know. I am getting married, the 27th to be exact. I want you to come and sit where my mother would sit if she were alive. You are the only family I have now; Dad died last year.

Love,
Teddy Stallard

Miss Thompson went to the wedding and sat where Teddy's mother would have sat. She deserved to sit there; she had done something for Teddy that he could never forget.

After telling the story, the principal conducted an activity in which staff members reflected on the legacy that they would like to leave with their students.

Once this story was shared with the staff, they frequently referenced it when speaking with one another; it had become a part of the culture. It became a constant reminder, in this school, about how fragile students are and in what small ways teachers can make big differences in students lives.

At report card time, the principal reminded the teachers about the Teddy Stallard story. The point was to emphasize how a comment that may at first glance appear to be insignificant may, in fact, have an enduring positive or negative effect on students and parents. A report card manual, prepared for the teachers, was distributed as a guideline to assist in the development of report card comments. The manual began with the following words:

This manual is made up of report card comments written by you and your colleagues. Often we read manuals that do not apply to our specific situation. This will not be the case with this manual. Different types of comments have been selected to provide you with a variety of ideas and styles for you to review. Overall, the quality of the comments is very impressive. It is easy to take pride in the sensitivity, care, and thoughtfulness that went into the report cards written by our staff.

The comments are divided into primary and intermediate sections and subdivided by subject area and general comments. I've culled through all the report cards so that each comment has a little different angle to offer. Interestingly, as I read through the comments, I recognized that some of the comments from the primary grade teachers have a lot to offer as suggestions to the intermediate grade teachers and vice versa. I would suggest taking an hour to read through the manual, marking comments that you find of interest—that address your class—before beginning report cards this quarter. Of course, thanks to everyone for writing comments that contributed to this project.

After reading hundreds of comments on previous report cards, I would like to make a few nuts-and-bolts suggestions relevant to our specific report card and concerning report card comments in general.

1. Consider relating comments in curriculum areas to specific curriculum issues as related to the student. Mention areas of strength and weakness that identify to the parents what is being studied in class. This should be considered, also, when discussing behavior.

2. If you want to make a general point, use the "additional comments" section on the back of the report card instead of the designated subject area section. Mentioning that "Beverly is a pleasure to have in class" or that "Steven is often late to school" should not be the primary point under the math section of the report card. Furthermore, summary comments about the student's overall performance belong in the additional comments section.

3. When discussing a problem, be specific and try to provide recommendations. For example, "Appu is not doing well in social studies and needs to try harder" gives very little guidance. Consider: "Appu's oral presentations in social studies should be organized more carefully. Please consider 'rehearsing' the presentations at home before the classroom presentation. I am sure her work will improve with this effort!"

4. Remember that the report card is a permanent record. Thus every comment should be meaningful: "Juan forgets to date his papers" can be mentioned at a parent conference instead of as part of the language arts comment section.

5. To preserve overall class confidentiality, it is not recommended to state, "Willy has the top math grades in the class." Furthermore, this tends to overemphasize competition.

6. Make sure your report card comment matches the grade. A glowing comment next to a "needs improvement" grade does not really make sense.

7. Comment areas should be used to describe important issues more than the number of assignments missed in a particular subject. Assignments

missed is important information, but it does not tell us very much about how the student is responding to the curriculum.

8. Avoid insensitive comments such as "Jacob is slow."

As you read through the manual, note which comments or ideas "strike you" and/or could be helpful in developing appropriate comments about members of your class.

Thanks,
Steve

Report card comments by grade level and subject area were included in the manual following the guidelines. The members of the culture of this school were, in this way, celebrated for their efforts to date and reminded of core values. Schools that share strong beliefs and values related to student outcomes can increase the attention, time, feedback mechanisms, and resources directed toward helping students learn. This occurs because the focus on the student and the quality of student-teacher relationships becomes a part of school's operating procedures, actions, rules, and reward systems.

Thus far, through anecdotal examples, we have discussed a framework of elements for thinking about school culture. In the pages that follow, we will consider how a culture might be transformed, if it is not a positive one, or if it is not in keeping with a school's vision.

Transforming or Shaping a Culture

Effective leadership must be both administrative and cultural in scope (Schein, 1985). Terry Deal and Kent Peterson (1993) suggest that the principal shapes a culture through a variety of means. They believe that it begins with "reading" the existing culture and then progressively moving to actions or behaviors that "mold or reinforce desirable core values and norms."

Reading a culture involves "reconstructing a school's history by listening to the stories of past events, examining artifacts, such as faculty meeting agendas and minutes, reviewing newsletter stories and school goals" (Deal & Peterson, 1993). Prior efforts at school improvement, crises faced by the staff, traditions, and information about the former principal's leadership style also yield valuable data for constructing a profile of the existing culture. Once this information is garnered, the principal, in concert with the staff, identifies specifics related to the vision of a quality school. In keeping with this vision, detailed plans are made to gradually transform the culture so that the rituals, rewards, routine activities, stories, and norms call attention to the values embedded in the new vision. Deal and Peterson (1990), in a series of case studies, noted that principals shaped culture in both formal and informal ways. They identified six major culture-shaping strategies:

Figure 3.3. A Planning Model

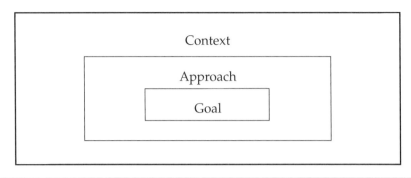

1. Developing a sense of what the school should and could be
2. Recruiting and selecting staff whose values fit with the schools
3. Resolving conflicts, disputes, and problems directly as a way of shaping values
4. Communicating values and beliefs in daily routines and behaviors
5. Identifying and articulating stories that communicate shared values
6. Nurturing the traditions, ceremonies, rituals, and symbols that communicate and reinforce the school culture

Georgea Mohlman-Sparks (1983) suggested that when setting out to implement an innovation that would require cultural change, one should first consider the goals of the change effort, then context factors, before deciding on the approach (see Figure 3.3). Implicit in this model is a realization that specific elements of culture could influence and shape the approach taken. If, for example, a school's cultural norms supported privacy and held that problem sharing meant one was "incompetent," these norms must be taken into account before a collaborative workplace could evolve as a goal. Perhaps faculty meetings could involve teachers in problem finding and sharing as an activity in order to erode these previous norms.

What one principal does will differ dramatically from another. One cultural transformation may take a year, whereas another may take 5 years. What is essential is that the principal holds the values and beliefs in focus as he or she conducts daily tasks, and that these values and beliefs are articulated widely. Continuous growth and improvement must be emphasized.

The following are some questions to ask yourself regarding leadership and culture building (Deal & Kennedy, 1982; Schein, 1985):

- What do you pay attention to?
- What do you react strongly to?

- What do you model, teach, and coach?
- How do you allocate rewards?
- What criteria do you use to recruit, select, and excommunicate teachers?
- What ceremonies, rituals, and traditions reinforce your vision?
- Who are the heroes and heroines of your school?
- What stories do you tell of the successes and accomplishments of the faculty and students?
- What school symbols communicate your vision?

You might also ask, "When do I have meetings?" "What items have priority placement on the agenda?" "How is time spent?" "Where are the meetings held?" "Is humor and smiling a ritual of daily life?" Each answer provides valuable data about the culture. For change to be effective, the "change masters"—whether they be the principal, teachers, students, or parents—must first sincerely examine the ceremonies, rituals, norms, values, stories, and traditions of the culture. Then culture-shaping techniques should be used to help the organizational culture reflect desired core values.

One faculty reflected that it was often the high achievers, or the students who got in trouble, who received the most attention. Wanting to change this trend, they asked one another, "Who are the students who get ignored? Who are the students who are likely to slip through the cracks?" They decided on a plan of action. Each faculty member collected pictures of the students who were in the categories they discussed. They published a compilation of each faculty member's students. The document was called "the vanilla kids." The name comes from the notion that vanilla, as a flavor, is not as "memorable" a flavor as blueberry, cherry, or butter pecan. Each faculty member was to reach out and communicate, every time they saw a vanilla kid. "You could see a difference in the students, and in the culture of the school within three weeks," one staff member reflected.

Final Thoughts on Culture

One principal noted, "culture is really the stage on which leadership gets played out. If, for example, the shared vision for a school is to be a 'home' for the heart and mind, one has to ask, 'to bring this to reality what will it take? What will be in the halls, on the walls, in the trophy case? What will the stories be like that are told to newcomers? What will be the traditions, celebrations?' And, what's more, as a principal I always have to be aware of how my behavior—what I attend to, put last on my priority list—what I participate in, what I don't—shapes the culture of the school." As Kent Peterson once reflected, "probably one of the most important things a leader does is to create, shape, and manage culture."

Note

1. The authors thank Tim Hansen, former director of the American School in Abu Dhabi, for sharing this story.

Reflections

This space provides for you a place to write in ideas that have been generated by this chapter, things you want to try, or adaptations of ideas presented herein.

1. Reflect on the school culture in your organization. What are the core values and beliefs? How are they depicted in traditional ceremonies, rituals, reward structures, artifacts, and stories? Are they consistent with the vision of the school? Why or why not?

2. Are there traditions or rituals in your school that are contrary to the values of the school? Why do you think this is the case? How might you transform them if need be?

3. Identify key "behind the scenes" staff members who play a major part in the school culture. What parts do they play?

4. What insights or new questions do you have as a result of reflecting on the ideas presented in this chapter?

PART II

CRITICAL SKILLS
FOR EFFECTIVE LEADERSHIP

4

The Art of Human Relations: Getting the Job Done

You must be able to deal with people and communicate with them, or just bag it . . . that's the crux of the whole thing.

A PRINCIPAL'S VOICE

Displaying effective and ethical human relations is a key to leadership on every level. It is a thread that runs throughout the organization and affects the culture, climate, personnel practices, and every individual who has contact with the school. It impacts the relationship between the school and larger community.

Human relations skills include working with people, building trust, creating a climate for teachers to comfortably discuss their own classroom practice, and helping individuals reach their potential. When positive human relations skills are manifested, people feel comfortable in taking risks, experimenting, collaborating, and communicating ideas and feelings; these behaviors enable students and staff to perform at high levels.

Task and Relationship Behaviors

One of the difficult aspects of the principal's human relations role is that task and relationship behaviors must be balanced simultaneously. If too much weight is placed on task behaviors as a measure of success, organizational members may feel stressed or pressured. If too much emphasis is placed on relationship behaviors, people may feel as if "it's all fluff, and no progress is being made." It can be helpful to reflect on key routine events—faculty meetings, newsletters, daily bulletins and announcements, meetings with the staff—and consider in planning for these how you might balance task and relationship behaviors. For example, one principal plans faculty meetings with a principal's advisory committee made up of teachers. This allows him to sense the attitudes of the staff toward key issues on the agenda. The agenda is constructed with time allocations for each item. It is distributed to the staff ahead of time so that items might be added prior to the meeting. During the meeting, in between every few agenda items, drawings are held or joke swapping is conducted for a brief period of time. On items that require staff input, table group discussions occur and collective group summaries are shared. At the very end of the meeting, feedback is requested. In these ways, attention to both task and relationship behaviors is modeled.

One principal brainstormed a list of things she could do to balance attention to task—getting the job done—with relationship-oriented behavior—taking care of people. Elements of this list follow.

Task Orientation	*Relationship Orientation*
Begin meetings on time.	Allocate time for congenial activities.
End meetings on time.	Plan interactive activities during faculty meetings.
When you ask for behavior change or products, give concrete examples of what you expect.	Protect faculty members from verbal attack when ideas are discussed.
Request feedback on agenda construction and coverage at the end of meetings.	Ask for input regarding decisions to be made; schedule time for discussion.
Take written notes on requests and follow up.	Schedule time for faculty members to work together (sharing ideas, trading lessons, integrating curriculum, developing curriculum, teaching one another instructional approaches).
Assign time limitations to agenda items. If additional discussion time is needed, request time from the faculty or permission to continue the discussion at the next meeting.	
	Follow up staff development experiences with opportunities for staff members to share how they have applied recent learnings.

Differentiated Support

As well as balancing the task and relationship roles, effective human relations skills include sensitivity to the individual needs of personnel. For example, teachers new to the profession may need very directive support as they struggle and triumph in the early stages of their careers. This assistance may begin with a tour of the school and a review of basic policies and procedures, with time to ask questions. Additional support can be provided through a variety of sources: the principal, a group of teachers, a mentor or lead teacher, or a combination of approaches.

Support might include consultation, modeling, feedback, and opportunities to visit other teachers or to talk with trusted colleagues.

Successful experienced teachers, on the other hand, may prefer reflective listening and coaching as opposed to directive support. The provision of opportunities to work on professional growth topics with colleagues may be a stimulating aspect of the support provided to this type of individual. (Refer to Chapter 10, "Maximizing Feedback About Teaching: Differentiated Professional Growth Options," for an extensive discussion about collegial support.)

Mind Styles

A principal's human relations skills may be enhanced by considering the impact of a staff member's "mind style" (Gregorc, 1985). School leaders would benefit from examining the literature on style and applying the lessons appropriately. For example, Gregorc identifies four basic mind or learning styles that affect how individuals think, what they value, and how they behave. The four styles reveal preferences for ordering information and perceiving information. Ordering preferences range from sequential to random. Perception preferences range from concrete to abstract. Thus a principal who, because of style, relates and perceives in an organized, concrete manner may have difficulty communicating with a staff member who operates through a more abstract, random approach. (Providing a workshop on style can be a lively, informative, and enjoyable staff development activity.)

"Style" represents one tool to enhance relationships among staff members. Focusing on style as a staff will also impact classroom practices as teachers become more aware of how their styles influence the lessons they design and, consequently, student learning. In addition, success in human relations may result as a consequence of interpreting how individuals are affected by the context of a particular situation and acting appropriately.

Recommendations for Skillful Human Relations

Following are some commonsense suggestions that should be considered as principals work to help the staff and students reach their highest levels of performance. These recommendations emerged as a result of observing and talking with many principals.

1. *Project yourself as a person first, principal second.* Show your human side. Let the staff know that you are approachable and genuine. This helps colleagues feel that they too can be themselves. When you show your "rough edges," it gives people permission to show theirs, and authentic relationships have a chance to flourish. While the leader strives to do the right thing, mistakes happen. In a sense, the

leader is saying, "We are all humans, we make mistakes, and through our human-ness, we learn."

2. *Be consistent about what matters.* Consistency on the part of a leader is a great asset if the leader's words and actions are communicating the important values of the school. Furthermore, matching actions with words helps create credibility and provides the staff with a sense of security about what can be expected of the princi-pal. Also, trust builds when the staff knows what to expect—what can be pre-dicted—in the principal's actions.

3. *Never lose sight of the vision and your role in fostering the vision.* Maintaining a focus on the vision while working with teachers, students, and parents in the work-place allows one to stay on course and create positive attitudes and perceptions among others in the workplace. Focus on the people side while working on the vi-sion.

4. *Take time to look at people; smile, respond, and laugh.* Taking time to interact sincerely, with a smile or meaningful "hello," shows others that you care. More-over, the nonverbal gestures that you make, and respond to, really count. Your abil-ity to "read" nonverbals can make the difference in communicating effectively with a staff member. The message may not always be obvious, but it is still there to be re-ceived.

5. *Use active listening so people sense that you are really listening and that you do care.* Active listening demonstrates that you are hearing what is being communi-cated. People are more likely to be motivated when they feel heard and under-stood. In addition, active listening tells the speaker that his or her time is also important and that a full explanation is welcome and can benefit the principal's un-derstanding. Active listening usually includes asking clarifying questions to en-hance understanding as well as paraphrasing. Unfortunately, we often listen only to respond, to speak. This often communicates a message that what we have to say is more important than the contribution of another.

6. *Dignify people and take the high road.* When you look for the best in people and communicate by dignifying them, you can expect that the best will come back to you. Additionally, dignifying people includes taking the high road in all rela-tionships. If you embarrass or insult someone, it is difficult to build bridges, and you will likely regret your actions later. Dignifying people shows respect, which can foster trust, and trust is the most critical attribute in building a learning organization.

7. *Walk a mile in your colleague's moccasins.* Taking another person's perspec-tive often reveals insights that we would not otherwise be privy to. This gives us a greater appreciation of the other's needs, viewpoints, and, possibly, an inside view of what that person considers when making important decisions. This can provide a measure of empathy as well. The ability to empathize is one of our most sophisti-cated and valuable human characteristics. Also, appreciating another's point of view enhances our capacity to fine-tune communication because of greater under-

standing. As the world and school become more global in their constituency bases, taking time for individuals to share the unique perspectives afforded by their cultures or experiences enriches understanding and adds a valuable asset to the organization.

8. *Respect, nurture, and celebrate diversity of ideas and people. Diversity brings richness to a school.* Encouraging and nurturing the diverse ideas of individuals can tap a new level of creativity that enables the staff to collectively face challenges. Diversity reflected in different ideas and cultural perspectives can enable the leader to see with many different eyes. This enhances one's overall perspective. Moreover, the person who might not share the leader's viewpoint, or the viewpoint of the majority, may be offering an important idea or thought that has been overlooked.

9. *360° Feedback.* One practice that capitalizes on the value of diverse perspectives is called full-circle evaluation or 360° feedback (Dyer, 2001). This process involves soliciting feedback from multiple and diverse sources so that the leaders can gather data about their performance from those who interact with the leader. Examples of data sources might include teachers, parents, students, classified staff, central office personnel, and community members.

10. *Be accessible, open, and supportive.* People have a need to connect with one another, especially during the change process when many people feel lost, needy, incompetent, vulnerable, and out of control. Be there for them. Support can help individuals make the transition from old to new practices. Support entails listening, problem solving, reflecting, clarifying, and helping people develop workable solutions. Support may also mean spending time with people when tragedy or medical emergencies occur. One's physical presence at difficult times is deeply valued. Research in intensive care units has shown that the comforting presence of another person not only lowers the patient's blood pressure but also slows secretion of fatty acids that block arteries (Goleman, Boyatzis, & McKee, 2002). Thus, one's presence not only provides emotional comfort but also has the impact of changing a physiological state!

11. *Take time to smell—and water—the roses.* One superintendent took 5 minutes to play catch with a lonely boy, and 2 months later learned it meant a great deal to the student. A principal walked into a small class of students receiving special assistance and asked a boy, "Jonathan, how are you doing?" Later, the principal was told that after he left, the child smiled at the teacher and said, "Wow, the principal knows my name!" Remember that in small ways we can make a big difference in people's lives. Portraying interest in student or staff member's work, for example, can be invigorating to the principal as well as the recipient. It communicates care.

The following Chinese characters for *ear, eyes, you, undivided attention,* and *heart,* when combined, make up the verb *to listen* and remind us of critical compo-

Figure 4.1

nents necessary for effective human relations. You may want to post this symbol near your desk, or near a table around which you frequently hold conferences.

The Role of Emotions in the Organization

Experience tells us that when organizational members perceive that they are genuinely valued as people, and feel recognized for their efforts, and are important because of the contribution they are making, climate is enhanced and productivity soars. Indeed, leaders have a profound role in affecting the emotions of individuals within the workplace, their commitment to work, school, climate, and, ultimately, productivity!

All of us, at one time or another in our lives, have been inspired by a great leader who brought out the best in us. Daniel Goleman, and his colleagues Richard Boyatzis and Annie McKee, in *Primal Leadership* (2002), suggest that "Great leadership works through emotions." These authors go on to say that "the best leaders have found effective ways to understand and improve the way they handle their own and other people's emotions. Understanding the powerful role of emotions in the workplace sets the best leaders apart from the rest—not just in tangibles such as better business results and the retention of talent, but also in the all-important intangibles, such as higher morale, motivation and commitment" (Goleman, Boyatzis, & McKee, 2002, pp. 4-5).

The leader who is skillful in human relations has the power to influence organizational members' emotions in a variety of ways. Goleman and his colleagues suggest that the leader acts as a "group's emotional guide." The leader's behavior literally influences whether staff members' emotions will be driven in a positive or negative direction. Staff will look to the leader for guidance, especially during times of crisis. In times of tragedy, they will look to the leader for emotional support. Goleman et al. explain that "we rely on connections with other people for our own emotional stability" (p. 6) and that "other people can change our very physiology." Citing research that documents this statement, they explain, "one person transmits signals that can alter hormone levels, cardiovascular function, sleep rhythms and even immune function inside the body of another" (Lewis, Amini, & Lannon, 2000). Reflecting on this research, a principal noted, "So that's why when negative information is churned out through the rumor mill people often complain of losing sleep and feeling grumpy! And, conversely, that's why when I give positive feedback to staff about their efforts with students that they seem to get all pumped up." Indeed, researchers have found that human beings tend to "mirror" the emotional states of one another—positive or negative—when they are together. For example, people who are in rapport during a conversation often even mirror one another's body language!

Using Emotions Intelligently

How skillfully and successfully a leader models human relations skills largely depends on his or her *Emotional Intelligence.* Goleman (1995) defines Emotional Intelligence as "a basic flair for living—being able to rein in emotional impulse; to read another's innermost feelings; to handle relationships smoothly." He identifies four dimensions of Emotional Intelligence (Goleman, Boyatzis, & McKee, 2002), and divides these into two areas. The first area has to do with personal competence—how we manage ourselves, and the second area has to do with social competence—managing relations with others. The personal competence component includes *Self Awareness* and involves knowing one's own emotions, and understanding their impact on others. It also means knowing one's strengths and limitations—and having a sense of one's self-worth. *Self Management* involves emotional self-control, being trustworthy, and having the capacity to be flexible when need presents itself. Having an internal performance drive, the capacity to take the initiative, and spirit of optimism are also competencies related to self-management.

The *Social Competence* areas include social awareness and relationship management. *Social Awareness* involves empathy for individuals and the organization, organizational awareness and a service commitment to recognizing and meeting follower or client needs. *Relationship Management* includes inspirational leadership, the kind that involves guiding and motivating others with a compelling vision. It also refers to the ability to influence others, which usually means possessing a wide range of strategies for persuasion. Another key area of relationship management is the capacity to develop others through feedback and guidance. The person who manages relationships well often functions as a change catalyst and is skilled in conflict management, building bonds with individuals and fostering teamwork and collaboration (p. 39).

Being aware of the dimensions of Emotional Intelligence and striving to model them as well as reflect upon them during and after daily interactions will enhance one's relationships with staff members, central office personnel, professional colleagues, parents, community members, and one's own family. These competencies will also inform actions that will contribute to the well being and productivity of the organization. When people feel good about their working relationships with others, they will be able to focus on the centerpiece of school activity: making a difference for students.

Reflections

This space provides for you a place to write in ideas that have been generated by this chapter, things you want to try, or adaptations of ideas presented herein.

1. What other "Recommendations for Skillful Human Relations" would you add to the list?

2. List things you do that have a task focus. Then, make a list of things you do that have a relationship focus. Examine the lists to determine which one is longer. Why do you think this is the case? State what you do to simultaneously "get the job done" and "take care of people."

3. Reflecting upon the four Dimensions of Emotional Intelligence, what are your areas of personal strength? What are areas you'd like to strengthen?

4. What insights or new questions do you have as a result of reflecting on the ideas presented in this chapter?

5

Managing Time

What you pay attention to, and spend time on, communicates what you value.

KENT PETERSON (personal communication, July, 1991)

Time is the one resource we all share. However, what we choose to do within the time we have, how we actually spend our time, differs widely across individuals. No one actually "manages time." However, we can manage our use of time by clearly identifying our personal and professional goals and scheduling our time to reflect that. Easier said than done! In a study of time use among new principals, a major discrepancy was apparent between the actual and desired time that principals wanted to spend in the areas of curriculum and instruction. These principals were very dissatisfied with the amount of time they were able to spend on curriculum and instruction versus such items as pupil problems and facility management (Alvy, 1983).

Brevity, Fragmentation, and Variety

Part of the difficulty associated with the principal's efficient use of time lies in the characteristics of principals' work lives. Peterson (1982), in a study of principals' work, noted three attributes of their work lives: brevity, fragmentation, and variety (Mintzberg, 1973). For example, related to brevity, he found that 85% of the principals' tasks lasted 9 minutes or less. Often there was a sense of fragmentation related to the work because frequently the principal was interrupted by forces over which she or he had no control, and often these interruptions were unexpected. Furthermore, in examining the nature of the tasks, there was tremendous variety. This variety demanded a wide range of emotions and technical skills, some for which the administrator had no previous experience or preparation.

Together these attributes of principals' work, from one perspective, make the planned work very difficult to get done. But from another perspective, the brevity, fragmentation, and variety present an opportunity to work effectively. As an example, when taking your morning walk through classrooms (an important professional goal), you may be interrupted by a parent who is picking up makeup work for a sick child. This brief encounter presents the principal with an opportunity to express concern for the child and share the purpose of the morning walk through classrooms. This simultaneously communicates the principal's interest in students and the school's commitment to instructional excellence. As you continue your walking, you collect information about the school culture and the climate of individual classrooms. So, in a sense, the brevity, fragmentation, and variety often allow you to do two or more things at once.

Time Study Strategy

Due to these attributes of the principal's work life, principals must work hard to take control of their use of time, or circumstances will control them. The first step to the effective management of the use of time is to decide what is important professionally and personally through a time study. (Additional time management suggestions may be found in Chapter 17.) For example, professional items of importance might include spending time in classrooms, in the halls, and on the playground; giving feedback; developing and conducting professional growth activities; and professional reading. Personal items of importance might include time with family, time for tennis, jogging, golf, or basketball, and time to weave, knit, putter, or read. After the lists of important things are made, think about other "mundane tasks" that you may not value but are required of you given your role. Create a list of these. Although these may seem mundane, ignoring them can lead to potential problems. For instance, this list might include reviewing student attendance records or fire drill procedures, or inspecting buses for possible safety hazards.

Then create three to four personal and three to four professional goals. Think about the activities associated with each. For instance, activities associated with a goal of spending quality family time might include a family game night, going to dinner, having discussions, reading together, or building something.

After your goals are developed, put them aside temporarily, and conduct a study of your use of time. Do this for 2 weeks. You may choose to do this reflectively, at the end of each day, or as you move from task to task. Some principals have used a minicassette recorder because it seemed easier than writing down each task. Another option is to look back at your calendar for the previous month. Note how you spent time. When your time study is complete, review your use of time against your goals. Try highlighting, with a marker, those events, tasks, or activities that relate to your goals. Looking for a match in this way will help you determine if you are spending time in accordance with your priorities. Now take out your list of "mundane tasks." How much time are you spending on these tasks? Carefully analyzing your use of time in this way will help you determine what you want to do more of and what you want to do less of.

Techniques for Time Management

One principal remarked, "It is important to take control of one's schedule. That means long-range scheduling. If you think something is important—like visiting classrooms—build it into your schedule. That's the only way it will happen. Take care of yourself, and don't shortchange yourself on personal goals. I know that may seem selfish, but if your personal life is 'together,' it will help your professional life."

Another principal remarked, regarding scheduling time, "If you don't build what's important to you into the schedule, it will never get done . . . because unimportant events always are there to fill the void. Everyone wants a piece of the principal's time, but if the slices are too small, then you can't taste the accomplishments!"

Many time management consultants have developed models to help us reflect on which responsibilities/tasks are essential and nonessential and to determine which tasks should receive our immediate attention and yet often wait on the back burner (see, e.g., Covey, 1989). Unfortunately, important activities such as long-range planning, building relationships, reflection, and self-renewal often receive little or no attention because of responsibilities that press one's time. To illustrate further, daily interruptions that are difficult to avoid (e.g., telephone calls, drop-in sales visits, some administrative meetings) frequently overshadow essential responsibilities to the organization and oneself (e.g., visiting students on the field or in the classroom, talking with teachers, or reading a professional journal).

Managing Bifocally

One way to use interruptions as leverage points to get more done is to manage bifocally. Kent Peterson, noted researcher on principal's worklives, suggests that bifocal leadership and management actions can actually help a principal accomplish two things at once. Here is how it works. Suppose you are working with a school improvement team on a budget committee. At the same time you are working on the budget, you may seize the moment to educate the committee about the reading program in the school—one of the budget line items. Or suppose you receive a phone call from an angry parent. Use the call as an opportunity to build positive bridges between the school and this parent, collaboratively problem solve, and gather data about how this segment of the parent population views the school. This approach uses the call as a leverage point for changing the perception of the principal and the school from a negative to a positive one. Another way to manage time with insight involves the use of a pocket planner. The box that follows outlines how this process works.

Managing Time With Insight:
The Pocket Planner

The "pocket planner" can be used so that the barrage of demands become leverage points for accomplishing tasks.

One may use 3 x 5 index cards or a personal digital assistant for pocket planners.

How They Work

1. To track progress towards realizing the vision:
   • Post the school's vision.
   • Identify key goals.
   • Anytime you are out and about; receive a phone call; interview a student, parent, teacher, community member; observe student work; etc., that relates to the vision, jot down the date, the event, and your perceptions regarding how it relates to accomplishing the vision.
   • When it comes time for report writing, take out the data you've recorded and examine it.

2. As a management tool:
   • Anytime you see something that needs to be done, jot it down on a 3 x 5 card.
   • Decide whether you need to delegate the task to someone or do the task yourself.
   • For those cards with tasks not delegated, carry them with you. When you have a few extra minutes, take out the card pack, select one that is doable, given your time. You'll be surprised how you can use fragmentation to your advantage.

3. For keeping track of supervisory visits, with a goal of distributing one's proximity across staff members, gaining a sense of classroom work, increasing story telling capacity and building schoolwide norms of practice:
   • List staff member's names down the left side of an index card or screen.
   • Write the months across the top—3 or 4 to a card.
   • Every time you visit a staff member, jot down the date, time, and what you did during your visit. (e.g., IS—interviewed a student, ESW—examined student work, LN—left a note, TOT—conducted a time off task scan, WT—walk through visit)
   • Every time you have a few minutes—perhaps due to a canceled appointment—take out your pocket planner and visit someone you have not seen in action this month.

Many principals have pointed to the importance of reflecting about the effectiveness of daily work routines to determine whether they actually help get things done in a time-efficient way or if their use tends to inhibit creative abilities. By abandoning or altering a routine, a principal will be presented with an opportunity to approach a familiar task in a new way and in doing so, possibly become more productive.

All of us probably have recognized that our performance tends to peak at certain times during the day. Some refer to themselves as "morning people." Others jokingly remark, "Don't even ask me to think before 10:00 a.m.!" There is a note of seriousness in all this talk. Sensitivity to one's most creative or best "thinking" time can help you schedule those tasks that require the greatest concentration at times when your performance is optimal. Of course, this will not always be possible. To support your plan for the effective use of time, communicate your priorities and philosophy to the secretary and the staff. This can enable them to assist and support you in sheltering peak performance time as well as provide a model for them. It might be appropriate to provide examples of how you would like the secretary to respond (e.g., Mr. Smith is visiting classrooms now, may I schedule an appointment or have him call you back?).

Furthermore, principals must be sensitive to the demands of the day, week, or year that constrain the time of others in the organization. When scheduling personal appointments and all-school activities, principals need to consider how time can be most effectively used to acknowledge the important role that others play in the organization and to send the message that time does not "revolve" around the principal. For example, personally asking a teacher about the best time to schedule a professional appointment, or directing the secretary to do the same, can go a long way in setting the proper tone for the appointment. In one school, no faculty meetings are held on Friday at the request of teachers, so they can take care of pressing professional needs before the weekend.

One final thought: When your behavior aligns with your values and beliefs, you will feel comfortable with yourself, your colleagues, and your environment. Professionally, you will feel better about your day because you will know that you have made every minute count.

Reflections

This space provides for you a place to write in ideas that have been generated by this chapter, things you want to try, or adaptations of ideas presented herein.

1. Think about your goals. Conduct a time study.
2. Is your use of time aligned with your goals? Are any changes necessary?
3. When are your peak performance times? What do you usually do during these times?

4. What are some effective use-of-time strategies that you can implement on the job?

5. Would you read a professional journal article during the school day? (Why or why not?)

6. Who needs to be aware of your goals in relation to time? How will you let them know?

7. How might you use the pocket planner?

8. What insights or new questions do you have as a result of reflecting on the ideas presented in this chapter?

6

Effectively Working With the Central Office: Forging Success Through Cooperation

What I learned is that it's easier to ask for forgiveness than for permission.

A PRINCIPAL'S VOICE

Schools do not operate in isolation but as part of a school district with a broad philosophy and set of goals and values emanating from the central office (Gorton, 1980). Reality tells us that a strong relationship between the school and the central office is necessary to implement any major change over a sustained period. It is not enough for a school to desire the change even if all the key human resources are in place at the school site. Funding and resources must be available and the central office can supply both. At a minimum, successful change will necessitate the availability of the following elements: inservice training, funding, and instructional resources for students and teachers. In fact, Fullan and Stiegelbauer (1991) have noted that "individual schools can become highly innovative for a short period of time without the district, but they cannot stay innovative without district action to establish the conditions for continuous and long term improvement" (p. 209).

Caught in the Middle

Principals often find themselves caught in the middle between staff and the central office. There is a need to follow district guidelines, policies, procedures, and time lines while accomplishing the business of the school. This often involves sheltering teachers from outside interferences. A first step for a principal to help teachers then, is to find out how the district is structured or governed so the principal can represent the needs of the school. And secondly, Schlechty (2001) reminds principals, "Learn to see yourself as a member of the district-level team as well as the head of your own team at the building level. Recognize that your school is not the only system you need to consider; it is part of a larger system. Other schools and other principals are not—or should not be—your competition" (pp. 213-214).

How Is the School District Governed?

Understanding governance can considerably enhance a principal's work life. Initially, principals must recognize that the relationship between a school and the central office will depend to a great extent on the structure of governance and size of the district. Developing effective strategies to work with the central office will depend on understanding how the district works. Concerning governance, there are many traditional and experimental decision-making models. For example, in one school district, the school may be largely autonomous with control of the purse strings in the hands of a site-based counsel that includes a principal, parents, teachers, and community members. Another district may still make critical decisions in the central office with little input from the school site. What about the role of the elected school board? In most districts, school board members see their roles as supporting and fine-tuning the broad policies of the district. Yet in other districts, board members are involved in the nuts-and-bolts activities of the central office and individual schools.

Communication Between
the School and the Central Office

Although gaining an understanding of the governance structure is important, a lot will depend on the personnel in the central office and the school and their mutual ability to communicate with each other. Communication should be a two-way street, and the school principal can be the key to orchestrating an effective relationship with the central office. Certainly, the central office views the principal as the primary contact person. Thus, from a practical viewpoint, it is easiest for a district office to say, "We need to get in touch with the Carver School; let's call the principal, Ms. Breyer." But the principal should not expect that it is the job of central office personnel always to initiate the contact. The principal's attitude must be, "It is my job to communicate proactively with the central office." Otherwise, the principal may hear from the central office only when something is wrong or when they have a new idea to be implemented without school input.

How can principals effectively initiate contact with the central office? Traditionally, central office personnel do not spend as much time in schools as they would like. Principals need to build occasions into the school calendar to bring central office personnel and school board members into schools. Invite them to major programs, and let them know when Senior Projects, Invention Week, or the Science Exhibition is taking place, or when the middle school is performing a play. Send them the dates of important events well in advance. Acknowledge their presence when they attend these events. Bring students to the central office to perform and to share their reports or math investigations. Bring or send videos to the central office so they see the kinds of activities taking place in the school.

Also, principals need to keep communication lines open concerning key district meetings and new ideas that are developing. They should either ask to attend the meetings themselves or have a school representative attend who has both expertise and practical knowledge in the area. Furthermore, if a principal brings an important idea to a central office meeting, he or she will obviously have much more clout at the meeting if the idea emanated from, and has the support of, teachers.

Communication also depends on knowing how the informal organization works (e.g., how things really get done). Fair or unfair, the image of a central office is often one of a bureaucracy that moves slowly and is dominated by red tape. How does one cut the time and red tape necessary to communicate an idea or jump-start a potentially rich innovation? As in other areas, school principals need to find out Whom should you really speak with? Who are the power brokers in the central office? and Who "hangs together"? The idea is not to "beat the system" but rather to institute effective programs for kids and teachers as quickly as possible. Getting in touch with veteran principals or others who have worked in the school district for a long time can be the best way to find out how the informal organization operates.

Fortunately, many central office personnel are working hard to change the traditional bureaucratic image. Leaders are viewing the central office as "service centers" to improve student achievement and support teachers, principals, and parents. Schlechty (2001) advises central office personnel to remember that their "most important job is to create and manage systems that will enable principals and teachers to concentrate on the core business of schools, the creation of intellectual activity that students find engaging and from which they learn. Only secondarily, if at all, should you [central office personnel] see yourself as a supervisor" (p. 212). The central office in Long Beach, California, has tried to cut the red tape by streamlining the process for employing qualified teacher applicants. The school district tries to complete applicant physical examinations, finger printing, and paper work in one day—and in one building. Their rationale for consolidating the process is simple, "If someone has a bad experience when they come in here, we may lose a good teacher" (Johnston, 2001, p. 18).

School leaders must develop ways to slow down or eliminate an idea from the central office that may offer little prospect for student success. Deal and Peterson (1994), in their book *The Leadership Paradox*, talk about the "bifocal principal" who needs to follow the "central office directives (yet) be creatively insubordinate" (p. 49). Also, principals should recognize that central office personnel are doing the same thing. The art of politely resisting an idea and hoping that it will go away is practiced on many fronts. This jockeying on the part of the school and the central office can be frustrating but also helpful, as it keeps both sides on their toes.

It is important to build a relationship of mutual trust in which successes and failures are shared. Acknowledging failures may sound a little dangerous, but the alternative is to worry always about hiding mistakes. That makes for an unhealthy relationship. Additionally, principals are bombarded constantly with new ideas and innovations. Developing a strong relationship based on trust is critical to responding honestly when an idea emerges. If a principal is unable to express skepticism or a lack of knowledge about an innovation (e.g., What is data-driven decision making anyway?), it can be a very long, uncomfortable, and superficial relationship.

Finally, when the central office does bring in a new idea of worth, or provides the support for a school-generated idea that is implemented successfully, it is the responsibility of the school leader to acknowledge the role played by the central office. The central office needs to know that they are valued by the school site and that they play an important role. Their efforts deserve to be validated. Central office personnel may not verbalize the idea, but they too often feel distant from a school. As one assistant superintendent noted, "How many articles and headlines have you read about central office leaders? I suspect you've read very few" (Grove, 2002, p. 45). When a school reaches out and recognizes the role of the central office, that act can greatly reduce the distance. So, invite central office personnel to the key ceremonies that celebrate an innovation. They will remember this. The next time an idea develops from a school in which a warm and effective relationship has been forged, implementation of a change just may come a little easier.

Management Tips for
Working With the Central Office

Based on the preceding ideas, the following tips gleaned from successful principals can be helpful in working with the central office:

1. *Request a district-level activities calendar* with key events identified by the district several months before a new school year begins. Post the appropriate dates in your office, on your calendar, and in the staff room. Ask the secretary to place the dates on her or his calendar. Color code events and dates that will affect the school. Keep these in mind when planning school-level events. One principal developed such a time line of events on butcher paper sheets in the staff room. Another used a software calendar program so new information could be added and the data used for planning.

2. *Get a hanging file box for your desk.* Establish folders for district-level projects and events by date. As you collect information or ideas for these, simply drop them in the appropriate file.

3. *Plan ahead to participate in district projects, but expect surprises.* One has to assume that emergencies and unexpected events will pop up and drain energy away from planned efforts. Although one should plan ahead, the plan will not be foolproof. The principalship is filled with unanticipated events. When you are unable to attend a meeting, ask the assistant principal or an appropriate faculty member to attend in your place.

4. *Keep the district informed.* Many principals send weekly memos containing information about activities at the school, illustrated with student writing samples

or art work, to the central office. Send copies of communications that the central office may ultimately need.

5. *Invite central office personnel* to celebrations, assemblies, class activities, and other rituals of the school (as discussed earlier in the chapter).

6. *Read memos from the district carefully,* using highlighters. Save them in a binder for 1 to 2 years. You never know when you will need them again! Share appropriate memos with building grade-level or department teams, or in the newsletter or bulletin.

7. *Make presentations to the board of education* to keep them informed about school-level activities. Use students, when appropriate, during presentations (if this concept is valued! In some systems, it may not be).

8. When the central office makes curriculum decisions that affect the local school, *try to ensure that school-level personnel have representation on the district committees.*

Managing in these ways affords the principal an opportunity to stay visible and keenly aware of what is taking place in the school, the district, and the community. This ability to "keep a finger on the pulse of the organization" is a key skill of the effective manager. In addition, these management actions and interactions will provide the school with significant information to make effective decisions. Leadership decisions will more likely be sound, and the leadership will feel more confident in making them when they are based on information gathered while "out and about," managing the school.

Management and Restructuring

Recognizing that the needs of individual schools vary, many districts are restructuring. The implications of this are profound. For instance, financial and management functions are being delegated to individual schools.

The restructuring movement has produced an increased need for training to enable school-level personnel to effectively take on the management function at the local site. A related consequence of more individuals being involved in site-level decisions and management is the impact on the school principal of delegating. Some principals are quite comfortable with delegation; others are not. For some, the notion of taking ultimate responsibility for decisions and/or growing up with models of "principal-in-charge" make the concept of sharing leadership and management tasks difficult to embrace emotionally or philosophically. In Maine, many staffs and principals have found it useful to generate lists of leadership and management decisions to be made. After each item, a notation is made indicating which parties might be involved in that particular decision and what type of input they might have (e.g., be consulted, provide input, make the decision). In this way, a principal can reserve for himself or herself those decisions that would be uncomfortable to share with others. Interestingly enough, many staffs that have taken on shared management and leadership responsibilities report taking these so seriously that they have revisited a decision three to four times before acting on it. Whether management is shared or not, keeping a simple log of the decisions that are made can be helpful for future reference.

Maintaining a Strong Relationship Between the Central Office and the School

The tug-of-war between the school site and central office is not new. Although it remains to be seen whether the movement toward greater local school autonomy will improve the quality of education for students, it does make sense that those closest to the client often have the most relevant data on which to base decisions. However, thinking about the relationship should remind us that the central office and the school need each other. As noted earlier, the central office can provide numerous resources to a school. The resources can include disseminating important information concerning state standards, frameworks, or benchmarks and sharing achievement data with the schools; helping with the hiring of administrators, teachers, and support staff; and setting policy for the district and schools, including how site-based management should be implemented.

To serve schools and teachers, the central office personnel of the Arlington, Virginia, public school system take responsibility for assisting new teachers and teachers having difficulties, developing and implementing grants, meeting with citizen committees, organizing student art exhibitions and science fairs, conducting the textbook adoption and ordering process, and designing and conducting staff development (Grove, 2002). Furthermore, school districts can serve to link the ideas of the various schools—to keep the schools in touch with one another, very similar to the role played by those organizing a consortium. And the school site can offer the district answers to questions about what is working and what is not. The school site is, of course, the laboratory in which important decisions can be judged as being on the right track or needing further work. We often lament in education the fragmentation of the curriculum and the need to integrate more. The same point can be made regarding schools in a district. Too much fragmentation of information among schools within a district can easily lead to the weakening of human relationships and resource sharing so necessary in a learning community.

Reflections

This space provides for you a place to write in ideas that have been generated by this chapter, things you want to try, or adaptations of ideas presented herein.

1. How is your school district governed? What are the organizational and individual sources of influence that need to be addressed to implement change?

2. How would you characterize your school's relationship with the central office? What are some strengths and weaknesses? Are there particular things you would like to change?

3. What are your views on site-based management? Central office "dominance"? State "dominance"? Federal "dominance"?

4. What insights or new questions do you have as a result of reflecting on the ideas presented in this chapter?

PART III

HONORING THE SCHOOL'S MISSION

7

Understanding, Planning, and Implementing Change

We rarely recognize that changes in the nature of work also create losses that trigger powerful individual or collective reactions. The costs may not be immediately obvious nor reflected directly in tangible ways, but left unattended over time, pressure builds up and can become a silent killer in organizations—much like hypertension in the human body. The unresolved loss of title or office can cause personal maladjustments, such as depression or excessive drinking; the substitution of a computerized system for manual procedures can create uncertainty, confusion, and a loss of identity. Wholesale changes in an organization can dramatically affect overall morale, productivity, and turnover. Most often, however, we fail to link these effects to the real cause. We attribute the blame to personal or other intangible sources, rather than to changes in the work setting.

DEAL (1985, pp. 293-294)

Change Brings Loss and Resistance

The downside of change so eloquently described by Terry Deal is often neglected when we present teachers with ideas that "must" be implemented. Yet one's individual enthusiasm for the change may be quite tempered by the experiences of other faculty. Staff experiencing change may feel loss and insecurity and show resistance and confrontation. In fact, these behaviors should occur. Resistance, in particular, should be expected and can be very helpful in straightening out the change process and improving the process. Resistance will bring questioning and the need to examine the direction of the changes being implemented. In the end, if real change is to occur, organizational members must feel that the change has been effective and meaningful for them.

Influencing Individuals and the Institution

It is critical that we go about change in a way that shows sensitivity to individuals affected by change and the institution that is transformed as a result of change.

Thus the purpose of this chapter is to review significant aspects of change from an individual and organizational perspective to enhance the prospects for successful change to occur. The ideas discussed offer the best of what we know from research and practice to equip practitioners with basic information to develop thoughtful plans of action.

Initially and throughout the process, it is important to view change simultaneously from both an individual and institutional perspective. That is, it is important to see the trees and forest at the same time. Change takes place one individual at a time but, if effective, positively affects the whole organization.

With this view in mind, this chapter will begin by providing ideas to create a trusting environment—the first necessary step to implement effective change. The chapter will then examine basic assumptions about the change process, review research-based stages that an institution should go through when implementing change, provide a meaningful framework to build individual support for change, and discuss levels of concern that individuals may experience when implementing change.

Principals should recognize the tremendous role they can play as change facilitators or obstructors. "Throughout our years of research and experience, we have never seen a situation in which the principal was not a significant factor in the efforts of schools to improve" (Hall & Hord, 1987, p. 1). Principals can contribute to educational change as they are acutely involved in the culture and structure of the school (Fullan & Stiegelbauer, 1991). For example, principals can make or break a school's effort to foster collaborative decision making or engage in a schoolwide professional development activity. A principal's willingness to listen and set up collaborative teams during faculty and parent meetings indicates a desire to share decisions and engage in change. Furthermore, if teachers indicate an interest in a professional development activity, such as peer coaching, the principal sends a clear message of support or opposition by how he or she responds to the initial idea and facilitates or obstructs the project. In both subtle ways—such as where an item is placed on an agenda—and grand, explicit ways, a principal's actions influence change. Also, Fullan and Stiegelbauer (1991) remind us that change and progress do not always go hand in hand. In fact, rejecting change may be a bolder move for a school principal than pursuing what appears to be a "quick fix" solution.

Building Trust for Successful Change

Because change is holistic, every aspect of the organizational system has the potential to be affected. This underscores the importance of systemic thinking, that is, that changes in one part of the system have an impact on others. For instance, new graduation requirements or longer class periods may have profound effects on curriculum and teaching practices. Principals have a key role in preparing an environment where potential change initiatives can be rigorously examined by all staff members and, if appropriate, implemented.

One major factor in creating an environment for change is building a climate of trust where risk taking and experimentation can occur. This is easier said than done, especially in cases where previously the norms in the building emphasized "playing it safe." Nonetheless, because change involves new ideas, new behaviors, new materials, and new ways of operating, people need a safe environment to feel comfortable embarking on a change journey. When implementing new ways of doing things, an individual's performance often gets worse before it gets better. We all have experienced this when learning a new move in a familiar sport, for example. Fullan and Miles (1992) describe this experience as the implementation dip: "Even in cases where reform eventually succeeds, things often go wrong before they go right" (p. 749). Therefore, trust—between individuals and within the culture of the school—is an essential ingredient in the change process.

In many change efforts, because the innovation required new forms of working relationships (e.g., site-based management, interdisciplinary units) among individuals, there has been so much of a focus on building relationships versus focusing on a specific end, such as achievement, that performance actually decreased initially (Robbins, 1991a).

Conflict Can Contribute to Positive Change

The environment must permit individuals to take risks and express different points of view. At Ford Motor Company, employees often comment, "Failure is the opportunity to begin again more intelligently." Hence failure becomes a source of knowledge. In the same way that failure comes to be viewed positively, the emergence of conflicting viewpoints often associated with a change effort can be positive as well. When different points of view are voiced, conflict often emerges along with lots of energy. This can actually fuel a positive change effort if it is harnessed to provide a function rather than be swept under the carpet or viewed as a negative. The function conflict provides is raising an awareness of some aspect of the change that had not been considered before. This may have an important influence on implementation of an innovation. In one school's change effort to move to grade-level teams, staff members had not considered the impact of teaming on specialists' positions. Conflict provided a source of knowledge that revealed a blind spot in the planning for teams. An important quality of the expression of conflicting viewpoints is that there needs to be an orientation toward resolution rather than merely expressing a gripe. Conflicting ideas should be welcomed as providing valuable sources of information and insight to assist in planning for change or enhancing a change effort once it is begun. It has been said that if a change is "deep enough," it should be accompanied by conflict because it upsets the status quo.

Finally, another reason to accept conflict is that it brings differences of opinion out in the open. More damage is done when saboteurs operate beneath the surface through covert interactions to obstruct change efforts. This approach uses the unofficial or informal communication network in the school—the system through which information travels faster than the speed of any written memo (and holds more credibility!).

Strategies to Promote Trust

Because risk taking, experimentation, and voicing conflicting opinions are essential ingredients for change and because they thrive in a safe, trusting environment, attending to how to create such an atmosphere for change is an important first step. Yet this step can bring good or bad news. The bad news is that there is no recipe for successful change. However, that is also good news because it provides the opportunity to create a plan of action tailored to one's school. How change and trust building will be addressed at a school site depends on such issues as a school's history, staff turnover, relationships among staff members, schedules and logistics, and degree of community support.

The following menu of options can help build trust:

1. *"Walk your talk."* When one's words and actions are consistently aligned, credibility will usually follow. When one is credible, it is easier to believe in that person as a leader.

2. *Lead by personal example.* Leading by personal example provides an impetus for others to follow. To illustrate, when one demonstrates trust in others, trusting behaviors become an essential thread to build relationships in which one can feel the confidence and trust extended by the school leader.

3. *Encourage people to talk about what it means to be trustworthy.* A simple activity that one can conduct at a faculty meeting is to ask individual staff members to list 10 behaviors that contribute to one being perceived as trustworthy. Then groups of staff members get together, share their individual lists, and come to consensus regarding their top three items. Groups then report their top three. The important attribute of this activity is that people have spent time talking about what contributes to trust. How you spend time communicates what you value.

4. *Invite staff members to have input into collectively determining what the change will be and how it will be implemented.* Adults have a rich reservoir of experiences that begs to be tapped. Moreover, adults like to have a sense of control over what happens to them. Collective involvement about desired change and strategies for implementation can lend a sense of comfort, ownership, and security to those who will be directly affected by the change.

5. *Encourage consensus-building activities.* Consensus building enhances trust and facilitates change in that it provides opportunities for individuals to shape what happens at a site as a consequence of sharing individual viewpoints, facts, and opinions. A critical consensus-building question is, Can you live with it?

6. *Keep lines of communication open.* This helps to dispel rumors and encourages dialogue and healthy interaction to engender mutual support. It also provides a fo-

rum for people to discuss the fears that often accompany change. People fear the unknown, losing jobs, and losing the familiar.

7. *Encourage disagreement.* Resistance usually stems from one's fear of being vulnerable or powerless. Information provided through resistance helps the facilitator of change realize what will help people feel less vulnerable and more in control. Hence change can be approached more graciously when such factors are considered.

8. *Celebrate small and large successes.* People have a need to be acknowledged. This builds morale, recognizes individual deeds that contribute to organizational growth and accomplishments, and propels change. Be consistent with acknowledgment.

Assumptions About Change

Creating a culture of trust is a prerequisite to implementing change. However, before examining the institutional and individual dimensions of change, it is important to review general assumptions that one should understand to maintain a perspective on change. Fullan and Stiegelbauer (1991) note several important assumptions about change.

1. Do not assume that your version of what the change should be is the one that should or could be implemented.

2. Assume that any significant innovation, if it is to result in change, requires individual implementors to work out their own meaning. Significant change involves a certain amount of ambiguity, ambivalence, and uncertainty for the individual about the meaning of the change.

3. Assume that conflict and disagreement are not only inevitable but fundamental to successful change. Because any group of people possesses multiple realities, any collective change attempt will necessarily involve conflict.

4. Assume that people need pressure to change (even in directions that they desire), but it will be effective only under conditions that allow them to react, form their own position, interact with other implementors, obtain technical assistance, and so on. Unless people are going to be replaced with others who have different desired characteristics, relearning is at the heart of change.

5. Assume that effective change takes time. Expect significant change to take a minimum of 2 or 3 years.

6. Do not assume that the reason for lack of implementation is outright rejection of the values embodied in the change, or hard-core resistance to all change. Assume that there are a number of possible reasons: value rejection, inadequate resources, or insufficient time elapsed.

7. Do not expect all or even most people or groups to change. The complexity of change is such that it is impossible to bring about widespread reform in any large social system. Progress occurs when we take steps that *increase* the number of people affected.

8. Assume that you will need a *plan* that is based on the above assumptions and that addresses the factors known to affect implementation. Knowledge of the change process is essential.

9. Assume that no amount of knowledge will ever make it totally clear what action should be taken. Action decisions are a combination of valid knowledge, political considerations, on-the-spot decisions, and intuition.

10. Assume that change is a frustrating, discouraging business. (pp. 105-107)

Finally, when one is intimately involved in a change effort, it is often easy to lose heart. Keeping these assumptions in mind helps us to remember that change is not neat, but rather messy, most of the time. Yet change is inevitable and a vital part of organizational and personal growth.

Three Phases of Change

In an ideal state, one would collaboratively plan prior to implementing change and consider the following question: Is the change consistent with the vision and mission of the school? Careful attention should be given to diagnosing needs, generating commitment, and developing an action plan prior to implementing change. One principal shared: "I know that you can't walk in and change everything in one year. I found that out the hard way. You have to walk in and look things over critically and find out what your priorities are" (A Principal's Voice). Another, commenting on how much time the planning process took, said, "You just have to face the fact, as frustrating as it might be, that sometimes you have to go slow to go fast" (A Principal's Voice).

Unfortunately, reality often does not permit us to look things over critically or to go slow to go fast. Often, mandates thrust an organization into an implementation stage without regard for a needed readiness stage in which understanding and commitment to the change might be built. By examining research-based observations in the RAND study (Berman & McLaughlin, 1978) of the phases that an institution should go through for successful change implementation, individuals responsible for the innovation can work to assure that the needed stages of the change process occur.

The RAND study "set out to characterize the process by which an innovation is translated into an operating reality within school districts" (Berman & McLaughlin, 1978, p. 13). The study uncovered an interesting phenomenon.

Rather than a single process, several different ones could be observed for different innovations and also for the same innovation at different times in its evolution. Although all change agent projects evidently encountered a similar sequence of events and activities, three characteristic phases could be discerned within the overall process. . . . These phases roughly correspond to the project's beginning, middle, and end; but we did not use this simple terminology because neither beginning nor end makes sense in the context of a constantly evolving local educational system . . . and because instead of a chronological sequence "from beginning to end," the activities defining each phase overlapped one another. Instead, we call them *mobilization, implementation, and institutionalization.* (p. 13)

Thinking about the change process associated with implementing an innovation in terms of these three phases is helpful. One example might serve to highlight some of the critical activities within each phase. Suppose a school was interested in examining cooperative learning as a way to foster the development of students' academic and social skills.

In the mobilization phase, types of cooperative learning would be studied. This could include readings, videos, and visits to sites where cooperative learning is routinely used. Enthusiasm, commitment, dedication, and support for cooperative learning would be rallied among stakeholders who would ultimately be affected by the decision to implement its use: teachers, parents, students, administration, and support staff. Planning efforts should include the development of a team of representative stakeholders. Plans would be made regarding needed resources such as training, follow-up, and implementation support.

In the implementation phase, training would be provided, follow-up would occur, and feedback would be solicited regarding the quality of training and support and the applicability of cooperative learning to the classroom curriculum and student needs. Appropriate modifications would be made based on this feedback. "Review and refinement" sessions would be conducted. Typical follow-up sessions might include video analysis, peer coaching, collaborative lesson development, and idea swapping and sharing.

The institutionalization phase is marked by acceptance or final rejection of the change project. Institutionalized change would occur, then, if cooperative learning became standard educational practice in the classroom and at the school level. That is, it would serve as one strategy within every teacher's repertoire that could be used, given its suitability to a given lesson objective. Newcomers to the school would be taught cooperative learning strategies, and cooperative learning would be a part of faculty meetings.

Just as the organization goes through stages associated with the change process, so do individuals. The degree to which they receive support during this process will have a major impact on whether they will adopt a particular change.

A Look at Change
From the Individual's Perspective

Federal and state initiatives, district goals, advances in technology, new curriculum frameworks, and a number of other forces are frequently requiring schools, and the individuals within them, to change.

The invitation, or in some cases, the mandate to change often asks the organization and staff members to abandon long-standing, familiar practices in exchange for new ways of doing things. This phenomenon often leaves people with a sense of loss, a longing to go back to the old ways of doing things, and a concern that being asked to do something differently implicitly means that what they had done before was not good. Frequently, a sense of denial emerges: "If we wait just long enough, this too will pass."

Individual responses to change differ. Some people welcome it; others greet it with fear or anger. Part of facilitating the change process involves understanding the individual's change experience. Organizations change only as the individuals within the organization change. Change is a highly personal experience. Essentially, it is an individual experience and takes place one person at a time. Meaning is one critical influence that will ultimately determine whether a person is willing to change. If the change effort holds meaning for an individual, that person may be more likely to change. Teachers need to say and feel, "Yes, I can relate to this idea and see how it can improve student learning and make the job more exciting for me." People are more likely to adopt new behaviors when their own values and beliefs are consistent with the values and beliefs that undergird the new behaviors implied by the change.

Often, people are asked to change behavior before they have developed the new beliefs or values implicit in the change. This brings a feeling of discomfort. For long-lasting change to occur, individuals must first be provided with experiences through which they will come to develop the values and beliefs that drive the desired behaviors. Experiences change beliefs. Beliefs do not usually change without experiences. Many teachers have to experience positive results with students before adopting a new way of doing something.

To build interest and meaning for individuals who will be affected by change, the California School Leadership Academy identified four factors as part of a framework that school leaders should tap. Each of the following factors in this framework should be considered before embarking on a change effort:

- Relevance—whether a change is relevant to one's life or work responsibilities
- Feasibility—whether people may view the change as "doable," given other demands on their time and their philosophical beliefs
- Involvement—whether the individual being affected by the change has input into what the change will look like, sound like, be like

- Trust—whether there is trust between the person being asked to change and the facilitator or initiator of the change

If staff members have collaboratively developed a vision that promotes quality teaching and staff and student learning, and if the proposed change is consistent with the vision, chances are it will be greeted with greater enthusiasm. It will be viewed as relevant; people will perceive it as feasible; it will have meaning because of the members' previous involvement with developing the vision; and an atmosphere of trust usually will have been established.

Stages of Concern

In addition to facilitating change by paying attention to creating individual meaning for the change process, change facilitators find it helpful to understand how individuals show their level of interest or concern for change. Hall, George, and Rutherford (1979) developed common characteristics that indicate one's interest or concern regarding innovative or change experiences. Hall et al. emphasized that how people perceive and understand change will be dictated by their personality and experience. One person may perceive a change as an outside threat, whereas others may view it as rewarding. The degree to which a concern may be assessed and responded to accordingly will facilitate one's understanding and experience of the change effort. Table 7.1, based on Hall et al.'s (1979) work, portrays these stages of concern.

One principal developed the chart shown in Table 7.2 after learning about these stages of concern to remind himself about how to respond to individuals' comments related to a change effort.

Some Final Reflections on Change

How change is perceived has a major impact on organizational response. Harold Storlien, superintendent of the Medicine Hat School District in Alberta, Canada, advised the authors to look at all problems as challenges and opportunities. The principal can set a personal example by viewing change as an opportunity and encouraging risk taking and ownership on the part of teachers regarding the changes. This will help to create the atmosphere of trust that will be necessary for success. Key personnel in the process must constantly ask, Who do we need to inform? Who needs to know about what we are doing: Teachers? Parents? Principals? District personnel? Students? Community members? The media? Inclusion of relevant groups is a critical factor in the change process.

For example, the central office must be actively involved; there should be no surprises. They can supply the trainers, resources, time needed, and monetary

TABLE 7.1 Stages of Concern: Typical Expressions of Concern About the Innovation

Stage of Concern	Expression of Concern
6. Refocusing	I have some ideas about something that would work even better.
5. Collaboration	I am concerned about relating what I am doing with what other instructors are doing.
4. Consequence	How is my use affecting kids?
3. Management	I seem to be spending all my time in getting material ready.
2. Personal	How will using it affect me?
1. Informational	I would like to know more about it.
0. Awareness	I am not concerned about it (the innovation).

SOURCE: Hord, Rutherford, Huling-Austin, and Hall (1987).

TABLE 7.2 A Principal's Responses to Concerns About Change

Stage of Concern	Response
6. Refocusing	Stimulate a discussion and provide a comfortable setting so teachers can discuss how this could be enhanced or improved.
5. Collaboration	Relate ways that individuals can work together and share ideas.
4. Consequence	Show how it might affect staff and students.
3. Management	Invite users to demonstrate how they manage the use of an innovation.
2. Personal	Share how it might affect student and teacher growth.
1. Informational	Explain what "it" looks like in practice; provide examples.
0. Awareness	Provide information.

support to implement the change. The whole system must be involved for the project to succeed.

Schools must also revisit their vision during the process and ask the following questions:

- Is the change on the right track?
- In what direction is the innovation going?
- If it appears to be going off track, is that okay?
- Is the project taking a direction that was unanticipated, but best?
- Has reality shown—based on actual classroom use—that the original plan was unrealistic?
- Do the new changes that appear necessary as a result of the initial experiments align with the vision?
- Should the vision be altered?
- Have the recommendations of the staff developers or previous examples of success of the innovation proved to be unworkable for this school? For example, a staff developer may recommend that student portfolios be implemented and required schoolwide after the training. Will that work for your staff?
- Should volunteers be enlisted to set examples and "massage" the project?

The ability level of staff developers brought into the school can obviously make or break the change effort. When staff developers are enlisted to start a program, are they operating on a level appropriate for the staff? Staff developers often know the ins and outs of an innovation and must remember that a staff member may know nothing about the proposed change. Staff developers must consider, If we listen but respond at a higher level than is appropriate, then we are not meeting needs. The track record of the staff developer must be considered. That is, has the staff developer been involved previously with the school district? Have they talked with the key individuals such as the principal, teachers, district personnel, parents, and students who may be affected by the change? Eventually, plans should be put in place to develop trainers at the local site.

A phenomenon to be aware of, and plan proactively for, is a state of entropy or running out of steam that occurs about midcourse in a change effort. Many change agents plan ceremonies to acknowledge progress to date and to recall critical events along the way in order to garner the enthusiasm and energy among organizational members to sustain progress in implementing the change. "Be aware of this reality, plan for it, but don't interpret it as losing the battle," commented one principal when discussing entropy (A Principal's Voice). Rosabeth Moss Kanter (1977) offers a helpful insight with respect to the notion that if a change doesn't immediately produce results, it is tempting to move on to the "next new thing." She writes, "The difference between success and failure is often just a matter of time: staying with the project long enough to overcome the unexpected developments, political problems, or fatigue that can come between a great sounding plan and actual results. A basic truth of management—if not of life—is that nearly everything looks like a failure in the middle. At the same time, the next project always looks more attractive (because it is all promise, fresh, and untried)."

Do not be overconfident if the process gets off to a smooth start; that may be an indicator that something is wrong. The change may have been implemented too fast. Or the staff members, in the beginning, may be holding back their opposition and just going along with a top-down directive. Phil Schlechty (2001) reminds us that "compared to sustaining change, starting change is relatively easy." He points out that that is why more changes are initiated in schools than are sustained. In writing about the challenge of sustaining change, he notes, "Two things sustain change: one is a leader or leadership group that acts as a change agent; the other is a system or group of systems that supports change." This explains why, when the school culture does not have the capacity to sustain a change effort, "the change rarely outlasts the tenure of the change agent" (Schlechty, 2001). A key leadership task then, is to study and then create those system conditions that will support and sustain a change.

One must also consider whether the school is providing for rituals and ceremonies to dignify and deal with the loss of previously used methods when appropriate. Often, when a new program is being implemented, previous ways of doing things are discarded before time is taken to see how they may still have a function or perhaps be integrated with new practices. For example, if whole-language instruction is implemented, are the basal readers just being junked and considered to be an educational failure? How can the work of teachers who spent 20 years with the basals be dignified? Can an innovation be brought into a school with an acknowledgment of the elements of success of past practice? Is there a possibility that the old can be combined with the new instructional or curriculum strategy? For example, one principal reflected,

> There are some things that are working in that school and you need to work with people in the school who know what it has been like before. . . . If we did something last year that works, you need to inservice me. If it didn't work, we need to talk about how we can make it different.
>
> (A Principal's Voice)

For an innovation to succeed, the change and the mindset for change must take hold in the workplace. If you want to know if the innovation has occurred, do not just ask the superintendent or the principal or the teachers—visit the classrooms.

Then visit the classrooms 2 years after the project was introduced. Are there now trainers in the school who can train staff new to the school on the innovation? That is, has the change been institutionalized? Also, how is the innovation working in other schools? How is the innovative practice (e.g., authentic assessment or interdisciplinary instruction) being modified and improved? Are teachers in the district who are teaching in high school talking with elementary staff at districtwide functions about the change? All personnel should be learning together throughout the system.

If the change is successfully implemented, eventual satisfaction should be observed throughout the system. The teachers should display satisfaction with the change, students will know of the change and talk about what has taken place, and site and district administrators will be a part of the process, as will the parents. A key characteristic should be more schoolwide interaction. In the end, change must be systemic; all elements that are affected by the change must be involved.

Kurt Lewin (1951) once said, "If you really want to understand something, try to change it!" Indeed, change is an all-encompassing experience that envelopes both the organization and its members, evoking a multitude of responses. The world is characterized by chaos, unpredictability, and change. The only way to keep up with the changes is by building change into the system. Guiding change so that it is successful is certainly an essential skill of an effective leader. On reflection, we should consider that the change process goes hand in hand with the notion of leader as learner. Indeed, the measure of a leader may well be his or her capacity to understand and work successfully with change—to stimulate it, shape it, nurture it, guide it, manage it, revise it, and keep the change journey going.

Reflections

This space provides for you a place to write in ideas that have been generated by this chapter, things you want to try, or adaptations of ideas presented herein.

1. Think about a change effort you are anticipating or are currently involved with. Which of the concepts presented in this chapter will be most relevant? Why?

2. Review Fullan and Stiegelbauer's (1991) assumptions about the change process. Select the assumptions that are most relevant to your school. Consider posting them on a bulletin board near your desk or in a file to which you frequently refer.

3. Practice listening to individuals as they express concerns about a change. See if you can determine the stage of concern and an appropriate response.

4. What do you see as the two or three easiest traps that a school leader can fall into when trying to implement change? How can these traps be avoided?

5. What insights or new questions do you have as a result of reflecting on the ideas presented in this chapter?

8

Building a Vision
and a Mission Together

The future belongs to those who believe in the beauty of their dreams.

ELEANOR ROOSEVELT

Are students, teachers, administrators, and parents hearing a consistent message about the school's purpose? How would students characterize their school? Would they say, "We have to go there every day—it's boring and not safe" or "School's okay, the teachers ask our opinions and it's helping me think and maybe get a job" and "If I need someone to talk to, I know I can count on my teachers"? Does the school have meaning in the lives of teachers beyond that of a workplace to make money? What do parents tell newcomers in the community about the school?

Why Have a School Vision?

The preceding questions all inquire, What does our school stand for? To answer this question with some clarity, a school must have a shared vision—a purpose that can be seen or will be seen in the daily activities of the school. Stephanie Hirsh (1995–1996), associate executive director of the National Staff Development Council, explains, "A school vision should be a descriptive statement of what the school will be like at a specified time in the future. It uses descriptive words or phrases and sometimes pictures to illustrate what one would expect to see, hear and experience in school at that time. It makes reference to the facility, the curriculum, instruction, assessment, the staff and the community." The vision should be collaboratively developed and reflective of the stakeholders it serves: staff, parents, students, and community members. Special care should be taken to assure that all students, special and regular education students, and students of *all* cultures be remembered, represented, and included in the vision. Hirsh continues, "In contrast to a vision, a mission statement is a succinct, powerful statement on how the school will achieve its vision. It provides guidance for actions on a daily basis. The mission statement answers:

- What is our purpose?
- What do we care most about?
- What must we accomplish?
- What are the cornerstones of our operations?"

There are as many definitions and descriptions of vision and mission as there are authors writing about the topic and schools trying to define their purpose. Although at first this may seem problematic, this may not be the case, as the process of creating a vision and mission building—which encourages participants to think about a school's purpose—may be more significant than an actual definition. For a vision or mission to be alive, the building process must be a participatory one. Being involved in the process brings both ownership and commitment to the vision. Furthermore, it provides the opportunity for faculty members to discuss their values and beliefs related to schooling. For instance, in one high school, teachers talked about the fact that while student performance on high stakes testing was important, given world affairs it was also important to educate the heart, as well as the mind, and develop competencies such as empathy and self-management. When considering the vision- and mission-building process, one should keep in mind several ideas that have emerged from the literature on the characteristics of a powerful vision, especially for a learning community. A vision must be shared by the organization, and the organizational members—the people who make up the organization—must personally believe in the power of the vision as a force for creative, continuous improvement and as a force that can give personal meaning to their lives (Senge, 1990; Wheatley, 1992). It should also be shared by those who are served by the school.

A school vision helps students, teachers, administrators, and parents have a sense of what is important in their particular setting. Knowing what is important helps those involved with the school make choices. It helps the administrator to set priorities, the teacher to direct a lesson, and the student to prepare for class. A vision brings commitment throughout the system as people work together to create a school in which they personally are stakeholders. They believe in their work.

The principal should play a major role in transforming the values and beliefs of the school into a vision. In fact, Roland Barth defines leadership as "Making happen what you believe in" (2001, p. 446). This is accomplished through both symbolic and expressive leadership behaviors. From the symbolic perspective, a principal models and focuses individual attention on what is important. From the expressive side of leadership, principals, talking with teachers, help to crystallize and communicate the rationale for a vision and mission and generate shared discussions about what is important in the school. This focus on the meaning of a school leads to the development of a mission statement grounded in the collective beliefs of the staff. The process creates a commitment to shared direction and an energy to pursue it. The shared meaning helps to create a team orientation: "Yes, we are working together!" Teachers can be confident that colleagues are working on the same key principles with students related to academic or social goals on each grade level. Interestingly, when school beliefs and values are internalized, teachers function more freely and effectively—with less supervisory intervention—because they know what is important in that particular school setting (Grimmett, Rostad, & Ford, 1992).

Moreover, given the many external pressures and expectations put on us, a school must remain focused on pursuing its vision lest it risk veering off in one direction after another. Unless we have a clear focus, we may be spinning our wheels yet remain under the false impression that we are productively moving ahead.

A vision helps members of an organization to identify what is important and avoid spending time on what is not. Drucker (1992), in reviewing the history of management, notes that we often fail to "work smarter" and only ask "How is it [the job] done?" instead of "What is the task?" and "Why do it?" When our mission is clear, we know what the task is and why we should do it. Thus a school leader, in a setting where a shared vision exists, should be able to answer questions such as

- What kinds of social skills are important to the culture of the school?
- Do the results of teaching and learning have meaning in the workplace once students complete their schooling?
- What are the best teaching strategies and schoolwide traditions to accomplish the intended outcomes?

Peters and Austin (1985) stressed that effective principals often are "obsessed" with outcomes that represent the beliefs and values of the school. They function as a galvanizing force that propels collective actions toward their accomplishment.

School Activities That Highlight the Mission

The mission should consistently emphasize commitment to students, a commitment demonstrated in both talk and actions. During the school day, effective principals discuss educational issues, not Saturday night's faculty party. Successful principals serve as models for teachers, work closely with them, and engage in conversations about teaching and about students. Committed principals ask about students: "Is Toby improving in math?" "Has Stacey's home situation settled down?" "How has Bobby adjusted to his brother's jail sentence?" They ask teachers, "Is there something I should be doing that I am not?" "How might I support you in pursuing the mission of our school through classroom and schoolwide activities?"

Bennis and Nanus (1985) emphasize that getting "the message across unequivocally at every level is an absolute key" (p. 43). The message—the school mission—should be reiterated as often as possible: orally, in memos, during faculty meetings, at parent gatherings, and in working in classrooms with children. At one middle school, students take a homework folder home every evening. The mission is printed on the inside cover. Sixth and seventh graders must have signatures from parents indicating that homework has been completed. Students in the eighth grade carry the same folder but sign nightly for themselves. Often a slogan is developed that encapsulates the mission. This short version of the mission might appear on stationery, binders, or T-shirts to remind all of the mission.

The most effective way to communicate the mission is by personal example. A principal should spend time with students (low, medium, and high achievers) when possible, know their names, and join in celebrating student achievement and good citizenship. To illustrate, principals should use their offices to hear third graders read and share lunch with the middle school student government, high school National Honor Society, service clubs, or varsity basketball team. Principals should spend time on the playground, in halls, and in classrooms. The vision or mission can also be seen through student recognition assemblies, complimentary notes to teachers, parent nights, bulletin boards that display student work in prominent places, and positive calls home to parents.

A note to faculty on the last day of school can emphasize the mission.

Dear Staff,

On this last day of classes, I just want to reaffirm how much I appreciate your professionalism and dedication to our students.

Reflecting on this year, I can't help but think—extending my thoughts back to last August—that we brought 10 new teachers into our elementary school program, yet we quickly became one unified, professional group. This is a tribute to all of you and our mutual desire to work as a team in the best interest of our kids.

Reflecting back on your expectations for the class, how did you do on your legacy (with the class)? What was the most enduring contribution that you made to your class? Will it change next year or remain the same? Regardless, a key must always be to continue our elementary school mission: Let's challenge each child, and let that child know that we care.

Thank you for your support. Have a special summer.

Sincerely,
Bonnie

When discussing school culture, Deal and Peterson (1990) provide additional examples of activities that can contribute to strengthening a school's mission.

School traditions such as alumni homecomings, holiday celebrations, end-of-year gatherings, and yearly recognitions of merit, when infused with core values of the school, can build a shared sense of community and purpose. Graduation ceremonies, retirement rituals, academic awards banquets, and ceremonies to celebrate the granting of tenure to teachers can solidify the values of teachers and others, signal school purposes, and provide a social event to tighten collegial bonds.

It is important to analyze whether these traditions match the school's mission or contradict it. For example, one principal noted, "We were emphasizing collaboration and teamwork. Yet I realized we still had a 'Staff Member of the Month' award!"

To clarify what a school stands for, faculty groups, students, and often parents work with the administration to build a school philosophy statement. As mentioned previously, the process aspect of this activity often is more important. The process will be slightly different in each school. Moreover, specific school (i.e., if there is a district mission statement), departmental, grade-level, or class goals derived from the mission statement will have stronger roots and a clearer mandate because of the mission-building and goal-setting process. The process and written results also help to keep the school leaders accountable.

Let us examine the end result of this process and then examine how a mission statement can be created by school groups. The following document, the philosophy statement of the American Embassy School, helps all involved to see the school vision:

The American Embassy School Philosophy

We believe in the dignity and worth of each student and recognize the importance of their responsibilities to their fellow citizens in the world community.

We believe that all youth should have equal opportunity for education consistent with their individual capabilities and with their personal and social needs.

We believe that change is a constant factor in life. Therefore, education should encourage in students the development of personal values and thinking processes which will facilitate their ability to adapt to a changing society.

We believe that learning is an unbroken activity, continued throughout an individual's life span. Therefore, education should foster independent thinking, exploration and experimentation as a lifelong process.

Based on this philosophy statement, the following goals of the American Embassy School, Elementary Division, were written by the teachers, administration, and school board:

Guided by the general goals of the American Embassy School, the elementary school will:

- Establish a firm foundation in the core curriculum of Reading, Language Arts, Mathematics, Social Studies, and Science
- Enrich the curriculum through age-appropriate exposure to subjects such as Physical Education, Art, Foreign Language, Music, and Computers
- Enable students to gain an understanding and appreciation of India and global issues
- Provide an environment that celebrates and promotes maximum growth and development of children
- Instill an interest in and an eagerness for learning, permitting children to realize their fullest potential
- Recognize and respond to the individual intellectual, aesthetic, physical, emotional, and social developmental patterns of children
- Develop a program of active, child-centered learning based on a progression from concrete to more abstract thinking

Joint Administrative and Faculty Mission Statement

An interesting variation on developing a schoolwide philosophy statement is for the administrative and teaching staff to create a joint mission statement to define their role as professionals. The following mission statement was developed on a voluntary basis by interested administrators and teachers during several sessions (including Saturday mornings). The statement was shared with the whole administrative and teaching staff for final approval. The results are as follows:

The professional staff of the American Embassy School strives to offer the best educational program possible in order to develop the mind and character of each student.

1. Based on the goals of the school, the professional staff determines curriculum and instruction.
2. Within available means, we prioritize and manage resources and programs to provide the best education possible for our students.
3. We work to effectively communicate goals, objectives, and strategies to parents, students, and each other.
4. We are committed to ongoing professional development for the benefit of ourselves, our students, and each other.

Slogans keep the mission statement alive in the eyes of organizational members. A simple school slogan, such as "AES—Where children are challenged in caring classrooms" or "Every person is a learner," can signal to a faculty what is important in a particular school setting. In a workshop with the support staff, the slogan "AES—Where every family will always feel welcome" served as a catalyst to institute a new registration procedure for student admissions.

Mission-Building Activity

Although there are several ways to acquire a mission statement—borrowing one, buying one, synthesizing one—the most powerful strategy is to create one. The following technique represents one approach to developing a mission based on the collective visions of the staff, students, and parents. This approach has been used successfully throughout the United States, Canada, Europe (including Great Britain), and Asia.

Materials needed:

- Chart paper
- Tape
- Markers
- Large Post-it™ notes
- Index cards

Steps:

1. Explain what a mission statement is. For example, "a mission statement communicates a vision of what the organization stands for, what its members believe, and what ends will be accomplished in keeping with the purpose and beliefs. It serves as a galvanizing force for action."

2. Build a rationale for a mission statement. This step might include explaining why mission statements are helpful (shared sense of purpose, common direction, energizer) and examining mission statements from other organizations. During this examination, the staff could be asked to analyze the values that seem to be implicit in the mission statement. Identify how a mission statement influences a staff member's life.

3. Invite the staff to take part in the development of the mission statement. Explain that this will allow the opportunity to synthesize individual staff member's dreams or visions into a statement reached through consensus. This statement will represent the ends to which all within the organization will strive.

4. Ask staff members to think for a moment about the place where they would like to send their own very special child to school. How would the child be treated? What would his or her experiences be like? How would he or she feel? Describe your thoughts on a Post-it™ note.

5. Now think about the place where you would like to go to work every day. What would it be like? How would you feel? How would people interact? Write this on a Post-it™ note.

6. Take your two Post-it™ notes and fuse them into one. Write your thoughts on an index card.

7. Individuals then meet as table groups of four to six people and share their index cards. After they are all read, the table group creates a composite of the individual cards to which all in the group can agree. This is written with markers on chart paper.

8. Pairs of table groups meet and share their charts. They synthesize their two charts into one.

9. Continue the process until one chart is created that represents the shared visions of all in the room.

10. If parents and representative students have not been involved in this process, this same procedure may be repeated and the products of their work brought to the faculty. At this point, the staff could incorporate these charts with the faculty work.

11. At another time, a contest could be held or the group could work together to create a slogan that would encapsulate the mission statement.

A mission statement alone, however, will not stay alive unless specific goals are created to accomplish the essence of the mission.

Developing Yearly Goals to Accomplish the Mission

Another excellent exercise to keep the school vision and mission in mind is to develop annual goals for a school that are congruent with the mission. The process starts near the end of a school year looking toward next year's opening of school. The process is very simple. The teaching staff look at last year's goals and divide into about five groups of teachers across grade levels, subject areas, and across friendships. (For the first year, initial goals can be set up using the topic headings such as those listed in the example that follows.) Each group reviews the goals to get the ideas flowing and then answers three questions: What are our major successes this year based on the goals? What are some areas that we still need to improve on? and What are the recommendations for next year? When the groups reassemble, they listen for common points (a recorder types in the common points or posts these ideas on butcher paper). When three or four groups make the same point, the teachers know that they are on to something (e.g., the following document includes wait time with questions and giving students responsibility because several groups indicated an interest in pursuing those areas). This energizes and begins focusing the staff for the next year. The faculty fine-tunes the goals during the first month of school and receives individual copies of the final document. The goals should be revisited often during the year by sharing experiences during faculty meetings relating to implementing the goals.

Again, it is important to stress that the process of writing specific school goals helps keep the principal and staff accountable. The school goals become the "checklist for success" for that year in the school—and ultimately the total staff is responsible for implementing the goals.

These goals were developed as a result of the process discussed previously.

Elementary School Goals

A. *Student Expectations*

1. *Focus on student responsibility to promote academic and social independence and acceptance of consequences. Stress student courtesy, caring, and tolerance.*

Implementation:

- Tailor the school rules to promote your classroom goals.
- Hold recognition assemblies with special themes (e.g., proper nutritional habits).
- Use "Citizens of the Week" awards to emphasize specific school goals.
- Stress importance of positive behavior on the school buses.

2. *In the classroom, maintain high expectations and challenge each child.*

Implementation:

- Encourage independent, critical, and divergent student responses.
- Encourage use of learning centers and enrichment resources or strategies.

3. *Raise faculty and student consciousness concerning environmental issues.*

Implementation:

- Model recycling, energy conservation, and "less is more" themes.

B. ***Curriculum and Instruction***

1. *Promote the new language arts program.*

   Implementation:

   – Stress the integration of the language arts.
   – Emphasize content area writing.
   – Recognize importance of public speaking.
   – Increase use of reference material.

2. *Continue the curriculum review process.*

   Implementation—Science Committee:

   – Principles adopted by the Science Committee emphasizing "Project 2061" will be shared with the whole faculty to make appropriate curriculum decisions.

   Implementation—Reading Committee and Fine Arts Committee:

   – Committees review important curriculum developments and adopt principles.

3. *Mathematics: Further work with NCTM standards.*

   Implementation:

   – Conduct a math investigation on each grade level.
   – Provide workshops for new staff on NCTM standards.

4. *Refine communication and resources used in elementary school library.*

   Implementation:

   – Work on research skills curriculum and library use for research projects in Grades 3-5.
   – Teachers should notify library of major reports and grade-level student needs.

5. *Raise consciousness concerning curriculum connections in all subject areas.*

6. *Social studies: Continue refinement of global studies curriculum.*

   Implementation:

   – Increase communication for regular classroom lessons on global studies in Grades 2-4.

- Curriculum resources should be easily available to all teachers.
- Work on time line for semester reports (in Grades 3-5) to avoid overload in library and end-of-year pressures.

7. *Place special emphasis on importance of curriculum pacing in all subject areas.*

8. *Pilot Telecommunication Computer Project.*

9. *Continue to challenge students with appropriate teaching strategies.*

   Implementation:

   - Refine questioning and feedback strategies to diagnose student needs and provide appropriate resources.

C. *Staff Development*

1. *Expand peer-coaching activity to include a variety of reflective teaching activities.*

2. *Teachers' Center: Continue to expand use.*

   Implementation:

   - With significant number of new staff, assist them to maximize use.
   - Highlight professional journal articles with all staff.

3. *Portfolios: Extend student options and teacher involvement.*

   Implementation:

   - Develop buddy system to support teacher dialogue about portfolios.
   - Expand portfolio project to include more science and math options.
   - Continue to develop core staff with portfolio expertise.

4. *Clinical supervision: Pursue variety of ways for teachers to assess their growth (video- and audiotape, teacher portfolios, various observation instruments).*

5. *Faculty meetings: Increase teacher input and participation.*

   Implementation:

   - Provide time for teachers to share ideas—especially successes.
   - Increase cross-grade-level exchanges.

D. *Assessment*

1. *Experiment with a variety of reading and math assessment that reflect curriculum and instructional strategies and the systematic assessment of progress.*

2. *Refine cumulative record card to reflect curriculum changes.*

3. *Early Childhood Education Center: Systematically use high-scope assessment instruments to observe students and tailor the curriculum to individual needs.*

E. *Parent-Teacher Relations*

1. *Increase communication with parents through the monthly coffees.*

   Implementation:

   – Assist more non-English-speaking parents who attend coffees.

2. *Emphasize effective proactive communications with all parents.*

F. *General*

1. *Increase communication between specialist and regular classroom teachers.*

   Implementation:

   – Both groups of teachers should take initiative regarding communication.
   – Use "look book" daily notes to inform specialists of field trips.
   – Increase involvement of specialists in grade-level meetings.

Leaders emphasize that what a school stands for should be celebrated and not become simply an idea that gets lost in a dusty file. Individuals working in a school should work to agree on what their school represents. In fact, to take the idea a step further, many individual educational professionals are now writing professional and personal mission statements to help them take greater ownership of their day-to-day school activities and personal lives. This also helps school leaders keep on track by fostering constant reflection about their personal and professional work and experiences.

Much of what we have stated is encapsuled in the words of Drucker (1992).

What distinguishes the leader from the misleader are his goals. Whether the compromise he makes with the constraints of reality—which may involve political, economic, financial or people problems—are compatible with his mission and goals or lead away from them determines whether he is an effective leader. And whether he holds fast to a few basic standards (exemplifying them in his own conduct), or whether "standards" for him are what he can get away with, determines whether the leader has followers or only hypocritical time-servers. (p. 121)

Reflections

This space provides for you a place to write in ideas that have been generated by this chapter, things you want to try, or adaptations of ideas presented herein.

1. Consider, given the school in which you work, how a mission statement and slogan might be created.
2. Should the mission statement be chiseled in stone, or should it be a flexible document? Explain.
3. Write a brief mission statement that exemplifies your vision of the good school. Provide two or three examples (paint an image) that show how the vision is realized in the day-to-day school activities.
4. What insights or new questions do you have as a result of reflecting on the ideas presented in this chapter?

PART IV

WORKING TOGETHER TO BUILD A LEARNING ORGANIZATION

9

Enhancing Teacher Growth Through Supervision and Evaluation Practices Designed to Promote Student Learning

I ask teachers, before observing, "How will you know that all students are engaged? How are you going to promote their engaged behavior? What kind of samples of student work do you want to bring to our postobservation conference?"

A PRINCIPAL'S VOICE

Issues and Dilemmas

If schools are to be regarded as learning communities, everyone in a school must engage in the study of what constitutes learning. Our vision of lifelong learning for students can hold greater meaning if teachers and administrators also have an ongoing conversation to improve their talents and skills. Yet, in many schools, teachers feel intimidated when principals walk into their classrooms and are especially fearful of the observation and conferencing process. This is a clear indicator that the traditional administrative evaluation process has failed. Ideally, principals should frequently visit classrooms to see, share, and affirm the important work of schools. Interestingly, teachers, when looking for a new job, often resent the glowing written recommendations from principals who never seriously visited their classrooms. This tells us that teachers feel "cheated" about the assessment of their performance and the missed opportunity for growth that could have been fostered by the principal.

As noted in chapter 2, Deming stressed that when employees are having problems, management must learn to take responsibility, for the system is likely failing the employees. Deming opposed performance evaluations, merit ratings, and annual reviews (Walton, 1986, pp. 90-92). Although we maintain that practical considerations relating to schools and present district, state, and national educational polices make it difficult to fully embrace Deming's view on evaluation, we strongly believe that the dialogue he has stimulated in education may have a profound impact on schools and the literature about schooling (e.g., English & Hill, 1994).

Moreover, Deming would certainly stress that the old administrative paradigm of intimidation and control lent itself to "snoopervising" and caused bitterness on the part of teachers as principals told teachers what they were "doing wrong." That model has no place in schools functioning as learning communities. Thus we need to move away from operating on fear so the notion of growth can be built in from day one. Teachers should know right from the start that supervision and the specific evaluation process are intended to help them—that is the principal's job. Risk-taking behavior cannot flourish in an intimidating environment.

In this chapter we will discuss the goals of supervision, the transformation of supervisory and evaluation practices, essential ingredients for successful supervision, effective instructional strategies, brain-compatible practices, clinical supervision strategies, tips for conferencing and observing, guidelines related to evaluation and legal concerns, and final thoughts on supervision and evaluation.

How should supervision be characterized by today's principals? The following definition of supervision can answer this question: Supervision is providing support for teachers so they become the best they can be. Implicit in this definition is the development and refinement of a knowledge base and craft practice regarding effective teaching and learning. To carry out this definition, supervisors provide resources and promote formal and informal conversations with and among teachers to affect curriculum, teaching, student learning, and professional development.

Although classroom observations and teacher conferences based on the observations are critical to the supervision process, the definition above is intended to expand greatly the possibilities of supervision to help teachers "be the best they can be" by employing additional methods of support. For example, recommending a professional journal to a teacher or sharing an article with the staff may be important contributions made by a school principal. Additionally, support for interdisciplinary planning, assisting teachers in developing an advanced-placement high school course, or facilitating a professional forum on assessment measures based on state standards are all activities that can be supported directly or indirectly by the school leader in an effort to foster professional growth.

Transformation of Supervisory and Evaluation Practices

Today we recognize that teaching, student learning, and assessment are interrelated components of the school experience. Further, curriculum standards or frameworks that focus the classroom journey guide these components. We recognize, also, that although the purpose of schooling is to direct student growth, the growth of the adults in the schoolhouse also must be of paramount concern. These "events" have transformed supervision and evaluation in the following ways:

- There is a shift toward observing student work; previously, supervisors concentrated primarily on the teacher delivery system.
- Supervision and evaluation is often specifically focused on teacher implementation of state standards, benchmarks, or frameworks.

- Data-driven decisions may influence supervision and evaluation.

- Differentiated supervision is specifically shaped for novice, experienced, and at-risk teachers needing intensive assistance.

- Continuous teacher growth, in contrast to mastery, is a more suitable approach to address the complexities of teaching, learning, and assessment.

- Teachers are initiating and directing professional development practices such as peer coaching teams, critical friends groups, teacher curricular and instructional breakfasts, and "Action Research Projects."

- The Clinical Supervision Model, traditionally focused on a conversation about teacher behaviors, is refocusing the conversation around engaged student behaviors during class, and postobservation conferences centered on student work samples.

Essential Ingredients for Successful Supervision

To maximize the impact of supervision, principals should develop an honest, caring, and trustful relationship with teachers. Essential to that process is acceptance of the notion that as adults we have innate needs and desires to improve, grow, and learn. These desires are essential characteristics in a healthy school culture. The early research of Herzberg and colleagues (Herzberg, Mausner, & Snyderman, 1959) and Maslow (1954) demonstrated that as lower level factors such as physiological needs and safety were satisfied, motivation came from "finding one's niche," the work itself, and the sense of achievement. These, in turn, fostered a sense of self-esteem that allowed risk-taking behavior so that the teacher became motivated to go beyond his or her competence, to stretch and grow. Additionally, teacher needs for assistance vary depending on one's life stage, teaching skills, gender, personal events, career expectations, and commitment to the job. Principals must honor and address these individual needs to help teachers develop professionally and personally (Glickman, Gordon, & Ross-Gordon, 2000; Herzberg et al., 1959).

As principals actively learn from the teachers and students around them, and acknowledge that learning, everyone in the school becomes empowered with the knowledge that his or her ideas are influential. This notion can help to create a risk-taking climate in the school. When teachers see that principals desire to learn and share ideas, it is a lot easier to reciprocate that trust. If we really mean that the "leader is a learner," then the principal should expect to learn a great deal through the supervision and evaluation process—especially as related to the particular context of a teacher's classroom decisions: "Why that decision, at that moment?" This gets into the ecology of individual classrooms and gives special meaning to each teacher decision and classroom event. Furthermore, the leader-as-learner model can be transferred to the student as teachers show students that as teachers, they are learning every day.

The ideal dialogue between principals and teachers can, in some ways, be seen as analogous to the process of scientific discovery. When old ideas are found to be ineffective or "mistakes" are discovered, the scientific community should celebrate, for an advancement has occurred. We need to celebrate risk taking, "mistakes," and the process of thoughtful risk-taking behavior.

A postobservation conference with an experienced kindergarten teacher effectively illustrated this process. The lesson objective was to help students identify a variety of animal coats (e.g., skin, fur, scales, feathers) and recognize how the coats protect the animals. The teacher opened the lesson, showing a variety of animal coats and had the students touch them. She then asked the following question: "What do you think the fur and feathers do in the rain?" The kindergartners answered as follows: "Get wet!" The answer she expected was "The coats or coverings protect the animals." The students did not see protection at all—they saw a lot of wet animals!

The principal listened carefully as the teacher expertly analyzed her lesson. This experienced teacher noted that regardless of how long one teaches, "We tend to focus in on the lesson objective from an adult's viewpoint, instead of thinking about what a child might say." As a supervisor, the principal was fortunate to be on the listening end of this conference as the teacher expressed an insight of universal meaning for all teachers.

A discussion of supervision would be inadequate without providing a model of evaluation that can be used in schools. However, an important issue should first be addressed. Practitioners are constantly advised to separate supervision from evaluation. Although conceptually it may be ideal to separate the formative and summative process (e.g., supervision and evaluation), the political reality and the day-to-day interactions between teachers and principals make this an unrealistic aim. Reality—for the principal practitioner—is that you can never fully separate supervision and evaluation. A helpful way to conceptualize the interrelationship between supervision and evaluation is to think of supervision as the formative process that allows for several "dress rehearsals." The evaluation is the summative process in which institutionalized schoolwide guidelines are used to assess teacher performance. In most cases, this process documents specific teacher behaviors in relation to stated school, district, or state guidelines. Although most supervisory textbooks remind us that the formative process is descriptive and nonjudgmental, again reality reminds us that it is almost impossible to avoid a degree of summative interpretation—we all seek to know if we are successful when teaching. Figure 9.1 demonstrates the interrelationship between these two concepts.

It is important not to make the supervision or evaluation process intimidating and to emphasize the growth orientation of both processes. This idea can be shared with the total faculty at the beginning of the year as well as during individual conferences with teachers. Most of our teachers are good to excellent, but we constantly talk about the problems of firing the 5%. Certainly, it is important to uphold standards of excellence. After assisting a marginal teacher, if no growth occurs, we should document his or her lack of progress, using a legally defensible approach. For the most part, these cases tend to be a small percentage of the staff. (See

Figure 9.1. Formative and Summative Evaluation Continuum

Formative evaluation ⟶ Summative evaluation

Formative evaluation: Formative, descriptive, growth-oriented experiences (direct supervision, readings, peer coaching, action research)

Summative evaluation: A check to judge if desired instructional and professional behaviors are being practiced (curriculum implementation, instructional repertoire, professional growth)

"Guidelines Related to Evaluation and Legal Concerns" later in this chapter.) We need to focus on the 95% and keep them motivated and excited about their growth. Even champions need coaches, and we need to continually provide feedback to all teachers, including the best ones. As Blanchard and Johnson (1983) stressed in *The One Minute Manager,* "Feedback is the Breakfast of Champions" (p. 67). Principals need to keep that idea in mind. Principals can model this notion by asking for feedback from teachers regarding the effectiveness of their supervisory practices.

By emphasizing the theme of growth, the supervisory climate is enhanced, and the entire school takes great strides toward becoming a community of learners. One principal reported,

> One of my most productive conferences was with an expert teacher who was trying specific cooperative learning techniques for the first time. My job with her was just as important as with the marginal teacher. I needed to do what I could to provide meaningful data, ask questions to foster reflection and analysis, and to keep her motivation high. What she gained in her experiment with cooperative learning was a clinic for both of us on what should be included in a good cooperative learning lesson. I gained insight into what supervisory approaches were helpful. I won't have to worry about burnout with that teacher for a long time, because she was engaged and motivated by the learning process related to the implementation of cooperative learning and the opportunity to reflect and analyze the lesson and its effects. Furthermore, her enthusiasm will hopefully stimulate other members of the staff, and her students! (A Principal's Voice)

A critical role of principals is to help teachers fine-tune their professional skills. A key is to encourage teachers to reflect on what is taking place in their classrooms, in relation to instructional and curricular decisions. Although we cannot assume that all teachers are reflective and feel a part of their own professional development journey, many are. Those who are not can be assisted by the principal's direct supervision. As growth occurs, the principal responds to the teacher's develop-ment by offering the teacher an increased menu of choices from which to select de-velopmental activities. "It is not the particular classroom practice but the reasoning behind the teacher's practice that marks the level of maturity of the teacher" (Glickman, 1990, p. 65).

The following example from Pat Puleo (1993) in the *California ASCD Newsletter* describes how powerful it can be involving professionals in self-evaluation:

> Over the last few years, Golden Hill has conducted meetings with the com-munity and school personnel to establish expectations for our graduates. During these meetings, student expectations fell into four areas. Students need to be able to communicate, define and solve problems, know how to do research and evaluate, and possess good interpersonal skills. To this end, school goals were established emphasizing these attributes across the curriculum rather than establishing goals and objectives aligned with iso-lated subject area competence. Teacher goals were then developed to ad-dress these new student goals.
>
> As principal, my observations were focused on the teachers' emphasis on the new goals and objectives. The staff member directed the observa-tion. The evaluation conferences were directed by the teacher. My goal was to move staff toward self-evaluation. I wanted to be the one to hold up the mirror. As I sat with individual teachers, they reflected on their progress. They brought evidence of their students' accomplishments. The most powerful part of the interview occurred when I asked teachers to identify their strengths and the areas on which they would like to work. Their thoughts were insightful and honest. Without exception, their reflections were what I would have identified as areas for growth and commendation.
>
> In order to bring the process full circle, I included a copy of the last year's final evaluation in each teacher's opening day packet. This gave each of them a chance to see what areas they had identified as strengths and what areas they had committed to work on for the new year. Unbeliev-ably, I had several staff members ask for a mid-year review. They found the process beneficial. Some even took the self-evaluation format into their classrooms and used it as a tool to assess student work!
>
> Aligning teacher goals with school goals and providing an environ-ment which encourages teachers to become self-assessors fosters greater professional growth. If we truly want students to become self-evaluators, it is critical that we offer teachers the same opportunity. Studies show that evaluation is ineffective for teachers after five years. Self-reflection and growth can last a lifetime.

It is our responsibility to expose teachers to a variety of useful, relevant instruc-tional ideas. Principals can serve as facilitators. In this role, they can foster teachers' reflective practices to assist them in their analysis of teaching and interactions with students. At other times, teachers may request direct intervention from the principal. One teacher noted, "What if I am missing something that is really a problem in my teaching? How will I know if I cannot determine that as an area of weakness in myself?"

Beyond the classroom, establishing a professional video library of effective techniques, important issues, or teaching episodes can also help. Showing episodes during faculty meetings or encouraging individuals or groups of teachers to view and share ideas can help professionals reflect on their decisions. As Glickman et al. (2001) suggest, in addition to direct assistance, individuals grow as a consequence of "curriculum development, professional development, group development and action research" (p. 9).

A workshop for teachers new to a school, reviewing the philosophy behind the school supervision process, can certainly help to provide the rationale and reduce teacher anxiety about the process. Moreover, principals who bring a "new system" owe an explanation to the staff. Also, longtime teaching veterans in a school can often use a refresher concerning how evaluation and growth are related, and the principal can benefit significantly from staff comments at a workshop on how the process is going. To illustrate, the following principles of supervision and the explanation of a clinical supervision model described later in this chapter have been shared successfully in workshops with all teachers new to an elementary division in one school system.

Supervision Workshop

Several principles concerning supervision can assist in fostering a win-win approach:

1. Effective human relations skills are essential to supervision.
2. The supervision process is used to enhance thinking about teaching, learning, and assessment.
3. Supervision should be used to facilitate reflection, self-analysis, and self-improvement.
4. Teachers have a right to grow.
5. It is the supervisor's job to set teachers up to win.
6. Supervisors must first build trust before they can expect teachers to become risk takers.
7. Teachers, because of their daily experiences, are the experts on teaching—supervisors learn from teachers about teaching and about effective supervisory behaviors.
8. Concentrate on the 95% and remember the champions.

Effective Instructional Strategies

The link between supervision and evaluation and effective instruction should be an inextricable one. That is, the supervision and evaluation process should be driven by an understanding of how the brain processes information and the necessary elements that contribute to learning. This focus on brain-compatible learning also broadens traditional notions of supervision and evaluation by including an affective dimension. Recent research on brain functioning seems to indicate, for instance, that when learners feel at risk, their capacity to learn is reduced considerably because much of the mind's focus is turned to the task of establishing a sense of well-being. Therefore, the learning environment and the attitudes and perceptions toward learning tasks should be included in any supervisory or evaluation focus.

Although many teaching strategies exist, it is helpful to examine some general themes that often characterize core elements of effective instruction.

Preparing the Student's Mind for Learning

The minds of the learners first need to be prepared for the learning about to occur. This requires a meaningful focus of the learner's attention. Once this occurs, it is important that an outcome be stated so that the student will know where the lesson is headed. Even with a discovery lesson, a general outcome can be stated; for example, "By the end of this lesson, you will be able to solve this mystery!" To begin instruction at the appropriate level of difficulty and resolve any preconceived misconceptions about what is to be taught, it is helpful to assess what students already know about the topic of the lesson to be taught and what they would like to know.

In addition, because the mind stores information according to whether it perceives there is a later, future purpose, it is helpful either to provide a meaningful purpose or engage students in identifying the possible reasons for the lesson. Furthermore, if there are prior learnings that may assist the student in this lesson, they should be recalled as well.

Instruction

Instruction usually consists of three parts: input, modeling or demonstration, and active involvement or rehearsal.

Input can be provided in several ways. The teacher may provide information, perform an experiment, show a video, assign a reading, or construct a model. Or input might be provided by students, such as explaining a math investigation to the class.

Following this, it is helpful to provide a demonstration or model so that the learners can see what was introduced during the input phase.

Finally, students should be provided with an opportunity to rehearse what has just been taught and modeled. The key to the rehearsal is that students should be able to demonstrate to the teacher that they comprehend the intended input and, as appropriate, that they can either recall the information or perform the task.

Practice

To develop fluency and accuracy, and to promote long-term remembering, students should practice the new learning under the teacher's guidance in the same manner that the skill ultimately will be assessed. When students have demonstrated that they can perform the skill independently, they should be encouraged to practice in a way that can be retrieved and recalled during assessment. Teacher guidance is essential to ensure perfect practice. (Errors practiced are difficult to eliminate.) This increases the likelihood that students will store or internalize correctly the information that has been taught. Students need opportunities to revisit previously taught content so that this content remains vibrant and accessible over time.

These core elements can be helpful as part of the framework for discussing lesson plans, observing a lesson, and assessing to what extent the teacher accomplished his or her desired goals, based on student understanding, using work samples as evidence of understanding.

Brain-Compatible Teaching Practices

In addition to these above elements, the following 21 brain-compatible teaching practices offer teachers specific strategies to maximize student learning:

- Immediately engage the attention of learners when they come into the classroom. The activities need to be of high interest and anchored in benchmarks or standards. They can be used to build readiness for a lesson about to be taught or review a previously taught concept. (The brain remembers best what comes first and next best what comes last. Information lingers in the sensory memory only ¾ of a second. Then information is either forgotten or sent to short term memory. If the teacher doesn't engage the attention of the learner, something else will!)
- Routinely post lesson outcomes, benchmarks, or standards in a specific place on the chalkboard so students can refer to these. An agenda for the day and homework assignments should also have a regular place on the board. (Advance organizers trigger attention and are linked to promoting memory.)

- Use state standards to design curriculum and instruction and assess student work. (Research indicates that high performing, high poverty schools implemented this practice with notable results. Making the brain aware of performance targets increases attention.)

- Involve students in active learning experiences that engage a variety of learning channels: auditory, visual, kinesthetic. Seek ways to structure activities so that students may have an opportunity to use a variety of "intelligences" (visual-spatial, mathematical-logical, verbal-linguistic, musical, bodily kinesthetic, interpersonal, intrapersonal, naturalist) (Gardner, 1995). (We remember only 10% to 20% of what we hear. Active involvement focuses attention and increases the probability that students will remember what they have "rehearsed.")

- Engage students in learning tasks, such as experiments or experiential activities that require them to actively construct meaning. (The brain actually forms new neural connections when it is actively engaged in "meaning making" based on experiences.)

- Chunk curriculum content appropriate to the developmental age of the learner. (The capacity of short-term memory appears to develop with developmental age. This understanding has major implications for the design and delivery of curriculum.)

- Change activities at least 4 or 5 times within the context of a lesson. For example, students may first be actively engaged in a warm-up activity, report out, experience direct instruction, create a graphic organizer to summarize learnings, stand, pair and share their work (with other students), and respond to a prompt in their learning journals. (The more "firsts" and "lasts" within a lesson, the more memorable its content.)

- Provide opportunities for meaningful "rehearsal" or practice after initial content has been introduced. Periodically provide review activities to distribute rehearsal opportunities over time. (The more opportunities a student has to meaningfully rehearse, the greater the chance that information will move from short-term to long-term memory. Providing rehearsal opportunities using a variety of learning channels will maximize the probability that long-term retention will occur.)

- Structure opportunities for movement during learning experiences. (Movement provides oxygen to the brain, increases attention, and in some cases, integrates communication between the right and left hemispheres.)

- Seek opportunities to integrate the curriculum. For example, in the *Dear America* series, students read autobiographical accounts written by fictional characters based on actual historical events. So history comes alive in a language-arts context. (Subjects are not found in isolation in the real world. Long-term memory stores information in networks of association. The more "associations" or connections a student has with a particular fact or concept, the more easily that information can be recalled.)

- Use humor related to content. For example, concepts may be taught using a cartoon lecture. (Humor increases retention up to 15%!)

- Engage students in a variety of tasks that require higher order thinking skills. (Analysis, synthesis, and evaluation tasks require students to access and use remembered information to foster new neural connections in the brain.)

- Provide for a variety of flexible grouping contexts that engage students in working with different classmates. (Much learning occurs through social interaction. Students can receive instruction appropriate to their learning needs and pace in small group settings. As students master academic content, they simultaneously develop skills in working with, and appreciating, others. For many students, a small group setting reduces anxiety. According to brain researchers Caine and Caine [1991] the brain functions optimally in a state of "relaxed alertness.")

- Assign and grade relevant homework that extends rehearsal opportunities and reflects how content will ultimately be assessed. (Students learn more when they complete homework that is graded, commented upon, and discussed by their teachers.) Whenever possible, engage students in developing rubrics to assess their work. This increases their awareness of key attributes of quality work, and lends credibility and authenticity to the grading process.

- Match instruction and assessment practices consistent with how standards and benchmarks ultimately will be assessed and the setting in which assessment will occur. (Research on "state dependence" indicates that content will be most easily recalled when it is assessed under the same conditions as when it was originally learned.)

- Use authentic assessment measures. Engage students in applying new and recent learnings in a real world context. (The brain remembers based on what is embedded in a particular context. For example, to remember what one had for dinner last Saturday night, most people will have to first remember where they were.)

- Provide opportunities for students to summarize their learnings in written or verbal form and communicate them to others. (Summarizing strengthens neural connections. When students "rehearse" through reciprocal teaching, retention is enhanced 65% to 90%!)

- Monitor and invite students to monitor their own progress. (Self-monitoring and feedback can be a source for intrinsic motivation and may increase attention and focus.)

- Select assignments that are challenging and interesting. Provide a support structure to help students achieve success in a psychologically safe environment. (The brain learns best in an atmosphere of "high challenge and low threat" [Caine & Caine, 1991].)

- Create a learning environment where students perceive that they are (1) safe from physical, verbal, or psychological harm; (2) free to experiment and take risks when learning; (3) "connected" in their relationships with others—including the teacher and other students; and (4) valued members of the class. (Sylwester, 1995, notes that "emotion drives attention which drives learning and memory." If students feel safe and cared for, if teachers and others are responsive to their needs, their ability to focus and learn will be enhanced.)

- Encourage parents to stimulate their children's intellectual development and to provide a caring, responsive climate in the home. For instance, teachers can ask parents to help their child rehearse a report presentation to be given in class, or discuss the results of a recent class science experiment. (Environment plays a key role in brain development and intelligence. Verbal interaction with children, for example, has a direct impact on language and vocabulary development. A caring responsive climate contributes to the development of a child's sense of self-esteem.)

In addition to these 21 practices, Marzano, Pickering, and Pollock (2001) have identified nine powerful research-based instructional strategies. These nine strategies can make a significant difference for students if employed effectively. The strategies were found to apply to all subject areas, all grade levels, and all socioeconomic groups. These strategies include comparing and contrasting, summarizing and note taking, reinforcing effort and providing recognition, homework and practice, nonlinguistic representations, cooperative learning, setting objectives and providing feedback, generating and testing hypotheses, and questions, cues, and advance organizers. These strategies could be reviewed during the supervisory process to support teachers in planning instruction, or as part of a small group or faculty-wide staff development initiative.

Increasing Teacher and Administrative Reflection Through Clinical Supervision

A four-step variation on the clinical supervision model that follows can be used to implement an examination of these teaching strategies. With this model, the emphasis moves from sole concentration on classroom observation to more important conversations and reflections about planning, teaching, student work, and assessment. Thus the model serves as a catalyst for talking about teaching and learning. A critical part of this model is the preobservation conference that precedes the teaching. As Costa and Garmston (1991) have stated, "A good preobservation conference is worth six observations." The preobservation conference provides an opportunity for the teacher to unpack the thinking behind the planning process. It also provides a reference point to compare expected and actual outcomes in the postobservation conference.

1. The Preobservation Conference

Usually the teacher will choose a lesson, the key points to be observed, and the desired type of data-gathering method. There needs to be a focus on building rapport, trust, and self-esteem.

Listening to the teacher during the conference is a key supervisory objective. If the teacher talks more during the conference than the principal, declare the conference a success. Why? Because the teacher is talking and thinking about the teaching and learning processes. Principals have to get away from the notion that it is their role to "run" the conference. This does not preclude asking effective questions to stimulate discussion. Possible questioning topics may relate to student work samples, addressing standards, brain-compatible learning, diversity, equity, problem solving, engaging all students, the complexity of group work, and valuing teacher decision making (e.g., one experienced principal often tells teachers during preobservation conferences, "I value your ability to make instructional decisions on the spot"). Specific questions may include, What are your expectations for the students? When teaching, how do you know the students are engaged? How do you know they are progressing? How do you know that the standards are being reached? How are you coping with the standards and the specific challenges of special needs students? The more specific the preobservation conference discussion, the more fine-tuned the lesson is likely to be. As the lesson unfolds, data is gathered, based on the focus identified in the preobservation conference. This provides feedback for analysis that will occur in the postobservation conference. Figure 9.2 is an example of a preobservation form that can be used by teachers to focus the preobservation conference and lesson.

2. Observation

Traditionally, this has been the key step. The supervisor must work to reduce a teacher's anxiety about this step and stress that the primary purpose of the observation is to provide student work samples and instructional episodes for discussion during the conference. Students may be informed about the observation so that they can see that adults also continue to grow. For example, "Mrs. Johnson will be coming in to watch our class today. She'll be interested in discovering what helps us to learn." During this step it is crucial to observe teacher behaviors, students, and student work samples. Schlechty (2001) advises, "Rather than observing the classroom to see how the teacher is performing, the principal observes the classroom (and perhaps interviews students and reviews assignments as well) to determine the extent to which students are engaged, persist, and experience a sense of accomplishment and satisfaction as a result of what they are asked to do" (p. 144).

Figure 9.2. Preobservation Conference Form

PREOBSERVATION CONFERENCE FORM

Teacher's Name_____   Today's Date_____

Subject_____

1. Lesson Objective: What do you want the students to know and be able to do as a result of this lesson? (If appropriate, please bring student work samples to our postobservation conference to support the objective that emerged during this lesson.)

2. How does this lesson "fit" into the course curriculum? Are there particular standards or benchmarks that will be addressed by this lesson?

3. What background knowledge/skills do the students have for this specific lesson, or the major topic/unit that includes this lesson?

4. Do you anticipate any particular difficulties that the class or specific students may encounter during this lesson?

5. What will be the key aspects/steps of this lesson? Also, what activities will the students engage in during the lesson to meet your expectations? Let's remember that the lesson may include surprises that we could not have anticipated that may alter the sequenced steps of the lesson. (If you prefer, attach your lesson plan to this form.)

Figure 9.2. (Continued)

6. What teaching strategies/techniques/issues do you want me to concentrate on during the observation for discussion during the postobservation conference? Suggested areas for feedback include teacher decision-making, motivation, providing feedback to students, reinforcing students, student participation, equity in the classroom, addressing the standards, lesson sequence/logic, questioning strategies, traditional and alternative assessment strategies, opening, closure, logic or difficulty of ideas, pacing, checking for understanding, atmosphere in the classroom, clarity, higher level thinking, problem solving, modeling new learning, use of technology, classroom management, variety of activities, "out of the box" teaching techniques, organization of the lesson, creativity and imagination in the classroom, risk taking, student discovery of ideas, lab procedures, engaging all students, cooperative learning, peer support, use of instructional resources, teacher-centered behaviors, student-centered lessons, brain-compatible learning, multiple intelligences, and addressing special-needs students. What have I missed that you would like feedback on? (It is recommended that only two or three strategies/techniques/issues are selected for the observation and for discussion during the postobservation conference.)

7. What else?

Date, room, and time of lesson_____

Please fill out this preobservation form before or, if necessary, during our conference. Your comments on the form will provide the basis for the preobservation conference, the observation, and the postobservation conference. I look forward to our discussions!

3. Reflections on the Observation

With this four-step model, solitary reflection is essential and critical to the success of the process. If a supervision model is used that includes a pre- and postconference, then it is important, vitally important, that the teacher has an adequate opportunity to analyze the lesson before the postobservation conference. Along with the student work, the principal should provide the type of data requested by the teacher. The teacher may then review the principal's script-tape (e.g., written play-by-play of the lesson), examine a principal's diagram of the verbal flow during the lesson, a video- or audiotape, or a principal's summary of the lesson. A principal will need time to prepare the observational material for teachers if both descriptive and interpretive data are needed. Another approach is to provide the descriptive data to the teacher immediately following the lesson without any interpretive supervisory comments so that he or she may analyze it before the conference. The teacher, however, should be invited to reflect on the lesson and make observations before examining the data. The teacher analysis of the lesson may include a wide range of comments, such as why spur-of-the-moment decisions were made or what surprises occurred during the lesson. It may also include a comparison between the reflective interpretive data and the descriptive observational data.

4. The Postobservation Conference

The goal of the postconference is to encourage the teacher to reflect on his or her decisions related to student learning (e.g., What happened as expected? and What happened differently?). The teacher should have an opportunity to verbalize a comparison between his or her recollections of the lesson with the actual data from the observation.

Again, the teacher should dominate the discussion and, in most cases, decide where to go next. Interestingly, when trust is established, teachers prefer to take the initiative in stating that a lesson was successful or did not go well. When the teacher spots a problem, he or she takes ownership and is in the driver's seat in recommending ways to fine-tune a teaching strategy. Moreover, the conference can provide the opening for the next observation or another professional growth activity.

Tips for Conferencing and Observing

Obviously, the preceding supervision model has many variations and depends greatly on the experience of the teacher, the experience of the principal, the context of the school and students, and most importantly, on the relationship between the supervisor and teacher. The tips that follow are intended to generate additional ideas to enhance the supervisory process.

Use student work. Use the student work from the lesson when discussing the lesson outcomes. When possible, it is very helpful (following an observation) for the teacher to bring student work samples from the lesson to the conference. This provides evidence to discuss, What did the students do? What did they accomplish? Were the objectives reached? Were students engaged in meaningful work? In most cases, this is very satisfying for the teacher and gives the principal a feeling for what is taking place in class. An experienced principal recommended addressing the following issues and questions during a post-conference related to student work: "Remember, all those wonderful activities may not show meaningful work. Prudently ask, during appropriate conferences, "What is the point of the lesson? What are the 'learnings'? Do the student products reflect the lesson objectives? Let's look at a range of products, good products, unsatisfactory products. What are the rubrics? Keep in mind that the products at the postconference will show if quality work has been going on all year, not just during the two or three conferences."

Videotape. If a teacher videotapes a lesson for an observation, consider taping only part of the lesson: the opening, the student group work, the teacher modeling, the questioning, or the closure. A 10-minute video can easily lead to a 45-minute conversation.

Include student input. Students can add an important dimension to the evaluation process. One principal videotaped the preconference, lesson, and postconference with an experienced member of the staff. The teacher was helping the principal refine his conferencing techniques as he provided feedback on her teaching. The lesson was on dividing fractions. The teacher was very disappointed with how she began the lesson, and she shared this sentiment with the principal and her students after the lesson. She felt that their difficulty during the lesson was due to a lack of clarity on her part. The students told her that she was "way off" regarding her feelings about the lesson and that this particular lesson was one of the most challenging and interesting lessons of the school year. The students explained that the lesson really made them think, helped them to actually see how to get the answers, and realize that more than one correct answer was possible. That experience helped the teacher and supervisor to reflect on how difficult lesson success is to evaluate.

Elementary versus secondary supervisory activities. On becoming an elementary principal, one of the authors was anxious to know whether his supervision skills, developed in a high school setting, would need a "major overhaul" to effectively support and enhance the professional learning opportunities for elementary school teachers. The following comments address this issue:

> I should have realized that, just as I used my supervision skills from one subject area to another in high school, the same principle would apply in the elementary school. There were, however, some important differences

that affected what I would see during a classroom observation. The elementary principal must be ready to observe classes that will usually undergo several activity changes within a 30 to 40 minute "period."

Furthermore, one is likely to see more activities during a specific "period" as one moves from the upper to the lower elementary school grades. As an elementary school supervisor, I have to remind myself that I should expect vastly different curriculum goals, teaching strategies, and performance expectations from the various elementary school levels. Moreover, one observes the application of different techniques (and, quite possibly, different education philosophies) on three general levels: kindergarten, primary, and intermediate. (Alvy, 1993, p. 29)

Guidelines Related to Evaluation and Legal Concerns[1]

The legal guidelines related to evaluation are really for only 2% of the faculty, but 100% of the headaches.

A PRINCIPAL'S VOICE

Although this chapter certainly emphasizes the professional growth component of supervision and evaluation, there are times when quality assurance necessitates nonrenewal of faculty who are not meeting the needs of students. Although it is impossible to provide specific legal guidelines that will meet the particular expectations for each state concerning work with marginal teachers and possible nonrenewal, the following broad guidelines can serve as a starting point for principals:

- Pay attention to deadlines! For example, keep track of observation dates, due dates for written summaries of observations, and employment status deadlines. Concerning dates, know whether the deadlines relate to specific school work days or all calendar days including weekends, holidays, and other non-teaching days. Deadlines will likely be different for new teachers, tenured teachers, and marginal teachers on probation engaged in an assistance/improvement plan.
- Know the union contract inside and out. For example, Are there restrictions on how you can use announced and unannounced observations? Are short observations, "walk thrus," or "drop-ins" permitted as part of the documented evaluation process?
- Know the district instruments for evaluation and observation. There may be different instruments for new teachers and experienced teachers, for successful teachers on professional growth plans, and for marginal teaches on assistance/improvement plans. Find out if your own customized observa-

tion instruments or forms are acceptable or if district guidelines mandate specific instruments and forms based on district and union agreements.

- Document, document, and document. A paper trail must be maintained if non-renewal may result based on classroom performance. The documentation should be tied to specific state or district expectations for teacher competency. Make sure the documentation is not vague.

- If it looks like a marginal teacher will be placed on a timeline for improvement, with possible non-renewal of a contract, then the specific teaching problems should be documented (described) with precise language that provides a rationale concerning why the behavior is detrimental to student learning. A clear and explicit explanation of instructional performance expectations should be presented with recommendations or suggestions for improvement.

- A plan for improvement/assistance should be based on state laws, providing an adequate warning and timeline for improvement (e.g., 90 days on probation). The union contract may also contain language in compliance with the state laws. Again, know the state laws and the union contract. The improvement plan should clearly indicate the problematic behavior, with suggested remediation interventions (e.g., mentoring, workshops, videos, observations of colleagues, and conferences), and opportunities to display improvement.

- Often, school district lawyers offer state legal workshops for principals concerning working with marginal teachers and legal issues related to dismissal. Although it is critical to attend these workshops, they should not be confused with quality supervision and professional development. Stay in touch with the district lawyers when teacher dismissal may result.

Finally, it is important to note that even when working with marginal teachers, one must always hope that the result will be successful for both students and teachers. As Tucker (2001) notes, "Every administrator committed to taking his or her school to the next level of excellence should provide assistance to struggling teachers. They have an ethical obligation to do so because successful remediation affects many people. Students and their parents benefit because it ensures a quality educational experience. For teachers, remediation reflects the school system's concern for its teachers' professional development. Dedicated administrators know that whole-school improvement won't happen unless everyone performs well, and helping each teacher do so is an integral part of an instructional leader's role."

Final Thoughts on Supervision and Evaluation

Certainly, an effective supervisory process makes a principal a better evaluator when summative evaluations are required. With a good process, there should be few surprises. Teachers most often respect the process because the principal is familiar with their teaching style, has engaged in conversations with them on teaching, and has seen student performance and work in their classrooms. Probably the most valuable part of the process in helping the principal reflect for the summative evaluation is the teacher analysis of his or her own performance and assessment of student progress, because the analysis reveals much about one's desire and ability to understand the classroom and grow as a professional.

The teacher evaluation process should assess to what extent a given teacher meets the standards identified by the state and/or local system. These standards should be developed collectively by teachers, administrators, and the board of education and be based on a working knowledge of what fosters learning. Although the evaluation instrument may be based on state expectations, these are usually minimal standards for quality assurance that can be extended for growth. The following document is an example of an evaluation instrument based on collective standards focusing on curriculum, instruction, and classroom climate. In addition, this instrument addresses another goal of the system: ongoing professional development. The instrument examines teacher relations and communications, professional competencies and qualities, and professional growth and development.

As you review the instrument, note the relationship between the elements assessed and what you know that promotes learning. Notice that the instrument is to be used yearly, which reminds employees of the ongoing growth process characteristic of a community of learners. For example, on the last page, teachers are invited to write, in concert with the principal, professional growth goals. A comprehensive evaluation instrument provides the professional community of educators a strategy to engage in dialogue about growth. As Danielson (1996) notes,

> A framework for professional practice offers the profession a means of communicating about excellence. Educators have learned the value of a common vocabulary to describe teaching. Because of Madeline Hunter's work, most educators know what is meant by "anticipatory set," "input and modeling," and "teaching for transfer." Now, as our understanding of teaching expands, we need a vocabulary that is correspondingly rich, one that reflects the realities of a classroom where students are engaged in constructing meaning." (p. 5)

It is important to note that Danielson's (1996) four domains of instructional practice (planning and preparation, the classroom environment, instruction, and professional responsibilities) provide a wonderful framework for a dialogue about the classroom experience and teacher growth.

Together, the supervision and evaluation processes work to focus both the teacher and the principal in an examination of what contributes to learning for both student and adult. Collectively, these processes can and should support the school's vision of professional growth and student learning.

Teacher Performance Evaluation Form[2]

This form will be used for teacher performance evaluation. The form is a definitive guide regarding performance expectations. Although the form is a summative evaluation instrument to be used annually, it should be considered throughout the year in conferences and observations between teachers and principals. It is recommended that a minimum of two observations, followed by conferences, be made annually prior to completion of the evaluation.

The model below graphically indicates key aspects of the form.

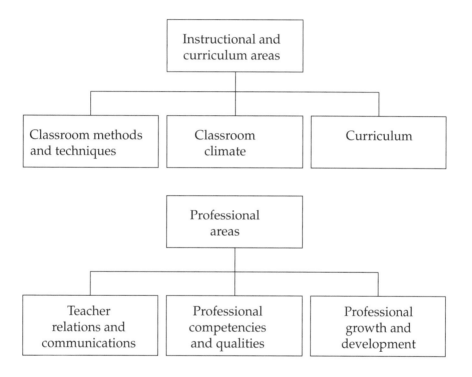

Since the evaluation of the teacher will be based primarily on classroom observations, the formal observation will serve as an important record for this evaluation instrument. A formal observation includes a follow-up conference.

Teacher Performance Evaluation Form

Teacher's Name _____

The competencies listed under the instructional, curriculum, and professional areas are considered important performance indicators. Thus, this evaluation form, with its performance indicators, serves as a guideline concerning expectations of teachers. The indicators are used as the measure for the overall comments in each area.

A. Instructional and Curriculum Areas
   1. *Classroom Methods and Techniques*
      a. Exhibits clarity and precision of oral and written language in lesson presentation
      b. Plans organized lessons at the appropriate difficulty level
      c. Remains focused on the lesson objective
      d. Uses a variety of instructional techniques and materials adapting to various learning styles
      e. Promotes activities that maximize time use and engage the whole class
      f. Provides the appropriate input or modeling to teach the new material
      g. Checks for understanding and, accordingly, varies the pace of instruction
      h. Provides guided and independent practice of new learning
      i. Demonstrates skillful questioning techniques
      j. Strives to achieve higher order thinking
      k. Uses a variety of traditional and alternative techniques to assess progress

      Comments:

   2. *Classroom Climate*
      a. Provides opportunities for all students to learn and experience success
      b. Fosters self-motivated learning and effective study practices in and out of the classroom
      c. Encourages and recognizes desirable behavior through positive-reinforcement strategies

    d. Uses techniques that help students develop a healthy self-concept

    e. Communicates often with students and encourages classroom dialogue

    f. Maintains a classroom atmosphere that motivates, challenges, and fosters high student expectations

    g. Displays interest in the whole child by encouraging both cognitive and affective development

    h. Demonstrates an appreciation of both individual and cooperative efforts

    i. Encourages tolerance for and acceptance of the various cultures represented by the student body

Comments:

3. *Curriculum*

    a. Displays breadth and depth of subject matter knowledge

    b. Develops age-appropriate content and skills objectives based on school philosophy and adopted curriculum

    c. Aligns curriculum content with appropriate teaching and assessment strategies

    d. Adjusts the pacing of instruction to meet the needs of the international student body

    e. Encourages content area competency through reading, writing, listening, and oral communication skills

    f. Works closely on curriculum planning and development with appropriate teachers and administrators

    g. Works to integrate the curriculum, as appropriate

Comments:

B. Professional Areas

1. *Teacher Relations and Communication*

    a. Seeks to improve the school program and climate through cooperation and constructive recommendations

    b. Demonstrates a valuing of peer differences

    c. Communicates effectively with appropriate staff when student concerns arise

   d. Projects a positive image of the total school program in
      the community
   e. Communicates effectively with parents
   f. Seeks advice and counsel when needed from super-
      visors and other teachers
   g. Shares experiences, ideas, and knowledge with staff
   h. Uses established channels of communication

   Comments:

2. *Professional Competencies and Qualities*
   a. Displays dependability in attendance and exhibits
      punctuality
   b. Shows, as a role model for students, good judgment, a
      professional attitude, and ethical behavior in all school-
      related matters
   c. Displays competency in oral and written expression
   d. Keeps accurate classroom records and submits reports
      and records punctually
   e. Adheres to Board policy, administrative procedures,
      and the organizational structure of the school

   Comments:

3. *Professional Growth and Development*
   a. Continues to develop skills and competencies
   b. Establishes goals for professional development
   c. Exhibits openness to suggestions, constructive
      criticism, and change
   d. Displays resourcefulness and initiative
   e. Engages in projects that strengthen the overall school
      program

   Comments:

Summary Comments:

Recommendations for Growth (based on administrative-teacher dialogue):

_____   _____
Date   Supervisor's Signature

Teacher Comments: (optional)

_____   _____
Date   Teacher's Signature

Notes

1. The authors wish to thank Sharon Jane, Les Portner, and Billie Gehres, three recently retired Washington State school administrators, for their assistance concerning these legal guidelines.

2. The original form of this document was developed at the American Embassy School, New Delhi, India.

Reflections

This space provides for you a place to write in ideas that have been generated by this chapter, things you want to try, or adaptations of ideas presented herein.

1. What are your thoughts regarding the broad definition of supervision provided in this chapter? For example, do you think the definition is realistic?

2. What would be the various considerations when observing and conferencing the new teacher? The experienced teacher? What other teacher profiles should be considered?

3. How do you feel about supervising teachers, specifically about their teaching?

4. What would be two or three of your individual goals as a supervisor?

5. For the veteran principal: How have you grown as a supervisor? What areas do you need to strengthen?

6. What are we doing for our best teachers to keep them at the top of their game?

7. Consider the pros and cons of using an evaluation instrument such as the one introduced in this chapter.

8. What insights or new questions do you have as a result of reflecting on the ideas presented in this chapter?

10

Maximizing Feedback About Teaching: Differentiated Professional Growth Options

Thinking improves when people interact with each other, when they break routine by experimenting, when they observe others at work, and when they assess and revise their own options. A cause beyond oneself becomes the norm, and the school becomes successful.

GLICKMAN, GORDON, AND ROSS-GORDON (2001, p. 74)

Reflections on Feedback

Invited feedback about teaching provides data to the teacher about the use of particular curricular, instructional, assessment, and classroom management practices and their consequences. The data provide a lens through which a teacher can reflect and examine his or her own behaviors in relation to their intended effects. It also provides the basis for a dialogue among colleagues about the thinking involved in planning and delivering instruction. Through the process of feedback, the teacher determines what might be done differently if the lesson was to be taught again. This analysis fosters professional growth, instructional excellence, and ultimately student learning.

Traditionally, feedback about instruction, other than student to teacher, has occurred during supervision. Carl Glickman, when addressing the topic of supervision, referred to a "super vision" of effective instruction. This play on words provides a helpful perspective on supervision and its ultimate capacity-building capability. Supervision is a growth-oriented process designed to enhance instruction curriculum, curriculum delivery, and assessment practices, primarily as a result of feedback based on classroom observation. Over time, it contributes to developing the teacher's thought process about teaching. Ultimately, it should result in enhanced learning for students.

The Situation:
Moving Toward Collaborative Feedback

In the past, the supervisory process has been conceptualized as occurring between a principal or supervisor and a teacher. Recently, however, with the focus on
the school as a "collaborative workplace" or as a "community of learners," many
have raised the question about whether the supervisory process should be limited
to occurring only between teacher and principal or if it should be collaborative as
well, to complement the cooperative goal structure of the school. The notion here is
that teachers, working closely with students on a daily basis, have the capacity to
provide one another with meaningful feedback.

Proponents of this belief point to the fact that in some settings, the individualistic nature of supervision, only occurring between principal and teacher, is inconsistent with the conceptualization of the school as a learning community, where
shared discussion and analysis of teaching among colleagues is valued and encouraged. There is much evidence to show that given the numerous demands on
the principal's role, there is limited time for supervisory visits. Hence, with the
exception of classroom visits that may occur during management by wandering
around, meaningful feedback about teaching, in many settings, becomes rather
spotty. If teachers have the option of seeking feedback from other sources—
colleagues, students, parents, and self, in addition to the principal—the process of
continuous improvement, based on frequent opportunities to receive feedback,
will be enhanced. Furthermore, a collaborative process provides an avenue
through which to tap the rich knowledge base about teaching that exists in individual classrooms.

However, in spite of the powerful argument for a collaborative approach, some
teachers have expressed a desire to maintain the option of receiving the more traditional form of supervisory feedback from one's immediate supervisor.

Together, these points of view about traditional and collaborative practices
have led to the accommodation of both in the development of a system of differentiated professional growth options. This approach is timely. Since most principals
are requesting that teachers differentiate learning experiences for students, it is important, for modeling's sake, that we offer teachers differentiated learning experiences rather than one-size-fits-all professional development.

Differentiated Professional
Growth Options: How the System Works

The process of differentiated professional growth options involves teachers
and administrative staff developing professional growth goals for themselves and
determining, from a menu of options, how they wish to pursue these goals. The

ultimate outcome of this process should be to enhance individual staff members' collective capacity to foster high levels of student learning.

The "menu" might include the following options:

- Clinical supervision
- 360° feedback
- Cognitive coaching
- Conversations about student work
- Video analysis
- Drop-in visit
- Archaeological dig
- Program planning and delivery analysis
- Reflective journals
- Portfolios
- Peer coaching
- Problem solving
- Action research
- Study groups
- Lesson study
- Professional book talks
- Individual professional growth plans
- E-learning

In some settings, where a high degree of trust exists, these professional growth goals are shared so that staff members become aware of others' interest areas and can support one another. This can become the basis for shared work and networking. In other settings, the principal may share his or her goals with the staff and then meet individually with teachers. Depending on the system and its policies, the principal usually has the final decision-making power in the process of determining how goals might be met. In the instance when a staff member needs more direct guidance, this should be provided, especially for nontenured staff.

The differentiated approach creates positive attitudes and perceptions about teacher-initiated professional growth and creates a schoolwide focus on what contributes to cognition and the development of affective skills. As faculty members experience an environment where reflection, professional dialogue, collaborative study of teaching, and self-analysis have become treasured values of the occupational culture, they experience learning about learning and learning about themselves. Collectively, these insights help to sensitize staff to the need to replicate, in the classroom for students, those same conditions they have personally experienced.

Sources of Feedback:
Categories and Approaches

There are several sources of feedback: supervisor, principal, peers, self, consultants, parents, or students. To address professional growth goals, one may select from a combination of these. The following paragraphs detail a variety of approaches to providing feedback. Who engages in each of these is largely a decision of the person defining how his or her professional goals will be addressed.

Clinical supervision. This approach, described in detail in chapter 9, involves primarily a preconference, observation, reflections, and postobservation conference. Discussion and analysis of teaching should be based on a common framework of language such as the Hunter Model, or brain research, using the information processing model. The goal of this process is to assist and support teachers as reflective classroom decision makers.

360° Feedback. 360° feedback allows staff members "to gather data about themselves from multiple sources in their circles of influence. The fundamental premise is that data gathered from multiple perspectives are more comprehensive and objective than data gathered from only one source" (Dyer, Feb. 2001, p. 35). The raters might include superiors, subordinates, peers, parents, students, and community members. The individuals being rated by others also rate themselves. 360° feedback provides an opportunity for staff members to compare their views of themselves with the views that others have of them. Karen Dyer, manager of the education sector of the Center for Creative Leadership in Greensboro, NC, writes, "The feedback is powerful because these data identify behaviors that leaders (and other staff members) can work either to strengthen or to diminish. In addition, 360-degree feedback assists them in comparing their performance to stakeholder expectations. The school district can also measure behaviors and characteristics that relate to the values, beliefs, goals, and strategies of the organization . . . Crucial to using the 360-degree process is trust." Hence, to assure overall quality, effectiveness, and integrity, Dyer suggests 5 key factors be addressed in the 360° feedback process.

- Feedback is developmental, not evaluative
- A coaching or mentoring session accompanies feedback
- The development of a goal or action plan follows feedback
- Feedback data belong to the receiver
- The process is confidential (Dyer, 2001, p. 36)

One teacher who chose this approach reported that the data she received from students, regarding which of her instructional behaviors helped them learn best, provided a compelling case for er to continue differentiating instruction.

Cognitive coaching. This is a

Non-judgmental process built around *a planning conference, observation, and a reflecting conference.* It is not dependent on a common language. Rather, it involves the use of clarifying questions, pressing for specificity, reframing, and other communication tools so that colleagues who don't share a common language can still communicate. Anyone in the educational setting can become a cognitive coach—teachers, administrators, department chairs, or support personnel. A coaching relationship may be established between teachers and teachers, administrators and teachers, and/or administrators and fellow administrators. (Costa & Garmston, 1994, p. 2)

In some districts, cognitive coaching skills are being used by school secretaries, counselors, bus drivers, aides, students, parents, playground supervisors, and cafeteria workers to enhance communication and establish trusting relationships. The goals of cognitive coaching, according to Costa and Garmston (1994), are "establishing and maintaining trust, facilitating mutual learning and enhancing growth toward holonomy [which is defined as] individuals acting autonomously while simultaneously acting interdependently with the group" (p. 13).

Conversations about student work. Conversations about student work engage small groups of teachers in examining the work they design for students and the results of student work. Phil Schlechty (2001), noted author of *Shaking Up the Schoolhouse,* writes, "Teachers do not cause learning. . . . Rather, they design activities for students from which students will learn (p. 83). Schlechty believes that when work is "designed right" and when the "right content" is addressed in the work offered to students, students learn. Hence, he says, "the primary source of variance in student learning is the quality of the work the teachers and the schools provide to students" (p. 84).

In conversing about student work, teachers usually follow a protocol. There are a variety available. Schlechty (2001) presents ten design qualities that are likely to make schoolwork more meaningful and engaging. Teachers in one district used these qualities as the basis for collaborative planning of student assignments and reflection, after the assignments were given and student work collected. They noted the positive impact this process had on staff and student learning.

Video analysis. This involves an individual videotaping himself or herself, either reviewing the tape alone or with colleagues, and reflecting on the thinking, behavior, and outcomes derived from the performance.

Drop-in visit. This activity usually occurs when an individual drops in to a classroom meeting or presentation and leaves a note containing an observation or probing question.

Archaeological dig. The "dig" involves examining artifacts from lessons, professional growth activities, programs, meetings, or other events and having conversations about them. The goal of the dialogue is to stimulate reflection and thinking about practice.

Program planning and delivery analysis. In addition to performance in the classroom, teachers demonstrate professional growth and expertise in planning and presenting sessions for others. For example, a team of teachers planned a professional development day for their colleagues. Another teacher coordinated the planning of a math, science, and technology exhibition. These "performances" can also provide a basis for observation and dialogue.

Reflective journals. Time for reflection fosters analysis. Writing about thoughts and perceptions after experiences causes one to think about behaviors and consequences. For example, when a teacher or principal thinks about instructional and curricular planning in relation to the outcomes derived, this activity promotes an analysis that adds to his or her own knowledge base about what promotes learning. The ability to think critically about one's professional performance is a cultivated skill that enables one to grow. This also entails, at times, exposing one's inadequacies and reaching out to other sources of knowledge (if journals are shared) within and outside of the school in order to solve instructional dilemmas. Journal formats may include a variety of forms: freewriting, mapping, interactive journals, reaction, contemplation, elaboration, or cause-and-effect. Once journal writing becomes a regular professional practice, one's mind will, as a consequence, usually increase its capacity to reflect. As one looks through past writings, often growth and insights are noted that become cause for celebration!

Portfolios. The portfolio approach is designed to promote reflection and analysis as well as to demonstrate professional growth. Portfolios are generally a collection of artifacts that represent growth in thinking, planning, delivering, and assessing teaching. They might also demonstrate growth in a particular area such as meeting planning or interdisciplinary planning. Portfolios should not simply be scrapbooks of lesson plans and student work, but rather they should demonstrate progress. Many teachers who have used this approach have elected to designate a portfolio focus such as literacy. Typical contents of a portfolio may be an audiotape, videotape, student work, lesson plans, samples of tasks, and snapshots. Sometimes student or parent letters or graduate work related to the portfolio theme are included.

Peer coaching. Peer coaching occurs when a pair or trio of colleagues with similar role status join together to preconference, observe, and postconference with one another. Often, the cognitive coaching model is employed. It is critical that the "inviting teacher," who requests feedback, steers the focus of the observation and determines the parameters of the discussion. The content of peer coaching activities should be confidential—shared only between the colleagues engaged in the process.

Problem solving. Sessions are designed to encourage staff to share problems and collaboratively problem solve in a way that fosters learning. A variety of problem-solving approaches may be used. Not only do staff members learn as a result of this process but they also use the problem-solving tools in their classrooms and meetings.

Action research. Staff members who elect to participate in action research select an area of focus, develop a research question, identify a data collection plan, and create a plan for analysis of data. They identify who will assist in data collection analysis and how findings will be posted and used. Data are collected and analyzed. Findings are described, summarized, and reported.

Study groups. This structure provides staff with the opportunity to select a topic or theme and identify ways that they will study it. For example, some study groups have identified the theme of "working with at-risk youth." Their mechanisms for studying included discussions of current practice, analysis of case studies, selected journal readings, a field trip to a local prison and dialogue with prisoners, and the reading of books. Members of the group kept journals about insights and experiences. As they learned and applied ideas and practices in the classroom, they frequently met to share experiences. Some teachers and administrators decided to begin student study groups as a result of their experiences as adult learners.

Lesson study. Lesson study engages teachers in co-developing lessons and reflecting on a lesson after it's been taught, in terms of teaching practices that fostered student learning. Catherine Lewis (2002), writing about lesson study conducted in Japanese classrooms, describes five characteristics of this process. "They are lessons:

- observed by other teachers
- planned collaboratively
- designed to bring to life in a lesson a particular goal or vision of education
- recorded
- discussed with co-teachers or planners and sometimes an outside educator or researcher" (pp. 59, 60)

Teachers report that this process is meaningful, on-going, helps them to see their teaching, and fosters learning.

Professional book talks. These talks center around a particular book or article series in which staff members voluntarily indicate interest. At one school, for example, a book talk was organized to meet once a week for a month using Jane Healy's book, *Endangered Minds: Why Our Children Don't Think* (Simon & Schuster, 1990) as a focus for discussion. At another school, a book talk was organized around Howard Gardner's *Frames of Mind: The Theory of Multiple Intelligences* (Basic Books, 1985). At another, Pat Wolfe's book *Brain Matters* (ASCD, 2001) was the focus of the book talks.

Individual professional growth plans. This growth option is to accommodate the individual who prefers to pursue an independent study. For example, one teacher wanted to increase his instructional repertoire. He chose to read a book by Bruce Joyce and Marsha Weil titled *Models of Teaching* (Prentice Hall, 1972). He visited classrooms where *Models of Teaching* was being used. He rented, watched, and analyzed videotapes of *Models of Teaching*. With this background, he began writing lesson plans to employ these models in daily teaching. He kept samples of his plans and student work associated with these lessons in a portfolio.

E-learning. This professional development activity engages individuals in taking online courses offered by a number of professional organizations and universities.

Self-Assessment:
Establishing Benchmarks of Progress

In addition to developing professional growth goals and identifying what approaches will be used to address them, it is important that each staff member who participates in a differentiated professional growth options program identifies benchmarks of progress with dates of completion. For example, an early portfolio benchmark might be the development of the case where artifacts are to be stored. Another might be the creation of a portfolio theme or goal. In addition to benchmarks, resources needed—human and material—should be noted. The benchmark target dates should be reviewed quarterly and progress celebrated.

Individual Reflection and Institutional Renewal

It has been said that an event does not become an experience until one has time to reflect. Reflection is a precious resource in settings where most of the activities are characterized as fast paced, involving a constant stream of decision making. The tools for differentiated professional growth options are many. They provide choice for different types of adult learners at a variety of stages in their careers with a variety of interests. What they have in common is the capacity to foster reflection, and, potentially, an enduring desire to learn more about educational craft. Ultimately, the result of these activities should be an increased capacity to serve students and foster high levels of learning.

Implementing a system of professional growth options provides a recognition of the need to nourish the professional growth of every individual in the school and to stimulate a collaborative effort to pursue learning about learning. Through this process, the entire institution becomes a richer knowledge source with increased capacity to serve its adult and student learners.

Reflections

This space provides for you a place to write in ideas that have been generated by this chapter, things you want to try, or adaptations of ideas presented herein.

1. How does the concept of differentiated professional growth options fit with your philosophy regarding professional growth?
2. What might be some advantages and disadvantages?
3. What professional growth options do you prefer? Would you add any?
4. How might differentiated professional growth options support teachers in their efforts to assist students in addressing challenging state and national standards?
5. What insights or new questions do you have as a result of reflecting on the ideas presented in this chapter?

11

Building a Collaborative School

What does ethical leadership mean? For me as a practitioner it means promoting democratic values and beliefs within the school community through collegiality and shared decision making. It also means showing respect for teachers and students, and recognizing that teachers are experts in curriculum and instruction. In the classroom, ethical leadership means encouraging respect for each student and helping students to do their best, share ideas, and take risks as they learn and work individually and cooperatively.

A PRINCIPAL'S VOICE

Portrait of a Collaborative School

Imagine a school where teachers work on teams to design curriculum; plan instruction; develop authentic assessment tasks based on specific, agreed-on standards; problem solve; counsel students; support each other; and teach. They collaborate in designing and participating in professional growth activities. As a part of this effort, they peer coach with one another—their focus is learning about learning. When one walks into the faculty room, the dialogue is about teaching and learning. There is a parent-teacher-student organization that meets regularly and has as a focus for their work, collaboration to support learning. When one visits classrooms, often cooperative learning is observed. The students experience, at a classroom level, the same type of collaboration that adults model at a building level. Teachers work with students on the student council. Support staff, including bus drivers, cafeteria workers, instructional and library aides, office personnel, and playground supervisors, frequently meet to receive training and to discuss how they can facilitate and enhance the learning process.

Administrators and instructional staff meet frequently and share decision making to promote better and lasting decisions about the quality of the workplace and learning. There is open communication at all levels. Trust exists. People are committed to values, beliefs, and activities that focus on learning.

This school or collaborative center for learning extends its activities to include partnerships with the community and local businesses. There is two-way dialogue about what skills students need to be successful in both school and life.

Community members attend school activities, and school community members take part in local civic activities. Business leaders and school staff attend shared professional development activities.

There are learning fairs where all who contribute to learning are recognized and celebrated for their efforts.

An Image of Reality

The above scenario is far from reality in most schools. The history of the teaching profession is rooted in norms of isolation, stemming from the original "school"—an isolated one-room schoolhouse.

Thus professional isolation is a condition familiar to many teachers. And so it is that in many of today's schools, this one-room schoolhouse structure is repeated every few yards down the corridor. In fact, Maeroff (1993) concluded that teachers go about their jobs as if each classroom were a separate building. Although classroom endeavors are largely communal—one teacher interacting with several students simultaneously—professional interactions within schools frequently tend to be one-on-one. A principal meets with a teacher in a supervisory visit or communicates about a particular student. A teacher inquires of another about a particular curricular issue. Teaching, in the main, tends to be a solitary, private act with regard to adult interaction. Total faculty gatherings, for professional interaction, tend to be infrequent. In many cases, there are agreements that time for total faculty meetings be limited to once a month, or in some schools, once a semester!

Sometimes perceived as an intrusion on planning time or, as a result of past experiences, not worthwhile, time for professional collaboration—joint work among colleagues—is limited within most workplaces.

Recognition traditions tend to be individualistic as well: for example, "Teacher of the Year," "Staff Member of the Month." Success is defined as making it alone. As a result of these conditions and traditions, teachers seldom have the opportunity to experience the benefits of collaborative work and, as a consequence, lack the values and beliefs necessary to sustain collaboration. It seems ironic that the very individuals who are being asked to foster cooperative learning experiences for the students in their classrooms are sometimes not encouraged to engage in similar experiences with their professional colleagues. This lack of personal experience, in some instances, limits one's awareness of some of the subtleties that influence collaboration as well as the feelings and opportunities it brings.

The Case for Collaboration

What is the difference between schools that are learning and making progress and those that aren't? Jan O'Neill and Ann Conzemius (2002), in *Four Keys to a Smooth Flight*, report that "schools showing continuous improvement in student

results are those whose cultures are permeated by: a shared focus, reflective practice, collaboration and partnerships and an ever increasing leadership capacity
characterized by individuals who focus on student learning, reflect on student assessments and learn as a collaborative team."

In addition to research, teachers report that for a variety of reasons, their work
is becoming increasingly difficult. Many report that students of today have different needs and problems than those who occupied classrooms during their
preservice years and initial years of practice. A large number of teachers speak of
increasing classroom demands and a discontented public. It would seem that these
difficult times point to the need for colleagues to join together in addressing them
to ease the individual burden they pose.

Moreover, research and experience tell us that collaboration makes a difference. Roland Barth, as director of the Principal's Center at Harvard University,
once shared with a convocation of principals, "Four years of public school teaching—and 10 years as a principal—convince me that the nature of relationships
among adults who inhabit a school has more to do with a school's quality and character, the accomplishments of its pupils, and the professionalism of its teachers
than any other factor."

Judith Warren Little (1982), in a keynote address to Napa mentor teachers in
Napa, California, observed that in collaborative settings, such as the teachers'
room, when the dialogue focused on teaching and learning, the school typically
was improving. This was not the case when the talk focused on griping about students, administration, or one another.

Similarly, Susan Rosenholtz (1989) studied 78 schools and characterized these
schools as "stuck," "in-between," and "moving." The moving schools were found
to be learning enriched. Their environments were characterized by a shared purpose and direction, teacher collaboration, teacher on-the-job learning, and teacher
certainty (efficacy). In these settings, there was evidence of teacher commitment
and student learning. In her study, Rosenholtz (1989) noted,

> In the choreography of collaborative schools, norms of self-reliance ap-
> peared to be selfish infractions against the school community. With teach-
> ing defined as inherently difficult, many minds tended to work better than
> a few. Here requests for and offers of advice and assistance seemed like
> moral imperatives and colleagues seldom acted without foresight and de-
> liberate calculation. Teacher leaders . . . reached out to others with encour-
> agement, technical knowledge to solve classroom problems, and
> enthusiasm for learning new things. (p. 208)

In the learning-enriched settings, Rosenholtz found that principals played a
critical role in contributing to "an abundant spirit of continuous improvement"
where no one ever stopped learning. They did this through "frequent and useful
evaluations which seemed also a powerful mechanism for delivery on the promise
of school improvement as they also served as guides for future work." In addition

to evaluation, these principals often orchestrated collaborative relations between more and less successful teachers. Teachers came to realize that these relationships helped contribute to classroom success. Having experienced the power of these alliances with other professionals, teachers desired to continue such relationships.

Collaborative principals were found who "uniquely rewove schools that had come altogether unraveled" (Rosenholtz, 1989, p. 208). In contrast, principals who seemed

> Unsure of their technical knowledge and concerned with their own self-esteem, did teachers and students an enormous disservice. In protecting their turf, even the smallest attempts by teachers to solve school or classroom problems were met by distance, intimidation, or defeat. Most often, it was here teachers learned the unassailable lesson that they must shoulder classroom burdens by themselves . . . no teacher could impose upon another. (p. 207)

In an article titled "How Our Schools Could Be," Deborah Meier (1995) emphasized

> When schools see themselves as membership communities, not service organizations, parents and teachers discuss ideas, argue about purposes and exercise judgement, because taking responsibility for making important decisions is at the heart of what it means to be well educated. Students can't learn unless the adults who must show them the way practice what they preach. (pp. 369-370)

Indeed, William Cunningham and Donn Gresso, in *Cultural Leadership* (1993), state "collegiality is the most important element in the success of and commitment to school improvement."

Thus proponents of the research on collaboration and those experienced in it purport "together, we are better than alone." Yet achieving the goal of collaboration is a distant target in many schools. Therefore, the movement toward it must be gradual. Gradual change allows for the provision of experiences so that individuals have the opportunity to participate in collective activities that will build the necessary values, beliefs, and desire for continued collaboration.

Moving Toward Collaboration

Because the collaborative experience tends to be an uncommon one, the initial activities designed to foster the development of values and desires for collaborative work and, eventually, the creation of norms for collaborative practice need to be introduced, facilitated, and structured by someone or some group outside or within the organization. Expect resistance. Staff members do not always perceive the need for this type of experience. Collaboration may be a foreign activity. People may not see a purpose for collaboration and view it as an invasion of privacy. Furthermore, adults have a lot to lose—especially their professional image and self-esteem. It is important that a staff's initial experiences with collaboration do not require them to put their professional selves on the line. Rather, the experiences should be designed to be "low risk," that is, activities that do not require the participant to expose professional knowledge, skills, or talent. Initially, these may be congenial activities, such as breakfasts, games, or potlucks; later, they should be more collegial in nature, such as planning a field trip, reading and analyzing articles from professional journals, suggesting implications for practice, or discussing curriculum. As individuals become more comfortable with one another, they will also be more willing to expose their professional selves. As they benefit from this type of collegial activity, they may come to value and seek additional opportunities for collaboration with colleagues. As individual values and beliefs within organizations begin to change, the organizations change. New traditions and collaborative practices will emerge as individual values that celebrate collective action develop.

An example of this comes from Central Park East Secondary School in New York City.

> Another priority for us was creating a setting in which all members of the community were expected to engage in the discussion of ideas and in "the having of their wonderful ideas," as Eleanor Duckworth (from Harvard University) has put it ". . . One of our most prominently stated, up-front aims was the cultivation of what we came to call 'Habits of Mind'—habits that apply to all academic and nonacademic subject matter and to all thoughtful human activities." The five we came up with are not exhaustive, but they suggest the kinds of questions that we believed a well-educated person raises about his or her world.
>
> • How do we know what we think we know? What's our evidence? How credible is it?
> • Whose viewpoint are we hearing, reading, seeing? What other viewpoints might there be if we changed our position—our perspective?
> • How is one thing connected to another? Is there a pattern here?
> • How else might it have been? What if? Supposing that?
> • What difference does it make? Who cares?
>
> In order to carry out our basic mission of teaching students to use their minds well and preparing them to live productive, socially useful and personally satisfying lives, we approach curriculum with these habits as a backdrop and specific 'essential questions' at the core. (Meier, 1995, p. 371)

Necessary Conditions for a Collaborative School

In a collaborative school, all staff members engage in the study of learning and those practices that facilitate the learning process. In a sense, the school becomes a learning community with a focus on continuous improvement. While no specific recipe exists to make this a reality, Rebecca Burnette and Rick Du Four described some key ingredients at the 2002 Association for Supervision and Curriculum Development Conference. These included, "shared vision, mission, values, goals, collaborative teams, collective inquiry, action orientation, commitment to continuous improvement, and results orientation." As Roland Barth and others have said, for profound learning to occur—whether by students or adults—an individual must

- Acknowledge areas in need of improvement
- Pose the problems
- Take risks
- Use humor
- Collaborate with other learners
- Demonstrate compassion
- Model learning
- Maintain a focus on learning
- Communicate well with colleagues

Yet, in some schools, individuals might not feel safe to demonstrate these behaviors. In schools where cultures of isolation exist, the path to collaboration requires that staff members change the way they think and relate to one another. One principal commented, "You want people to feel 'Hey, I'm part of this,' but it's hard to do when what is modeled is 'dog eat dog.'"

Additionally, *time* for collaboration, *training* in strategies and guidelines for collaborative work, *trust* among all involved in the collective enterprise, and *tangible* support (in word and deed) must be provided for norms of collaboration to develop and thrive. "Teachers are more likely to cooperate when barriers to common action are removed and they feel their problems are shared" (Little & Bird, 1984). When this is the case, teachers, inspired by a common purpose, may be able to bring about change at both the classroom and school level.

Critical to the development of a collaborative school is the notion that collaboration cannot be forced. Therefore, groups of colleagues who desire joint work should be supported with resources to pursue it. Others, who have not yet developed values for collaboration, may be exposed to opportunities for collective action without the expectation of participation. One school developed a norm that proposed, "Everyone has the right to participate. No one must. If you choose not to, however, you must go along with decisions of the collective group. If you choose to disagree verbally, we will take time with you to work out the disagreement" (Wells Junior High School, Wells, Maine).

The focus of collaborative work must be its ultimate impact on the student. To that end, colleagues must engage in work that ultimately leads to a heightened awareness of the conditions necessary for learning to occur. Maeroff (1993) asserts that a faculty can be renewed intellectually if it views change as a team or collaborative endeavor. Moreover, as staff members gain comfort with the process of change, the actual process can become as natural as the desire to improve one's teaching and student learning. In a collaborative workplace focused on learning, all staff would assume some responsibility for the professional welfare and growth of both students and colleagues. For this to exist, however, requires—for many schools—a fundamental change in the school's culture.

In a collaborative culture, the core values, which are reflected in the practices, reward structures, rules, sanctions, and traditions of the school, must be characterized by a spirit of curiosity about teaching and learning and a belief in joint work. When such a culture exists, staff members join together to share the responsibility of integrating the curriculum, working with special needs of at-risk pupils, problem solving classroom frustrations, developing reflective and analytical skills of students, and creating meaningful academic tasks. They also celebrate one another's accomplishments and share the learning implicit in these feats. This recognition also serves as an intrinsic motivator, creates synergy, and perpetuates the belief that together we are better than alone. Cooperative goal structures are, as a consequence, reinforced and advanced.

Each school differs in how it evolves to become a culture characterized by collaboration. Leadership, the history of professional development, experiences of the staff, and existing norms, values, and beliefs will influence how the development of a collaborative workplace begins. However, there are some specific activities that tend to take place in a developmental way. Collaboration tends to emerge as staff members move from relationships characterized by congeniality, to cooperation, and then to collegiality. How much time is spent in each of these stages will be a function of the existing characteristics of an individual school.

For example, the collegiality that exists when staff members collaborate is not created overnight. In fact, the building blocks for collegiality go beyond work and take considerable time. Thus, when a school principal visits a teacher or other staff member who has experienced a family crisis or is recovering from a serious operation or accident, he or she often finds that sharing the moment of crisis is invaluable in building professional trust. At times, several activities—some congenial, some cooperative, some collegial—might go on simultaneously.

A teacher and principal reflecting on how their staff grew to become a collaborative one noted, "We had come to know each other as human beings . . . sharing about our families, interests, and sports. This was essential to build the trust so you can bare your soul with your colleagues and say, 'Here's the problem.' To be intellectually honest requires a foundation of trust." They described a continuum:

Congeniality   Cooperation   Collaboration

This continuum is significant in that it reminds one that if a basic respect for one another as human beings does not exist, people will experience a more difficult time collaborating.

Hargreaves and Dawe (1989) provide a useful typology for considering the impact of school culture on the development of a collaborative workplace. They suggest that there are four types of cultures:

- Fragmented individualism—the traditional form of teacher isolation
- Balkanization—consisting of subgroups and cliques operating as separate subentities
- Contrived collegiality—leading to a proliferation of unwanted contacts among teachers that consume already scarce time with little to show for it
- True collaborative cultures—"deep personal enduring cultures central to teachers' daily work" (Hargreaves & Dawe, 1989, p. 14)

Thinking about these cultures, one could assume that if the nature of relationships among adults in a school was characterized by Individualism or Balkanization, it is very probable that individuals would not take much of a risk when it came to revealing their professional selves in working with others. Therefore, when planning activities to foster the development of a collaborative workplace, low-risk activities in which individuals' professional knowledge was not at stake would be more likely to engage staff members than high-risk activities in which individuals might be asked to display their knowledge publicly. Cultures in which Contrived Collegiality exists might be transformed by inviting staff members to come together and share activities that have personal meaning for each of them. Here the matter of creating choice versus delivering top-down mandated initiatives, such as interdisciplinary curriculum or peer coaching, is essential.

The following portrays a range of activities and examples as well as illustrates the difference between congenial tasks and collegial tasks.

Congenial activities. These are designed to create a sense of comfort with one another as human beings. The experiences typically are not professionally focused. Examples might include potluck lunches, volleyball games, swap meets to exchange educational resources, or Friday afternoon gatherings.

Collegial, professionally focused experiences. These develop interest, respect, and cooperation among and between individuals as colleagues. The focus of these interactions tend to be the curriculum, instructional practice, and assessment. These are represented by a broad range of activities.

1. Low-risk activities that do not require participants to expose their professional knowledge and skills. Rather, these activities are designed to raise an awareness of the value of multiple perspectives and a realization of the resources that may exist beyond one's classroom door in neighboring classrooms. These tend to create a desire for collaborative work. Examples might include a cooperative learning activity where small groups of teachers read different journal articles, then meet to discuss them.

2. Group process and communication skills sessions, during which staff members build their own ground rules regarding how they will treat one another while working collaboratively, learn about how to facilitate collegial work, and learn about the subtleties of communication. These sessions would also include information about group development, conflict resolution, consensus building, and problem-solving models.

3. Medium-risk activities that require professionals to expose some of their professional knowledge and skills. These activities generally occur outside of one's classroom and may include such tasks as professional sharing of successful practices, problem solving, or curriculum mapping, articulation, or integration. These tend to build a desire for more knowledge about content areas or teaching practices.

4. Professional development sessions that provide information about either content areas or instructional practices and their consequences. Examples of these might include workshops about teaching reading or writing across the content areas, using technology in the curriculum, research on the brain, or specific instructional strategies that are associated with fostering student achievement.

5. High-risk activities that require professionals to expose their professional knowledge and skills. These might include the rigorous examination of teaching, curricular, or assessment practices and their consequences. Training to prepare staff members for this type of collegial work might include sessions on conferencing skills, classroom observations, and data collection. An example of a high-risk activity might include peer coaching, mentoring, or conversations about student work.

6. Study groups focused on shared interests to ensure the ongoing nature of collegial work.

7. Collaborative action research projects in which professional colleagues formulate research questions, develop a plan to collect and analyze data, collect data, analyze them, summarize and publicize their findings, and identify new questions that may have emerged.

Because there is an intrinsic similarity between the goals of the activities discussed in the previous list and the goals of supervision—the development of knowledge and practices regarding staff and student learning—in some schools that have actualized true collaborative cultures, these activities have become a way of addressing the professional growth goals of individual teachers identified during the initial supervisory conference. This concept is discussed at length in Chapter 10.

Differentiating professional growth experiences for staff increases staff members' understanding of the value of providing differentiated learning experiences for students. Collectively, this fuels the school's capacity to serve students.

A Spectrum of Activities

The descriptions that follow provide more detailed examples of low-, medium-, and high-risk activities designed to build the values necessary for a collaborative school. Principals, teachers, and support personnel have used these activities during faculty meetings, team department meetings, job-embedded learning experiences, and inservices. The broad goal of their use is to provide experiences to develop values for collaboration that will lead to joint work among professionals versus seeking to "infuse" these values.

Listening posts. In listening posts, staff members are asked to generate professional topics about which they would like to chat. For example, some may wish to talk about authentic assessment; others might want to converse about brain research, interdisciplinary instruction, or behavior management, to name a few. Each topic is assigned to a specific area or "post" in the room by the facilitator. Staff members gather by the topic area of their choice and have a discussion for 15 to 30 minutes. At the end of this time, the individuals who have discussed each topic develop a 1- to 2-minute summary of their discussions and report back to the larger group. In this way, the entire group benefits from hearing about the separate topic area discussions. In fact, seeds of interest across topic areas are often planted as a consequence of such sharing.

Article sharing. Another out-of-classroom activity that brings teachers together for dialogue, sharing, and learning is a collaborative learning strategy in which articles are selected to be read. These articles usually reflect a common theme. Suppose there are five articles to read about "Closing the Achievement Gap." Staff members form groups of five. Each person in a group numbers off one through five and reads a different article. Then people who have read the same article across groups (all the "ones," for instance) meet and discuss what they have read, decide on the critical points, and plan how they will share their articles with colleagues who have read different articles. Colleagues then gather in their one to five groups and each teaches about his or her article. Hence, through this activity, staff members realize that a richness exists when colleagues work together that is not possible when individuals work alone. Further, colleagues discuss how ideas and strategies gleaned from the articles might be integrated into their classroom practices.

Carousel brainstorming. As trust begins to develop and values for collaborative work are created, staff members become more comfortable sharing professional knowledge. Carousel brainstorming promotes this type of sharing within a relatively safe context. In carousel brainstorming, four to six sheets of butcher paper are posted around the room. Topics are assigned and written on each sheet. For example, one sheet might be titled "Motivation Techniques That Work." Staff members are then divided into groups and position themselves in front of one of the sheets. They brainstorm for 3 minutes, writing onto the sheets their brainstormed ideas. They then rotate to the next sheet, taking the colored marker that has been assigned to their group with them. The process continues until each group has brainstormed at every chart. At this point, the group members walk around the entire room, reading the completed charts. Frequently, when this activity is conducted, there are requests to have the charts typed and distributed.

Helping trios. As staff members feel increasingly comfortable and trust one another, they are willing to let their rough edges show, resulting in greater adeptness in joint problem solving. Helping trios lends a structure to the problem-solving process. Peers form groups of three and designate a person as "A," another as "B," and the third as "C." During round 1, which lasts 5 minutes, A shares a problem while B and C listen. During the next 5 minutes, B and C ask clarifying questions about the problem. Finally, during the last 5 minutes, B and C offer solution ideas to A, who writes the ideas down. The process is repeated so that B and C have a chance to discuss their problems as well.

Pinwheel activity. Another problem-solving strategy that engages larger numbers of faculty is the pinwheel activity. Groups of six are formed and stand in a pinwheel configuration. That is, three people stand in the center, each facing a person in an outer circle. The three individuals in the center each pose a professional problem or dilemma they are experiencing to the person facing them. The people they face generate possible ideas about how to address the specific problem posed. After they brainstorm solution ideas for 3 minutes, the people on the outside rotate. In this way, the individuals in the center are able to gain additional ideas about how to address their problems or challenges. The process continues until each person in the center has three different sets of ideas from the three outside "consultants." Then the pinwheel is "turned inside out," and the outside people who had brainstormed solution ideas previously have a chance to share their problems and garner ideas from professional colleagues. This process makes the staff aware that others share similar problems or challenges and that a tremendous amount of expertise exists among faculty members that begs to be tapped.

What's your bag? Teachers post questions about curriculum, instruction, special needs students, resources, or assessment on the outside of a brown lunch bag (one question per bag). The bags are stapled (leaving an opening on the top) on a bulletin board in the staff room. Blank 3″ x 5″ index cards are also put in a container on the bulletin board, along with a pen. Staff members are invited to respond to the bag questions using the index cards. They write ideas on the cards and drop them into the bags. Question owners read the ideas in the bag and redeposit the cards in the bag so others may read them as well.

Once a foundation of trust, comfort, and risk taking is created, the opportunities for peers to support one another through collaborative exchanges are limitless. Some additional activities might include co-planning lessons, developing curriculum materials to address standards, creating cross-age learning opportunities for students, devising interdisciplinary units, sharing lesson plans, creating differentiated units of instruction, examining artifacts of student work, developing authentic assessment tasks, participating in study groups, portfolio sharing, or engaging in collaborative action research around teacher-generated questions.

As joint work among colleagues continues, norms of collaboration evolve. Working together becomes "the way we do business around here," as one staff member put it. Eventually, governance structures may reflect collaboration as well. For instance, one school designed a structure called the Principal's Advisory Committee (PAC). The PAC was made up of three teachers elected by the staff and the principal. Together, they met and planned faculty meetings. The PAC members rotated responsibility for conducting the meetings as well. The teachers on the PAC provided a bridge for communication with faculty members at large. In the process of serving on the PAC, they received training in meeting management, problem solving, decision making, conflict resolution, effective staff development, and communication skills. Hence, in addition to serving their colleagues, they developed critical leadership skills. Other collaborative schools have adopted site-based management or shared governance structures and practices. In these collaborative structures, staff members apply a variety of skills to make school-level decisions.

The Principal and Collaboration

As noted earlier, a key factor in the development of a collaborative school is the principal's role. The principal must truly believe in and value professional collaboration for this type of work to be sustained over time. This must be reflected not only in what is said but in the actions of the principal as well. For instance, if opportunities for professional collaboration are provided, do they occur during prime time, or are they placed at the end of a meeting's agenda? Does the principal collab-orate as well? Is there a budget item to support this type of endeavor? For many principals who have not experienced collaborative efforts heretofore, such activi-ties may be uncomfortable. Some principals, for example, have indicated a discom-fort with shared governance because they felt, from the district's perspective, the principal still had accountability for decisions. In these cases, many principals solved the problem by requesting staff input but reserving the right to make the fi-nal decision. So that the staff did not feel "sold out" by this, one principal first facili-tated a session in which the faculty brainstormed all the decisions to be made, and these were recorded on butcher paper. The principal and the staff then labeled who would have primary responsibility for input for each one.

In other instances, although the principal sensed a degree of discomfort, it was simply acknowledged, and the principal expressed the belief that this was part of the learning process that everyone, at one time or another, experienced. Staff sup-port for this new role was requested. In other settings the principal shares leader-ship responsibilities for creating a learning community with teachers. Speaking of this at the 2002 National Association of Secondary School Principals Conference, Jo and Joseph Blase stated, "It's time to craft a new kind of educational leader, whether principal or teacher. This new leader is capable of building a constructivist, data driven, dialogic, inclusive learning community in which the development and achievement of all is pre-eminent."

Some Final Thoughts on Collaboration

Creating a collaborative culture has been described as "the single most impor-tant factor" for successful school improvement initiatives (Newmann & Wehlage, 1995).

Regardless of how a collaborative organization develops, schools that are able to reach such a state report a sense of synergy, creativity, and a capacity for innova-tion and learning uncommon to those who function in isolation. Moreover, in true collaborative cultures, joint work among teachers has developed as a daily norm for operating. It is reflected in daily work habits, meetings, and ongoing, planned, job-embedded professional growth experiences. In these cultures, staff members are willing to put their professional knowledge and practices on the line to be scru-tinized by their colleagues. They view one another as sources for learning.

Time is a precious resource in schools. Therefore it is essential that collabora-tive time in schools is focused on capacity building to assure high levels of quality student learning. There should be strong links between core beliefs, vision and mis-sion, data analysis, goal setting, and site level collaborative work. Planning in this way enables the realization of excellence.

Reflections

This space provides for you a place to write in ideas that have been generated by this chapter, things you want to try, or adaptations of ideas presented herein.

1. Thinking about the goal of enhancing student learning, what additional collaborative activities would you add to those offered in this chapter?
2. Thinking about the staff of which you are a part, how would you characterize their capacity to engage in risk-taking behavior (low, medium, or high risk)? What activities might you share?
3. What insights or new questions do you have as a result of reflecting on the ideas presented in this chapter?

12

Asking the Right Questions About Curriculum, Instruction, and Assessment, or Getting to Know the C.I.A.

Today you are immersed in curriculum.

A PRINCIPAL'S VOICE

Keeping the Curriculum Relevant

The notion of teachers closing the classroom door and deciding for themselves what should be included in the curriculum is no longer acceptable. Previously, research and experience indicated that many teachers taught what they were comfortable with, and what was expedient. A middle school principal described it this way: "Teachers have to focus more on curriculum. They have to adopt texts that meet standards, and focus on competencies and skills. I used to love to do my 'moon unit.' Today I could not do it. It does not meet the state standards." Many principals and teachers are still learning how to best implement their state standards and the high stakes assessments that often accompany the standards.

Teachers are feeling pressure and some anxiety about meeting federal and state high stakes testing expectations and state standards. Ironically, local schools are expected to implement the democratic ideals of site-based management, and yet embrace federal and state expectations related to curriculum and high stakes testing. Principals must ensure that the pressure and anxiety that some teachers might be feeling does not overflow into the classroom. For example, most teachers are uncomfortable with "teaching to the test" if the test does not meet the curriculum expectations and needs of the students in their classes. This cannot be stated too strongly as a teacher's attitude and enthusiasm for the curriculum sends a subtle but strong message to students about the importance of learning. The process or strategies that we use teach children and adults how we feel about learning and how we learn. If lifelong learning is the vision, then what is taught and how it is taught must be considered in tandem. Generating the momentum toward accomplishing this goal is perhaps one of the greatest challenges for the principalship. To help address this challenge, we will examine both curriculum and instruction by raising significant questions throughout this chapter.

Asking the Right Questions

Principals, because of their daily interaction with students, teachers, and parents, may be in the best position to reflect on how the curriculum is affecting the total school community. From this vantage point, the principal must consider and facilitate discussion concerning the following questions and issues as curriculum and instructional decisions are made. By promoting these questions and encouraging dialogue among the staff, principals can do a great deal to keep teachers thinking about curriculum, their students, and ways of teaching.

How Should Curriculum Be Defined?

There is no one definition of curriculum that is universally accepted. For example, curriculum can mean a sequenced plan to educate students or a broad field of study (e.g., examining various curriculum models). Yet defining curriculum is a very difficult and important task, for the definition says much about the scope of school experiences that one believes has a direct impact on student learning. For example, a narrow definition of a curriculum plan usually focuses on specific classroom content and skills that can be objectively tested, whereas a broader definition moves beyond specific classroom content and skills and involves activities that have long-range implications and sometimes are not easily tested. Additionally, a broader definition implies that almost all of the actions of a classroom teacher and activities within a school may have far-reaching curriculum implications for a student.

Based on the comments and connections made in this book about a school's overall mission as a learning community for continued adult and student growth, a broad definition of curriculum is appropriate. Thus curriculum is defined as *planned and unplanned concepts, content, skills, work habits, means of assessment, attitudes, and instructional strategies taught in the classroom and the variety of school activities in and out of class that influence present and future academic, social, emotional, and physical growth of students.*

What Kind of Authentic Student Work and Results Are Essential to Prepare Students for Successful Living in a Democratic Society?

Moving from our definition of curriculum, it is important to consider student work and anticipated outcomes that go beyond school-related tasks and expectations. Each proposed outcome should answer satisfactorily the question: Will this learning help students when they are not in school, as citizens and in the work-place? According to many educators and business leaders, we must identify the skills that will be needed in the future and how to best teach those skills. For example, if we accept Drucker's (1992) view that to work successfully in an organization one must have "the ability to present ideas orally and in writing; the ability to work with people; [and] the ability to shape and direct one's own work, contribution and career" (p. 5), then we must teach the appropriate content and skills to foster these competencies.

Thus a multicultural curriculum, cooperative learning activities, independent and challenging thinking activities, and multidisciplinary and interdisciplinary activities (that include oral, written, and cross-subject analyses) become important, not because they are fashionable but because they provide essential skills that must be transferred to the workplace. Moreover, when deciding on key student learnings, it is essential that one asks, What are the specific instructional techniques and activities (e.g., cooperative learning, drafting several versions of a report, debating) that best teach specific curriculum expectations and foster applications of these learnings in the workplace? To illustrate further, in the elementary, middle, and high school-level community service programs and in the middle and high school-level courses, workplace experiences become essential links to support and highlight the connections between school and real-life experiences.

To develop relevant curriculum expectations, a structured approach that covers essential questions is very helpful. The classical Tyler Rationale still provides us with four essential questions that should be addressed by individuals and committees when developing curriculum. These questions are as follows: "a) What educational purposes should the school seek to attain? b) What educational experiences can be provided that are likely to attain these purposes? c) How can these educational experiences be effectively organized? d) How can we determine whether these purposes are being attained?" (Hyman, 1974, p. 40). Add to this model what we now know from research on the human brain and developments in teaching methodology, and we have the key elements to engage in a meaningful dialogue on curriculum, instruction, assessment, and learning within a school setting. An approach close to Tyler, but subtly different, is expressed by Wiggins and McTighe (1998) as they effectively tackle curriculum "backward" with a design strategy that initially may appear counterintuitive. "This backward approach to curriculum design also departs from another common practice: thinking about assessment as something we do at the end, once teaching is completed. Rather than creating assessments near the conclusion of a unit of study (or relying on the tests provided by textbook publishers, which may not completely or appropriately assess our standards), backward design calls for us to operationalize our goals or standards in terms of assessment evidence as we *begin* to plan a unit or course. It reminds us to begin with the question, What would we accept as evidence that students have attained the desired understandings and proficiencies—before proceeding to plan teaching and learning experiences?" (p. 8).

A different approach is taken by English and Hill (1994), who suggest that because of the injustices of our society, we should go beyond the present or futurist thinking when developing curriculum because we will just perpetuate the existing order: "The place to begin creating a curriculum is the world as we would wish it to be" (p. 61). Although English and Hill recommend some of the same innovations noted above (e.g., multidisciplinary curriculum), their approach is very different as they believe that our traditional curriculum models are too closely linked to the injustices fostered by the present school setting. They reject school as we know it and the traditional curriculum units and themes as too value laden and reductionist. English and Hill (1994) would move toward "arena planning," which embraces the ideas and experiences of the learner when planning curriculum and, to promote learning, is centered on personal meaning, experiences, and activities of children (pp. 65-70).

What Are the Instructional Considerations to Effectively Communicate the Curriculum to Students?

One of the keys to assuring that the curriculum content is communicated well is through sound instructional approaches. Caine and Caine (1991) present a very strong argument for basing instructional considerations on recent discoveries in research on the human brain. Central to their thesis is that the brain is constantly making connections; thus curriculum and teaching models and methodologies should emphasize learning based on an integrated curriculum, thematic teaching, thematical orchestration, and cooperative learning (pp. 118-122). Furthermore, Caine and Caine stress that as the human brain is both an emotional and a cognitive organ, it responds to motivating stimuli that immerse the learner in a variety of engaging experiences such as reading, listening, and talking (p. 6).

The recent findings from cognitive learning theory echo the work of Caine and Caine. The following seven concepts (Herman, Aschbacher, & Winter, 1992) can be extremely helpful as teachers and principals consider the development and implementation of instructional strategies to deliver curriculum:

1. Knowledge is constructed. Learning is a process of creating personal meaning from new information and prior knowledge.

    Applications: Encourage discussion of new ideas. Encourage divergent thinking and multiple solutions, not just one right answer. Use multiple modes of expression; emphasize critical thinking skills. Relate new learnings to past experiences.

2. Learning is not necessarily a linear progression of discrete skills.

    Applications: Engage students in problem solving.

3. There is great variety in learning styles, attention spans, memory, developmental paces, and intelligences.

Applications: Provide choices in tasks and how mastery is demonstrated. Provide "think time." Do not overuse timed tests. Provide opportunities for revising and rethinking.

4. People perform better when they know the goal, see models, and know how their performance compares to the standard.

Applications: Involve students in defining and discussing goals. Provide a range of examples of student work; discuss characteristics. Provide opportunities for student self-evaluation and peer review. Solicit student input into standards.

5. It is important to know when to use knowledge, how to adapt it, and how to manage one's own learning.

Applications: Give real-world opportunities (or simulations) to apply or adapt new knowledge. Have students self-evaluate: How they learn, how they set new goals, and why they like certain work.

6. Motivation, effort, and self-esteem affect learning and performance.

Applications: Encourage students to see the connection between effort and results.

7. Learning has social components. Group work is valuable.

Applications: Provide group work. Incorporate heterogeneous groups with a variety of student roles. Consider group products and processes. (pp. 19-20)

In their classic book *Models of Teaching,* Joyce and Weil (1972) identify a wide range of teaching models. These models represent "approaches to creating environments for learning." More than 90 different strategies are identified by Joyce and Weil. They describe four different "families" or approaches to teaching into which these strategies can be categorized.

Although there is much overlap among families (and among models within families), the four are: 1) those oriented toward social relations and toward the relation between man and his culture and which draw upon social sources (The Social Family); 2) those which draw on information processing systems and descriptions of human capacity for processing of information (Information Processing Family); 3) those which draw on personality development, the process of personal construction of reality, and the capacity to function as an integrated personality as the major source (The Personal Family); 4) those developed from an analysis of the processes by which human behavior is shaped and reinforced (Behavioral Systems Family). (Joyce & Weil, 1972, p. 8)

Examples of the social family of instruction include cooperative learning strategies such as the jigsaw or Learning Together. Information-processing strategies include such techniques as concept attainment or concept formation. An example from the personal family is synectics, designed originally as a problem-solving tool, but one that can also be used to add interest and vitality to writing. Finally, mastery learning or programmed instruction serve as strategies from the behavioral family.

In addition to *Models of Teaching*, others have developed effective tools to enhance the impact of the delivery system and curriculum content. For example, Gardner's (1995) eight different types of intelligence, Marzano et al.'s (1992) work, *Dimensions of Learning*, and Gregorc's (1985) and Butler's (1992) works on mind styles of teachers often influence the selection of teaching approaches.

Although each approach varies as to its central purpose, all contribute to enriching the toolbox from which teachers can draw to communicate curriculum effectively. Teachers are encouraged to develop a wide repertoire of teaching strategies and use a variety of techniques in their classroom to enhance the curriculum delivery system and meet the varying needs of students.

How Can Data Driven Curricula, Instructional, and Assessment Decisions Help Educators Foster Student Academic Growth?

Background

In the past, when student test scores on national norm-referenced tests were shared with faculty or parents, few changes were made based on the testing results. The tests may have given us some insight into how a particular child, school, or district was performing, but there was little concern about teacher or student accountability. Today the situation has changed. The standards movement in most states is accompanied by assessment systems that align the standards with high stakes tests in specific disciplines.

Purpose of Data-Driven Decision Making

Quite simply, data-driven decision making takes an analytical and hard look at the question, How are the students doing? This question is grounded in state and national expectations for student achievement (i.e., standards) that hold administrators and teachers accountable in each school. These standards target areas in which students and schools are expected to show progress over time. Both quantitative and qualitative trends and patterns of student progress are monitored and interpreted, often related to the standards deemed essential within a particular state. As Manobianco (2002) notes, "Interpreting data in isolation is useless without linking the data to what we want students to know and be able to do as well as looking at our instructional strategies" (p. 17).

In addition, effective data-driven decision making implies that teachers will use multiple sources of data to fine tune their teaching in order to meet various student needs. Scherer refers to this important assessment responsibility as the examination of "multiple data waves" in which teachers might use data collected from portfolios, reading records, classroom observations, and audio recordings, in addition to norm-referenced or criterion referenced tests and standardized tests (2001, p. 15).

Creating a Culture That Supports Data-Driven Decision Making

To create a school culture that embraces the examination of testing data is not easy. Yet, it is occurring in numerous schools. Often these schools include principals who are "effective school leaders [and] are hunters, gatherers and consumers of education" (NAESP, *Standards for What Principals Should Know and Be Able to Do,* 2001). These schools willingly examine curricula, instructional, and assessment practices that may account for strengths, weaknesses, and puzzling student scores without blaming or pointing fingers because of testing outcomes. Instead, teachers comfortably ask, How can we use the data to target difficulties and improve teaching and learning? This reflects a climate in which accountability is balanced with honest analysis in a nonthreatening manner.

School leaders can set a positive tone in schools by promoting a dialogue about assessment. To illustrate, principals can encourage data analysis during faculty meetings, pre- and postobservation conferences, and during actual teaching, grade level meetings, and other professional development activities. One middle school assistant principal stated, "The most exciting activity that we encountered as a faculty concerned data driven decision making related to sharing writing samples across the curriculum during a faculty meeting. During the meeting we established rubrics aligned with state standards as we scored student work together. This activity made all of us aware of the writing expectations that students should be held accountable for within each discipline." Also, faculty meetings can provide forums for inviting representatives from other schools, with demographic profiles similar to your own school, to share information about progress and concerns with their curricular standards and assessment measures. Principals can help teachers with purposeful scheduling to provide time for teachers to diagnose data together and more effectively plan teaching and learning.

Recently, a retired teacher shared the following observation: "When I was teaching I did not worry about standardized tests because the tests were not given till the following year. Today, with standards and the increased testing and accountability, teachers cannot ignore how the progress in their class might affect testing the following year." Consequently, opportunities must be provided that allow teachers to "compare notes" with grade level or department colleagues to review standards and benchmarks and discuss effective instructional strategies. During these meetings teachers can remind one another to concentrate on essential curriculum elements, pinpoint areas that need greater emphasis, identify strengths, and explore grade level or subject area trends (e.g., "How are our students doing on word problems in math? The data indicates that we are accomplishing our goals in this area. Let's continue to use these curricula and instructional practices—and use some of these practices in other areas too").

This horizontal articulation must be complemented by vertical articulation with grade level or subject area colleagues above and below a particular grade to reduce curriculum repetition and share successful teaching strategies. These horizontal and vertical grade level meetings provide opportunities for critical friends and Action Research activities to occur, linking state standards and state assessment with actual classroom performance.

Pre- and postobservation conferences and class observations should also be used to promote data-driven decision making. During preobservation conferences, principals need to ask teachers about targeting standards, benchmarks, and assessment data with student work in particular classes.

Types of Data

The risk of using scores on one high stakes test to make important decisions about a child has encouraged educators to examine various ways to measure success. Thus, both qualitative and quantitative assessment measures, also referred to as soft and hard data, are being explored to make better curricular and instructional decisions about student needs and teaching strategies (NAESP, 2001).

Hard data. Hard data sources include norm-referenced and criterion-referenced tests, usually externally developed and graded. Often, these tests are given once a year, or once every few years. Traditionally, these tests have *not* been aligned with state goals and objectives. Today, however, criterion-referenced tests measure student success based on state expectations. Disaggregating testing data (discussed below) helps schools examine trends and diagnose specific strengths and needs.

Soft data. Soft forms of assessment include a variety of alternative assessment measures and teacher-generated tests. These forms of data are usually internal, that is, developed at the school site or in the classroom and often carry greater meaning for teachers, students, and parents. Common forms of alternative assessment include portfolios, senior projects, exhibitions, performances, audio recordings of student progress, group presentations, lab experiments, and teacher observations.

A portfolio, as a record of student growth over time, is especially promising as a rich source of student data. When a teacher, parent, or community member can look at a specific student's work, generated during a year or over several years, one can see progress right before one's eyes. Hard copy evidence of student work as artifacts of progress is very powerful. Hearing and/or seeing a brief audio- or video recording taped over several months, of a first grader learning to read, is equally powerful.

Data-driven decision making also uses feedback generated from student, parent, or community surveys. For example, data revealing how present high school students or recent graduates are succeeding in the job market can help schools with curricula and instructional decisions.

Disaggregating Data

Data-driven decision making seeks "to look deeper into the surface data" to help schools identify why some students are doing better than others (NAESP, 2001, p. 64). Because of the electronic data resources available to schools, disaggregating information is much less difficult today than even ten years ago. Principals can lead this effort, along with guidance counselors, school psychologists, technology teachers, and central office assessment specialists.

Multiple demographic variables can be examined by disaggregating data. Examples of demographic variables include gender, attendance patterns, ethnicity, race, student mobility, teacher mobility, teacher tenure, free or reduced lunch eligibility, tardiness, behavioral referrals, and second-language learners. It is critical to engage in a dialogue when disaggregating data to examine trends or patterns that emerge as variables are considered.

One cannot exaggerate the importance of analyzing data demographically. For example, a majority of students in a particular school may have achieved outstanding results on the state's math assessment test. However, disaggregated data may reveal that 75% of the students in the school, who are eligible for free or reduced lunch, scored below the minimum expectation on the test. Clearly the school needs to target this population to help these students improve their test scores.

Finally, a cautionary note. Disaggregating data helps principals, teachers, and parents examine whether schools are succeeding with their various populations. However, whenever we separate groups and highlight differences, there is a risk that data might be misinterpreted or misused—leading to stereotypical remarks and possibly racist or prejudicial generalizations. Unfortunately, the history of standardized testing, going back to the 1920s and the original intelligence testing movement, is filled with prejudicial use and abuse of data results that led to limiting school and career opportunities for both indigenous and immigrant American populations (*Lessons Of A Century*, 2000). School leaders must guard against this abuse of data.

What Is the Best Way to Determine Whether Students Have Grasped the Key Curriculum Goals?

This question presents one of the most difficult and controversial issues in education: the eternal debate over standardized tests and alternative assessments. This debate centers around finding the best way to judge what students know and are able to do. Unless we are satisfied with the ways of assessing students, curriculum accountability will always be questioned. Standardized tests give us some insight into how students in each school rate when compared to each other and to students in other schools. Thus, state assessments, based on curricula standards, serve as a crucial and very public source of information for comparison and accountability purposes. This is especially true when high stakes tests are used to make decisions for promotion and graduation. However, we need to go further if each teacher's expertise about his or her class is to count—and if we are to identify the diverse strengths and needs of each student. The nature of assessments may need to vary in each class. Thus a major part of a school's discussion on curriculum must be related to the learning tasks on each grade level that indicate whether students have grasped the essentials of the curriculum. Clearly, assessment is not separate from curriculum and instruction.

Probably one of the richest activities for a teaching staff is to develop acceptable performance standards and performance tasks to be assessed. To illustrate, let us assume that an 11th-grade American history class has just studied the governmental system of checks and balances. Instead of giving a traditional essay exam to assess their knowledge of the system, why not try a simulation activity in which groups of students represent the three branches of government (e.g., executive, congressional, and judicial) and debate over which branch or branches of government should be responsible for handling scenarios presented by the teacher? Before beginning the activity, a teacher should have a strong sense of which concepts are critical for understanding. The activity should be structured so students have an opportunity to display and reinforce their understanding of the concepts. For example, When does a police action by our military become a war? or What role does each branch of government play if America is fighting a war? This will give students an opportunity to really wrestle with issues, debate, think on their feet, and see the different interpretations that are possible. This type of performance task adds some credibility to those trying to address the following concern: The focus should be on developing student tasks that can give us insight into how students in 5 years may apply what they have learned today. Such a task also presents opportunities for students to practice critical thinking, decision-making, public speaking, and listening skills in addition to demonstrating knowledge about branches of government.

The positive response of so many teachers to alternative assessment strategies probably indicates a realization that the search for ways to authenticate learning has brought greater meaning to both teachers and students. Principals would be wise to encourage these explorations if teachers are taking ownership of the various strategies to pursue meaningful curriculum goals. Portfolio assessment, for example, has enabled teachers to see significant growth over time and has encouraged students to take greater ownership and reflect more on their work (Tierney, Carter, & Desai, 1991).

Gardner's multiple intelligence theory has increased interest in various assessment strategies to give students an opportunity to display their talents. To illustrate, Armstrong (1994) has cited anecdotal records, work samples, audiocassettes, videotapes, photography, student journals, sociograms, informal tests, and student interviews as suitable ways to demonstrate understanding through a multiple intelligence approach (pp. 116-123). Finally, having students write their own homework or test questions or use learning logs, webbing, and semantic mapping are all indicators that teachers continue to search in creative ways to help determine how best to find out whether students have grasped the curriculum goals.

How Can a Principal Help to Keep a Conversation on Curriculum Active?

Principals can promote this process by providing a forum through monthly grade-level or department meetings devoted at least partially to answering questions already raised in this chapter and others, such as the following: Is our curriculum relevant? Are we accomplishing our primary curriculum objectives? Are we behind? Ahead? What can we leave out without hurting the program? The idea is not just to "cover" the curriculum but to address the essential components of the curriculum necessary for students to succeed in present and in future grades—and more important, in life. We hear often that "less is more." If we accept this notion, then selecting key learning objectives and focusing on those objectives should be a much greater concern than "touching" on each chapter recommended in a textbook.

The principal needs to facilitate the development of a forum so teachers interact across grade levels to align and articulate the curriculum. First-grade teachers must meet with second-grade teachers and ask about expectations and how they can meet student needs across grade levels. In middle school and high school, subject area specialists should do the same so important content skills and concepts are not overlooked and subject area fragmentation is minimized. Discussions of this kind across the curriculum can facilitate interdisciplinary planning and highlight key concepts that individual teachers can emphasize to reinforce students' prior experiences with the same concepts. At one school, the principal allocated time so that teachers could identify key themes that they taught. For example, one teacher taught the Civil War; another, the "war" on poverty; still another, the Vietnam War. The key theme was the concept that all oppression brings resistance and conflict. By teaching this concept, students could make connections across classes and enhance understanding regarding the connectedness of knowledge. The discussion also increased the amount of future dialogue about curriculum among professionals at this school.

The development of statewide curriculum documents that describe important student learnings is of paramount importance. To help guide teachers and enhance the conversation on curriculum, teachers should work with principals, curriculum specialists, or grade-level leaders to develop locally relevant and brief curriculum guides based on state expectations that may include key concepts and skills, essential questions, and assessment components. Pacing charts with general timelines to meet unit or thematic goals can also be helpful. Furthermore, the guides should include a list of instructional resources, textbooks, and enrichment material available for each subject. These documents should be brief, maybe three to five pages.

Otherwise, there is little chance that they will be read. The written curriculum should be a living document frequently reviewed and discussed by teachers. What good is a curriculum that remains in a desk drawer gathering dust? By having teachers involved in refining the state-, district-, or school-developed curriculum to meet the needs of particular students, the principal can help to facilitate and maintain a dialogue on curriculum and teaching.

How Much Should Curriculum Change?

Before addressing the issue of curriculum change, it is important to consider a school's overall belief on whether curriculum is dynamic or unchanging. Without getting into a major discussion of various curriculum philosophies, let us remember that a classical education is very different from John Dewey's notion of curriculum as process and experimentation in a democratic society—adjusting to changing world needs. The classical ideal maintains that there are essential skills and classical works that are enduring regardless of how the world changes.

If one accepts the notion that curriculum is dynamic, then there is always something new to add to the curriculum. Changing societal needs, technological innovations, national security concerns, and political realities all mean curricular changes. For those who accept the changing curriculum, the crucial questions are, What do we need to do to prepare students for the future? What should be added to the curriculum? and What should be removed from the curriculum?

It is not easy to differentiate the latest fad from a meaningful curriculum innovation. What new curriculum ideas should be adopted? Which traditional ideas should be discarded or revived? Again, staff dialogue is a key. How can the school principal help the staff to determine what ideas are worth examining? Which state standards and benchmarks should receive greater or less emphasis based on the local setting? Encouraging teachers to read professional journals, using time during faculty meetings to discuss innovations, sponsoring brown bag or study groups, and encouraging professional growth experiences beyond the school (e.g., conferences, workshops, and courses) are all ways that principals can help the staff examine the changes that are taking place. Ideally, the principal should empower the teachers to take the lead regarding an innovation. When necessary, principals can productively contribute to innovative projects by sharing research with the staff and revisiting the school vision and mission. Principals can then provide the support to encourage an innovative or pilot program in a class, grade level, or throughout the school.

States, school districts, or individual schools with institutionalized curriculum review cycles (usually 3-6 years) go a long way in making sure that systematic decisions are made when innovations come down the pike. (Schools should try to have representation on the district committees to assure that curriculum decisions are relevant to site-based needs.) The review cycle, which provides for an examination of different subject areas in a systematic way each year, can bring productive change, thoughtful decision making, and exciting curriculum discussions to a district office or school. Furthermore, the process "puts the skids" on those who try to pressure a change without a comprehensive review. The most refreshing aspect of a review cycle may very well be that the process institutionalizes change by building change into the structure of the organization. The very nature of the cycle encourages renewal because teachers examine the recent research in the curriculum area and other curricular and innovative instructional methods. This is essential in keeping an organization on the cutting edge.

An excellent project for a school to stay abreast of curricular innovations is to collect articles on various curricular or teaching trends and conduct a jigsaw activity at a faculty meeting to discuss the ideas. Various topics might include

- Assisting special needs students
- Whole-language instruction
- The "backward" approach to curriculum design (Wiggins & McTighe, 1998)
- Alternative assessment
- Integrated curriculum
- Pros and cons of national or state standards
- NCTM standards
- Multicultural education
- Using technology
- Developing rubrics for student work samples

A variation of this activity might be to revisit the ideas of curriculum innovators such as John Dewey or Robert Hutchins or possibly discuss the ideas of more current theorists such as Howard Gardner or Elliot Eisner. This activity might encourage staff members to review what these educators propose and then reflect as to whether the ideas are right for the school.

To pilot a curricular idea, a school might decide to tackle a topic, such as integrated curriculum, as an innovative project. For example, an integrated environmental education activity could result from this curriculum project. Students could write poems about the environment, conduct scientific experiments examining the environment, use rainfall percentages in math, and discuss the social implications of Earth's changing environment. These activities could culminate in a schoolwide Earth Day activity.

What Can We Learn From the Differences Between the Elementary and High School Curriculum Expectations That Can Help Us Develop Effective Interdisciplinary Practices?

Relating the above question to an interdisciplinary curriculum approach can help to shed light on how we can do a better job teaching across disciplines.

A high school principal, observing an elementary school classroom, is immediately struck by the variety of subjects that elementary teachers are expected to teach within their classes. High school teachers face a considerable challenge because of the number of courses one teaches in a major discipline and the depth of knowledge one is expected to master for each course. On the other hand, the elementary school teacher, and often the middle school teacher, must maintain broad knowledge in a variety of disciplines. An elementary school teacher cannot be an expert in every discipline; the principal must accept this reality yet work with the teacher to ensure that each core subject is addressed competently in the elementary classroom. The various expectations of high school, middle school, and elementary school teachers can be discussed at grade-level meetings, during conferences with teachers from different schools, on inservice days, or as a focus of peer-coaching activities. Some schools regularly schedule vertical articulation days.

It is important to note that the traditional high school master schedule dictates how subjects are taught and the time frame of a class period. Until we take a hard look at the schedule, and exchange and pilot ideas—as many schools are now doing—it is difficult to try interdisciplinary strategies. In recent years, hundreds of high schools have "rejected" the traditional schedule and have moved to instructional blocks of approximately 80 minutes, with many block schedule variations. These new designs have enabled many high school teachers to experiment and succeed with interdisciplinary activities either alone or with colleagues. These interdisciplinary strategies rely heavily on planning time as well as class time.

Interestingly, elementary teachers may have a clear advantage in making curriculum connections because one teacher is assigned to instruct students in a variety of core subjects. Thus elementary school teachers can capitalize on the common subject area concepts and the interests of students across the curriculum. This can be a powerful motivator and, of course, sets the stage for understanding that the various disciplines should be integrated, not fragmented. We must recognize relationships and connections among the academic disciplines. Focusing on key interdisciplinary concepts is one way of doing this. If one teacher teaches about the circulatory system and another the solar system, the key concept is that of "system." If the concept of what a system is is taught well, then other teachers can capitalize on adding to this existing student understanding. Elementary school principals have a unique opportunity to promote this important educational principle with the teaching staff. They also need to allocate time for planning across classrooms and grade levels and for teachers to share their interdisciplinary approaches.

A major challenge for high school principals is working with the staff to develop more integration among the various disciplines. Approaches can range from paralleling a couple of courses, to teaching common themes when possible, to complete integration of two or more courses through team teaching and the synthesis of a variety of subject or thematic areas. In addition, providing a forum for secondary teachers to discuss what they teach and when they teach it can enable them to reinforce one another's subject area themes. For instance, in one high school, teachers in history and English were teaching World War II topics. By discussing the curriculum and how and when it was being delivered, they were able to emphasize and parallel key themes across their two classes for students. In another high school, dialogue led to the discovery that the English teacher was teaching *The*

Diary of Anne Frank in November, whereas the history teacher addressed the Holo-
caust in March. By coordinating the time frames in which these were taught, the
student experience was enhanced. At another school, staff members selected the
theme of the Baroque period and used this as a backdrop for their particular areas
of specialty.

Continuing the Curriculum Discussion

A principal's most important responsibilities regarding curriculum may be in
providing the forum or setting to facilitate teacher curriculum discussions and ensuring that state curriculum initiatives can be implemented into a practical living
and working document for the local school setting. In this way, the curriculum of
today can be kept dynamic and can excite teachers. Most important, it will prepare
students for an ever-changing world. As one teacher summarized, "We should be
aiming to help children become caring adults, builders of communities, sharers of
learning, lovers of the printed word, citizens of the world, and nurturers of nature"
(Teeter, 1995).

Reflections

This space provides for you a place to write in ideas that have been generated
by this chapter, things you want to try, or adaptations of ideas presented herein.

1. Do you agree or disagree with the definition of curriculum provided in
   this chapter? Discuss your ideas with a colleague.

2. What are the most important curriculum issues that currently need to be
   addressed in your school? Why are these issues important? How can you
   begin energizing the staff to address these issues?

3. Speculate on some of our societal trends that could affect the curriculum.
   Are schools addressing the curricular areas necessary to cope with the
   trends?

4. Should the curriculum reflect current societal trends or ideal societal possibilities?

5. What steps would you include in directing a curriculum review cycle?

6. How might staff interest in curriculum review, development, or implementation be enhanced?

7. What are the pros and cons of the federal and state initiatives related to
   high-stakes testing and curriculum standards?

8. What insights or new questions do you have as a result of reflecting on
   the ideas presented in this chapter?

13

What Principals Need to Know About Technology

By D. D. Dawson

"I think there is a world market for maybe five computers."

IBM CHAIRMAN THOMAS WATSON, (1943)

"Computers in the future may have only 1,000 vacuum tubes and perhaps only weigh 1 1/2 tons."

POPULAR MECHANICS (1949)

"Get your feet off my desk, get out of here, you stink, and we're not going to buy your product."

JOE KEENAN, PRESIDENT OF ATARI (in 1979 responding to Steve Jobs' offer to sell him rights to the new personal computer he and Steve Wozniak developed)

"The real problem is not whether machines think but whether men do."

B. F. SKINNER

More than 92% of public schools access the Internet (Market Data Retrieval, 2002, www.schooldata.com), and more than 80% of U.S. schools report that the majority of their teachers use computers daily for instructional purposes. This is quite an accomplishment considering the fact that few in education circles had even heard the words *computer technology* as recently as the 70s and early 80s. Those who had, associated the words with super computers used by the government to control space missions and to manipulate large quantities of data. Almost no one envisioned the potential of computers in the classroom.

Even though physical access to technology has become more prevalent in education, there is too little attention being devoted to the effective and efficient integration of technology into the curriculum and to the important role principals must play in assuring that this happens. This chapter provides an overview of technology skills principals should possess as well as providing an evaluation framework for assessing the effective use of technology in the classroom.

Technology Standards for School Administrators

The International Society for Technology in Education (ISTE) and its National Educational Technology Standards (NETS) Team announced its National Education Technology Standards for Administrators (NETS•A) Project in 2002. A significant beginning to the NETS•A Project was the publication of the *Technology Standards for School Administrators* (TSSA) document. The intent of the document is to identify knowledge and skills that constitute the *core* of what every K-12 administrator needs to know regardless of specific job role. These standards are indicators of effective leadership for technology in schools. They do not define the minimum or maximum level of knowledge and skills required of a principal, but rather represent a consensus among educational leaders of what best indicates effective school leadership for the effective and efficient use of technology in schools. The standards and accompanying performance indicators are as follows:

I. **Leadership and Vision**—Educational leaders inspire a shared vision for comprehensive integration of technology and foster an environment and culture conducive to the realization of that vision.

    Educational leaders:

    A. facilitate the shared development by all stakeholders of a vision for technology use and widely communicate that vision.
    B. maintain an inclusive and cohesive process to develop, implement, and monitor a dynamic, long-range, and systemic technology plan to achieve the vision.
    C. foster and nurture a culture of responsible risk-taking and advocate policies promoting continuous innovation with technology.
    D. use data in making leadership decisions.
    E. advocate for research-based effective practices in use of technology.
    F. advocate on the state and national levels for policies, programs, and funding opportunities that support implementation of the district technology plan.

II. **Learning and Teaching**—Educational leaders ensure that curricular design, instructional strategies, and learning environments integrate appropriate technologies to maximize learning and teaching.

Educational leaders:

A. identify, use, evaluate, and promote appropriate technologies to enhance and support instruction and standards-based curriculum leading to high levels of student achievement.
B. facilitate and support collaborative technology-enriched learning environments conducive to innovation for improved learning.
C. provide for learner-centered environments that use technology to meet the individual and diverse needs of learners.
D. facilitate the use of technologies to support and enhance instructional methods that develop higher-level thinking, decision-making, and problem-solving skills.
E. provide for and ensure that faculty and staff take advantage of quality professional learning opportunities for improved learning and teaching with technology.

III. **Productivity and Professional Practice**—Educational leaders apply technology to enhance their professional practice and to increase their own productivity and that of others.

Educational leaders:

A. model the routine, intentional, and effective use of technology.
B. employ technology for communication and collaboration among colleagues, staff, parents, students, and the larger community.
C. create and participate in learning communities that stimulate, nurture, and support faculty and staff in using technology for improved productivity.
D. engage in sustained, job-related professional learning using technology resources.
E. maintain awareness of emerging technologies and their potential uses in education.
F. use technology to advance organizational improvement.

IV. **Support, Management, and Operations**—Educational leaders ensure the integration of technology to support productive systems for learning and administration.

Educational leaders:

A. develop, implement, and monitor policies and guidelines to ensure compatibility of technologies.
B. implement and use integrated technology-based management and operations systems.

    C. allocate financial and human resources to ensure complete and sustained implementation of the technology plan.

    D. integrate strategic plans, technology plans, and other improvement plans and policies to align efforts and leverage resources.

    E. implement procedures to drive continuous improvement of technology systems and to support technology replacement cycles.

V. **Assessment and Evaluation**—Educational leaders use technology to plan and implement comprehensive systems of effective assessment and evaluation.

Educational leaders:

    A. use multiple methods to assess and evaluate appropriate uses of technology resources for learning, communication, and productivity.

    B. use technology to collect and analyze data, interpret results, and communicate findings to improve instructional practice and student learning.

    C. assess staff knowledge, skills, and performance in using technology and use results to facilitate quality professional development and to inform personnel decisions.

    D. use technology to assess, evaluate, and manage administrative and operational systems.

VI. **Social, Legal and Ethical Issues**—Educational leaders understand the social, legal, and ethical issues related to technology and model responsible decision-making related to these issues.

Educational leaders:

    A. ensure equity of access to technology resources that enable and empower all learners and educators.

    B. identify, communicate, model, and enforce social, legal, and ethical practices to promote responsible use of technology.

    C. promote and enforce privacy, security, and online safety related to the use of technology.

    D. promote and enforce environmentally safe and healthy practices in the use of technology.

    E. participate in the development of policies that clearly enforce copyright law and assign ownership of intellectual property developed with district resources.

An underlying assumption of the TSSA is that administrators should be competent users of technology tools. The K-12 principal is a hands-on user of technology. Many benefits of technology are lost to the principal who relies upon an administrative assistant, school technology teacher, or computer lab coordinator to check his or her e-mail, create spreadsheets, and search the Internet. To that end, the development of specific professional technology skills is essential for principals.

Developing Administrative Capacity Through Technology

Technology Terms and Acronyms

Professional jargon is all around us—no more so than in the area of technology. As school leaders, principals should be able to identify, understand, and use technical terminology on a daily basis. A few of the more commonly used acronyms include

- *ISP* - Internet Service Provider
- *OS* - Operating System (Windows 95/98/XP, Apple Operating System)
- *IP Address* - Internet Protocol Address
- *WAN* - Wide Area Network
- *LAN* - Local Area Network
- *NIC* - Network Interface Card

Terms like *infrastructure* (the wiring and hardware included in a school LAN), *hardware* (computers, hubs, switches, printers, etc.) and *software* (the programs used to perform specific functions) should be familiar to the principal.

Online sources for additional technology terminology include

- www.instantweb.com/D/dictionary/index.html
- whatis.techtarget.com/

Word Processing

Word processing is the creation of written documents—letters, memos, reports, newsletters, and so on. Sample word processing software programs include Microsoft® Word, Corel® Word Perfect®, and the word processing feature of integrated software applications like Microsoft® Works and Apple Works®. Principals should be able to create, edit, save, and print written documents. Most word processing programs

---

MEMORANDUM

TO: All Teachers
FROM: Ms. Andrea, Principal
DATE: October 2, 2002
SUBJECT: After School Staff Development

The workshop, *How to Effectively Utilize Technology in the Classroom,* will be held after school on Wednesday, October 16, 3:30 - 5:30 p.m. in the second floor computer lab. This is the second in a series of workshops designed to assist teachers with technology integration in the content areas.

include templates that provide formatting and design elements for the basis of the document. For example, if the user selects File/New from the menu bar in a Microsoft® Word document, they are presented with templates to create brochures, letters, faxes, and memorandums.

Spreadsheets

An electronic spreadsheet uses a computer's ability to perform numeric calculations rapidly and accurately. Like traditional paper-based spreadsheets, an electronic spreadsheet contains a worksheet area that is divided into columns and rows that when intersected, form individual cells. Each cell can contain text, numbers, or formulas. A unique advantage of electronic spreadsheets is their ability to perform *what if* analysis. For example, a principal may want to know how much profit can be made from the sale of yearbooks based on different selling prices. By inputting estimated values and appropriate formulas, the principal can change the variables (number of yearbooks sold, cost to produce the yearbook, etc.) to determine the profit.

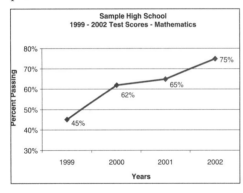

It has often been said that "a picture is worth a thousand words." Likewise, graphically depicting data in the form of a chart illustrates a powerful message. What better way to show increased test scores from one year to the next than to depict that information in a line graph? Once data is entered into a spreadsheet, with just a couple of mouse clicks, the administrator can visually portray that data.

Popular spreadsheet programs include Microsoft® Excel, Lotus® 1-2-3, and the spreadsheet component of integrated software applications. Templates to assist the user in creating a spreadsheet are also available in the software.

Presentation Graphics

School administrators are often required to present information to school boards, instructional supervisors, teachers, students, and the community. The ability to create meaningful presentations is essential. In the recent past, principals would create (or have created) transparencies for use in presentations. These transparencies were typically black and white and used on an overhead projector. Electronic presentation software gives the principal the ability to create professional-looking presentations with color, sound, and animation. Presentations can be made using overhead transparencies or using a projection device (multimedia projector) attached to a personal computer. Presentation graphics software also has features designed to print out the presentation in different formats—full page slides (for transparencies), speakers' notes, audience handouts, and outlines.

Hyperstudio and Microsoft® PowerPoint are commonly used presentation graphics software programs.

Database

A database is a collection of information that can be sorted and queried. An example of a database is a student information system. All the information about one student (demographics, class schedule, discipline, etc.) is called a record. While most school divisions have a centralized student database, the school principal should know how to utilize that database by performing searches (find where an individual student is located in the morning, find all seniors, or find all those students who have fourth block English) and create reports (How many girls are taking computer science classes? or How many students ride bus 43?).

The Internet

The Internet, sometimes called *the Net*, is a worldwide system of computer networks where users can exchange information via computers. Parts of the Internet include electronic mail (e-mail) and the World Wide Web (often abbreviated *WWW*) or called *the Web*.

The Web is the most widely used part of the Internet. Its most outstanding feature is *hypertext*, a method of instant cross-referencing. On most Web sites, certain words or phrases appear in text of a different color than the rest; often this text is also underlined. When the user clicks on the word or phrase, he or she is transferred to the site or page that is linked to that word or phrase. Sometimes there are buttons, images, or portions of images that are hyperlinked. If a mouse pointer positioned over a word, button, or image changes into an icon that looks like a hand, this indicates a hyperlink to another site.

To access information on the Internet, a software application called a *browser* is used. Popular browsers include Netscape®, Microsoft® Internet Explorer, and America Online (AOL).

To specify the location of a Web page on the Internet, a *uniform resource locator* (URL) or Web address is used. The URL contains the name of the protocol required to access the resource, a domain name that identifies a specific computer on the Internet, and a hierarchical description of a file location on the computer. Sample URLs are www.oreo.com or www.iste.org. The "com" or "org" part of the domain name reflects the purpose of the organization or entity.

.com commercial
.org non-profit organization
.net originally for Internet Service Providers; now used for many purposes
.gov U.S. federal, state, and local government agencies
.mil military
.edu educational institutions

In November 2000, the Internet Corporation for Assigned Names and Numbers (ICANN), a Los Angeles-based nonprofit group that oversees the distribution of domain names, approved seven additional domain names.

.biz	restricted to businesses
.info	open to anyone
.name	for personal registrations
.pro	for licensed professionals such as lawyers, doctors, and accountants
.aero	for anything related to air transport
.museum	for museums
.coop	for co-operative businesses such as credit unions

The Internet has rapidly become the primary research tool for teens. In fact, it is estimated that "94% of teens use the Internet to do research for school; 71% relied mostly on Internet sources for the last big school project" (The Internet and Education: Findings of the Pew Internet & American Life Project, www.pewinternet.org). Administrators, too, are quickly becoming advocates of the Internet for professional reading, research, and communication. With all the information on the Web, it is essential that administrators know how to both search the Internet and evaluate the results of searches.

When locating Internet resources, a *search engine* or a *directory* can be used. A directory takes the user to the home page of a Web site. A search engine locates pages on which appear the words and phrases one is looking for. A directory should be used when the user has only a vague idea of what is wanted (great music sites, list of major newspaper sites). Use a search engine when the aim is to get to a particular piece of information quickly (song title from a particular movie, quote from a newspaper column). A review of major search engines and how to effectively search the Internet can be found at searchenginewatch.com.

With the plethora of Web sites contained on the Internet, how does the principal know what is a reliable source and what is not? When evaluating Web sites, the credibility, accuracy, reasonableness, and supporting documentation of the site should be considered.

- *Credibility:* Is it a trustworthy source? Are author credentials listed? Is it a known or respected authority? Is there organizational support?

- *Accuracy:* Is the site up to date? Is the information factual? Is the site comprehensive? Do audience and purpose reflect the intentions of the Web site?

- *Reasonableness:* Is the site fair? Is the site balanced? Is the site objective? Is there any conflict of interest? Are there fallacies (obvious untruths)? Is the tone of the site balanced?

- *Support:* Are sources listed? Is contact information listed? Can the information be verified elsewhere? Are claims supported? Is documentation supplied?

Adapted from Robert Harris, "Evaluating Internet Research Sources," www.virtualsalt.com/evalu8it.htm. Accessed April 28, 2002.

A Web site with links to other resources used to evaluate Web site content can be found at home.socal.rr.com/exworthy/eval.htm.

Cyber Safety

With such easy access to information via the Internet, principals should be aware of the dangers associated with the Internet and take proactive steps to ensure the safety of children using this resource. The Children's Internet Protection Act (CIPA) was signed into law on December 21, 2000. This law places restrictions on the use of funding that is available through the Library Services and Technology Act, Title III of the Elementary and Secondary Education Act, and on the Universal Service discount program known as the E-rate (Public Law 106-554). These restrictions take the form of requirements for Internet safety policies and technology that blocks or filters certain material from being accessed through the Internet. The Internet safety policy must protect against access, through computers with Internet access, to visual depictions that are obscene, including child pornography, or are otherwise harmful to minors.

Additional information about the Children's Internet Protection Act and compliance measures can be found at www.cybertelecom.org/cda/ cipatext.htm.

Electronic Mail

Electronic mail (e-mail) is quickly replacing the postal service for informal communication. Programs used to send and receive electronic mail include Microsoft® Outlook, Microsoft® Outlook Express, Netscape® Communicator, and America Online (AOL). The layout of an e-mail message looks similar to that of a memorandum. The following elements are included:

To:	e-mail address of the recipient (johndoe@emailaddress.com)
From:	e-mail address of the sender (johndoe@otheremailaddress.com)
Subject:	topic of the e-mail
Message:	text of the e-mail

Documents, photographs, and other file types can be sent with the e-mail in the form of what are called *attachments*.

In the interest of effective communication, the following e-mail guidelines are offered:

- Indicate a topic in the subject line so the recipient can quickly discern the subject of the e-mail. Subject lines can be used to categorize e-mail or quickly locate an e-mail.

- When replying to an e-mail, include the original message with the reply. The use of color when replying to specific questions is useful.

- Many e-mail programs use templates or *stationery* to enhance the appearance of an e-mail. Keep in mind that not all e-mail programs are able to properly display the template; therefore, limited use is encouraged.

- When replying to an e-mail, use the *Reply* button versus the *Reply to All* button. Reply to All sends the message to everyone listed in the originally received message.

- When attaching files, be aware of the size of the document. The larger the file, the longer it will take the recipient to download the file.

- Spell check the e-mail before sending. Make use of the *drafts* folder to save an e-mail that is incomplete.

- Acknowledge e-mail as soon as possible. Principals may want to designate a specific time during the day to respond to e-mail. This can be done when there is less demand for the principal's time, and can help them focus on the e-mail communication. Some e-mail programs offer an *auto response* feature that allows the user to customize a reply to be sent to the sender as soon as an e-mail is received. It may be preferable to customize the auto response message to let the sender know that their e-mail has been received and will be responded to fully at a later date/time.

- Use folders to categorize e-mail. A principal may want to develop e-mail folders for PTA, teachers, school board, personal, and so forth.

- Use filters to categorize e-mail. For example, an e-mail filter can be defined that will automatically highlight in a certain color those e-mails from a certain person (or persons) or containing specific words in the subject line.

- Avoid spreading e-mail "spam" ("Win $100 by sending this e-mail to five of your friends") or hoaxes ("There is a deadly computer virus circulating that will wipe out your hard drive"). Some Web sites used to investigate spam or hoaxes are:
    www.datafellows.com/virus-info
    www.urbanlegends.com
    www.symantec.com/avcenter/vinfodb.html
    www.viruslist.com/eng/index.html

- Send a copy of an e-mail to people who are mentioned in your e-mail. For example, if you are advising the recipient to contact a certain person for additional information, send a copy of that e-mail to the person to be contacted.

- Assume the messages you send and receive are permanent and public. Do not write anything in an e-mail that you would not want to be accessed by others.
- Do not use ALL CAPS when writing an e-mail. The use of ALL CAPS can be interpreted as shouting or anger.
- Some people use "smilies" or "emoticons" (emotional icons) at the ends of sentences to convey the emotion of the writer. Emoticons are "facial" expressions made by a certain series of keystrokes, most often producing an image of a face sideways. Acronyms are frequently used to save time when composing a message. A list of common acronyms and emoticons can be found at www.pb.org/emoticon.html.

Technology in the Classroom

Some technology skills essential for the principal or administrator have been identified. However, with the proliferation of technology throughout the curriculum, how does the principal know if it is being used effectively to teach students? To promote teachers' effective and appropriate integration of technology into the classrooms, principals should "inspect it and expect it" on a regular basis. But what exactly should principals look for when observing in the classroom? Models to evaluate the use of technology by teachers in the classroom have been developed and utilized in many school districts.

The International Society for Technology in Education (ISTE) has identified standards and performance indicators that classroom teachers should be prepared to meet in order to demonstrate effective utilization of technology in the classroom.

I. *Technology operations and concepts*
   a. Demonstrate introductory knowledge, skills, and understanding of concepts related to technology.
   b. Demonstrate continual growth in technology knowledge and skills to stay abreast of current and emerging technologies.

II. *Planning and designing learning environments and experiences*
   a. Design developmentally appropriate learning opportunities that apply technology-enhanced instructional strategies to support the diverse needs of learners.
   b. Apply current research on teaching and learning with technology when planning learning environments and experiences.
   c. Identify and locate technology resources and evaluate them for accuracy and suitability.
   d. Plan for the management of technology resources within the context of learning activities.

e. Plan strategies to manage student learning in a technology-enhanced environment.

III. *Teaching, learning, and the curriculum*
   a. Facilitate technology-enhanced experiences that address content standards and student technology standards.
   b. Use technology to support learner-centered strategies that address the diverse needs of students.
   c. Apply technology to develop students' higher order skills and creativity.
   d. Manage student learning activities in a technology-enhanced environment.

IV. *Assessment and evaluation*
   a. Apply technology in assessing student learning of subject matter using a variety of assessment techniques.
   b. Use technology resources to collect and analyze data, interpret results, and communicate findings to improve instructional practice and maximize student learning.
   c. Apply multiple methods of evaluation to determine students' appropriate use of technology resources for learning, communication, and productivity.

V. *Productivity and professional practice*
   a. Use technology resources to engage in ongoing professional development and lifelong learning.
   b. Continually evaluate and reflect on professional practice to make informed decisions regarding the use of technology in support of student learning.
   c. Apply technology to increase productivity.
   d. Use technology to communicate and collaborate with peers, parents, and the larger community in order to nurture student learning.

VI. *Social, ethical, legal, and human issues*
   a. Model and teach legal and ethical practice related to technology use.
   b. Apply technology resources to enable and empower learners with diverse backgrounds, characteristics, and abilities.
   c. Identify and use technology resources that affirm diversity.
   d. Promote safe and healthy use of technology resources.
   e. Facilitate equitable access to technology resources for all students.

Source: cnets.iste.org/TeacherStandards.html

An observation tool based on the ISTE standards and performance indicators can be developed to assist the principal in determining the degree to which teachers are integrating technology into the classroom and their professional lives. A quick observation tool in the form of a checklist may look like this:

Checklist for Observing Technology Use and Integration in the Classroom

Technology Standard and Performance Indicator	*Observed*	*Not Observed*
I. *Technology operations and knowledge.*		
A. Uses technology terminology in the classroom in a way that is understand able to students.		
B. Encourages student use of technology terminology and concepts in the classroom.		
II. *Planning and designing learning environments and experiences*		
A. Uses technology to deliver developmentally appropriate learning opportunities for students.		
B. Integrates technology with current research on teaching and learning.		
III. *Teaching, learning, and the curriculum*		
A. Lesson plans show evidence of technology and content integration.		
B. Instructional materials (worksheets, study guides) show evidence of technology and content integration.		
IV. *Assessment and evaluation*		
A. Teachers use technology as an integral part of classroom assessment.		

B. Students use technology to track progress toward academic goals.		
V. *Productivity and professional practice*		
A. Communicates with colleagues, parents, and/or students via e-mail.		
B. Produces instructional materials using appropriate technology (word processing, spreadsheets, Web sites).		
C. Uses technology for administrative tasks (grading, lesson plans, etc.)		
VI. *Social, ethical, legal and human issues*		
A. Models and teaches legal and ethical technology practices in the classroom.		
B. Displays and/or discusses legal and ethical practices of technology with students.		

Another tool to observe the types of technology being used in the classroom or lab is presented below. This observation tool provides space for comments and feedback based on lesson observation.

Instructional Technology Integration Observation Form

Teacher _____ Observer _____

School _____ Grade _____ Date/Time _____

Setting: ☐ Classroom   ☐ Computer Lab   ☐ Mobile Lab

Technology Used—Software/Application:

☐ word processing   ☐ graphics/drawing
☐ presentation   ☐ database
☐ hypermedia   ☐ spreadsheet
☐ graphing   ☐ tutorial software
☐ simulation software   ☐ drill/practice software
☐ other (specify) _____

Technology Used—Internet:

☐ research   ☐ Web page creation
☐ online course   ☐ cyberhunt or Web quest
☐ online simulation   ☐ electronic fieldtrip
☐ other (specify) _____

Standards Addressed:

```
┌──────────────────────────────────────────────────────┐
│                                                      │
│                                                      │
└──────────────────────────────────────────────────────┘
```

Sequence of Instructional Activities During the Lesson:

```
┌──────────────────────────────────────────────────────┐
│                                                      │
│                                                      │
│                                                      │
│                                                      │
│                                                      │
└──────────────────────────────────────────────────────┘
```

O = Observed   **N** = Not Observed   **NA** = Not Applicable to Lesson

_____ Demonstrates the ability to plan and organize using technology in the lesson.

_____ Identifies and uses appropriate technology (hardware and software) in the lesson.

_____ Provides for individual student differences when using technology.

_____ Integrates technology appropriately into the content lesson.

_____ Demonstrates enthusiasm for the use of technology in the content area.

_____ The lesson uses higher order thinking skills (e.g., analysis, synthesis, evaluation).

_____ The lesson encourages all students to be active participants in the learning process.

_____ The teacher effectively sets up, configures, and utilizes technological components in the lesson.

_____ The teacher provides appropriate technical support/assistance to students.

_____ The lesson assesses student use of technology.

_____ The teacher effectively troubleshoots technological problems with hardware and software.

_____ The teacher demonstrates the ability to provide alternate instruction in case of technological problems or failure.

_____ Students have an opportunity to summarize their learnings at the end of the lesson (content and use of technology).

Comments:

Signature of Observer _____ Date _____

Signature of Teacher _____ Date _____

Conclusion

Technology is an important component of today's schools. The appropriate and efficient use of technology is to enhance school improvement efforts, facilitate staff learning, build positive home-school-community relationships, and ultimately foster high levels of student achievement. To reinforce these purposes, school principals should discuss with teachers how technology can best be utilized in a school to assist with the teaching and learning of students while, at the same time, protecting students from harmful content. Staff development should be made available to principals to develop their skills. The identification of in-school or division "experts" should be explored for classroom instructional support and for one-on-one professional development. In addition, there are many online tutorials and distance learning opportunities available for principals.

Learning about technology is an ongoing process. What better way to model effective use of technology than by using it on a daily basis?

> *Computers are magnificent tools for the realization of our dreams, but no machine can replace the human spark of spirit, compassion, love, and understanding.*
>
> Louis Gerstner, CEO, IBM

Reflections

This space provides for you a place to write in ideas that have been generated by this chapter, things you want to try, or adaptations of ideas presented herein.

1. What is your assessment of technology integration in your school?
2. Create a plan for assessing and developing your own technological proficiency.
3. How can you assist teachers in developing technology skills?
4. What questions do you have as a result of reading this chapter?

14

Fueling the Learning Organization Through Staff Development

It takes a whole village to educate one child.

AFRICAN PROVERB

Why Staff Development?

Educating a child begins with a village of elders who themselves model and find their lives enriched by the quest for lifelong learning. Students learn as a result of what they see modeled within the school. Building-based staff development and other professional growth activities are, by design, opportunities for members of the school community to grow professionally in ways that will ultimately benefit both teacher and student. In the process, the entire system improves because of its increased capacity to influence productivity. Echoing this notion, Margaret Arbuckle, from the Western Maine Partnership, addressing a group of principals, stated, "Schools that support the continuous learning and development of students also support the continuous development of the educators for them. Schools must be places of learning for both students and educators. You can't have one without the other. Building a culture of professional learning in schools is a necessary condition for sustained learning and particularly critical if we are to link professional development with reformed concepts of teaching, learning, and schooling."

Staff Development Defined

Staff development consists of any activity that directly affects the attitudes, knowledge levels, skills, and practices of individuals that will assist them in performing their roles—present or future. Ideally, such development will not only make the individual a visible learner and responsive teacher but it will ultimately affect the student as learner. Research and experience suggest that the principal plays a vital role in collaborating with staff members to create and maintain a climate friendly to staff development and in ensuring that staff development activities address specific needs

180

and that activities are assessed for impact. Creating attitudes among the staff of "good but growing" is a critical first step. This is important because some staff members feel that when they are invited to attend training, there is an implicit message that they "need it" because of an inadequacy related to their performance.

Creating an Atmosphere for
Staff Development to Thrive: Some Guidelines

Creating an atmosphere for successful staff development involves attending to the following guidelines:

Provide opportunities to create a sense of purpose for professional development. This purpose should reflect the school's vision, organizational members' professional growth needs, and student needs, as evidenced by performance on outcomes valued by staff members. For example, the staff can share professional growth goals and discuss student performance in relation to desired levels of achievement. Then, relevant staff development activities can be identified to address these need areas.

Encourage and support collaboration and mutual respect among all in the school community. This can be a critical source of support and will contribute to the implementation and institutionalization of staff development practices. Keeping all individuals informed, inviting people to participate in support group activities following training, and recognizing and celebrating collaborative efforts are essential events.

Focus on continuous improvement in quality. When precision training is developed that matches both staff and student growth needs, both individual and organizational performance is enhanced. Time should be taken to discuss and analyze needs according to responsibilities associated with roles. Student performance and desired skills should be examined. Training should specifically address the needs identified in this process.

Conduct readiness-building activities and plan collaboratively prior to training and implementation. Include maintenance activities to assure institutionalization of staff development. Wood, Thompson, and Russell (1981) suggest five stages for a staff development program (see Table 14.1).

When training is designed, attention should be paid to five key components (Joyce & Showers, 1981).

1. Presentation of material
2. Demonstration of skills

TABLE 14.1 Planning Guide for Staff Development

1.	Readiness	Awareness, identification of broad goals, gaining commitment to innovation
2.	Planning	Goals translated into comprehensive, detailed plans; planning team representative of staff
3.	Training	Plans are translated into practice; effective staff development procedures followed
4.	Implementation	Support provided for posttraining activities, adaptation, and assessment
5.	Maintenance	Continuous monitoring, reassessment, and adaptation of innovation

SOURCE: Wood, Thompson, and Russell (1981)

3. Practice
4. Feedback
5. Coaching in the correct use of the new skill

There should be a focus on providing frequent opportunities for staff members to revisit staff development content, share successes, problem solve, and refine skills. This ensures opportunities for staff members to adapt new behaviors and learnings to their own situations. It assures that training can be designed to address teacher concerns (mentioned in Chapter 7) that initially focus on how the staff development will affect them personally; then, how they will manage a new program's implementation; and later, it may develop into how the programs will affect students (Hall & Loucks, 1978).

Design training for a variety of skill levels. Choose the appropriate one given staff needs. Training may be delivered to provide awareness, knowledge, skill development or application opportunities, or to foster internalization of concepts. Also, training should be spaced over time to promote the integration of new ideas, approaches, and behaviors into the classroom or workplace.

Design training that addresses learner needs and context variables. Susan Loucks-Horsley, in an interview with Dennis Sparks, executive director of the National Staff Development Council (1999), reflected, "We recognize that young people learn in different ways, but often don't acknowledge that this applies to teachers as well when we plan learning experiences for them." Loucks-Horsley, describing contextual learning strategies for teachers, emphasizes that,

Selecting strategies is really the process of designing staff development. It is a dynamic process similar to one teachers go through in designing lessons for their students.

Staff development leaders have to ask themselves which strategies make sense to use at that particular time with that particular set of teachers for a particular set of outcomes.

Context variables are important in making these decisions. What are the district or school standards and goals for student learning? What do teachers already know and what do they need to know? What current policies and practices influence student learning? What is the school culture? What is the nature of the student population? Teachers' levels of content understandings are also very important, especially at the elementary level where teachers may not have a deep understanding of content, as is often the case with science and mathematics. A lot of different aspects of the context come into play when selecting the right combination of strategies.

Training activities need to reflect and model those attributes of good teaching that we want to promote in classrooms: active learning, a brain-compatible approach, time for reflection, and tasks that respond to multiple intelligences. To illustrate:

1. Active learning opportunities can include cooperative learning tasks, small-group work, role playing, simulation, direct instruction, reciprocal teaching, videotape analysis, discussion, e-learning, and microteaching. Emphasis should be on teaching that engages the whole class. For example, questioning strategies should be modeled to increase participants' awareness of the power of questions to engage the entire class and give all students the opportunity to respond to a variety of thinking and skill levels. These would include the skills of convergent and divergent thinking and the use of wait time to enhance the quality of student responses.

2. The brain-compatible approach recognizes the need for active involvement of the learner with the learning task and with fellow participants. It also highlights the need for participants to rehearse new learnings. It underscores the importance of not teaching too much too fast and linking new learning to previous experiences where applicable. Finally, it acknowledges the need to develop schemata or frameworks into which new information or knowledge fits.

3. Time for reflection allows the mind time for rehearsal and analysis. Reflection fosters the development of new neural connections. Insights can be gleaned as a result of providing time for thinking. Reflections may be recorded in logs or journals. They may be shared or remain confidential.

4. Multiple intelligence theory (Gardner, 1995) suggests there are at least eight "ways of knowing." These include verbal-linguistic, mathematical-logical, visual-spatial, bodily-kinesthetic, musical, interpersonal, naturalist, and intrapersonal. Designing staff development tasks with these in mind lends credence to the importance of highlighting the multiple ways we perceive and respond to the world.

Effective staff development programs use what is known about adult learning. Adults are more likely to be motivated when there is a relationship between staff development and their on-the-job responsibilities. Adults come to any learning experience with a rich background that begs to be tapped. Also, adult learning is ego involved. Learning a new skill may promote a positive or negative view of self. There is always a fear of external judgments that we adults are less than adequate, which produces anxiety during new learning situations.

Adult learners need to see the results of their efforts and have accurate feedback about progress toward their goals.

Staff development programs should be voluntary. Respecting staff members as professionals and treating them accordingly means providing each individual with the right to set meaningful professional development goals and allowing them the freedom to choose how they will meet those goals. These goals should be related to building a staff member's capacity to serve students in areas identified by assessment data and other qualitative data. Expect that not all staff members will embrace wholeheartedly the notion of staff development. Often, however, when key individuals seek such experiences, peer examples and peer pressure are more powerful influences than mandates. Influence, pressure, and support will play important roles in generating participation among those staff members who do not "jump on board" immediately.

When training is a "required opportunity" associated with implementing a new program or using new materials or equipment, provide the staff with choices regarding when training might be scheduled, the format, or the time frame. When staff development is designed for new staff members or beginning teachers, it is helpful to consult staff members who joined the previous year. They can lend valuable suggestions regarding their first-year needs that will contribute to planning responsive staff development.

Involve the staff in planning for staff development. One way to increase participation or "buy in" to staff development is to create a forum where teachers, support staff, administration, and classified staff can talk about the tasks associated with their roles and define areas that training would enhance. In addition, desired student outcomes could be examined in relation to current levels of performance. Training topics and approaches might then be identified that would provide all staff members with the knowledge, skills, and strategies to support students in reaching their potential.

Provide opportunities for the staff to learn about classical pedagogical knowledge and "current practice." It is important to provide staff members with information about current trends and developments in education such as the standards movement, process writing, interdisciplinary curriculum approaches, and authentic assessment. Equipped with knowledge, understanding, application opportunities, and the chance to analyze and evaluate how these developments affect or fit with one's work, the practitioner then has the background to distinguish between fleeting fads and sound practice when confronted with staff development choices.

When staff development occurs away from the school site, encourage school teams to attend. This provides a building-based system of support when colleagues return from training sessions and begin to implement new practices.

Demonstrate administrative support for staff development. Strategies include attending training with the staff, using the techniques or approaches, and allocating time for planning and implementing new learnings. Discussion time should be allocated to provide opportunities to problem solve and share examples of practice. As the principal conducts "management by wandering around" visits, taking time to write a note regarding a teacher's implementation of a strategy learned in staff development is a great way to celebrate learning. It also fosters the development of school-wide norms of practice.

Use staff development as a public relations tool. With limited time, energy, and financial resources, using staff development as a public relations tool while it is being used to develop the individual and the organization provides the chance to get the most out of the investment. In some settings, the public relations venture might be an awareness session for parents about a new instructional, curricular, or assessment trend such as cooperative learning, differentiated instruction, emotional intelligence, or student portfolios. Providing information in this way also takes the mystery out of what the school is doing. In other schools, the public relations effort might be an invitation to businesses or key individuals from the community to attend training along with faculty members. One district typically shares training with the local college, university, and industry personnel, for example.

Avoid jargon. One way to diminish the possibility that staff development will become threatening is to eliminate the use of jargon and acronyms as substitutes for phrases or structures. A principal recently commented, "It's like alphabet soup around here . . . 'the SST will meet to develop IEPs in accordance with PL 94-142.' Why can't they just say, 'The student study team will meet to develop the individual educational plans for students in accordance with public law 94-142'?" Using language that a person on the street can understand helps to make the staff development activity "user friendly."

Build local school capacity. Once a staff has received training in a specific area and has applied it in classrooms, that often represents the end of the particular staff development effort. One way to continue the development of individuals while creating a local resource is to provide opportunities for staff members to participate in training for trainers. This fosters the development of presentation skills and helps a school build site-level support. Ultimately, this enhances the prospects that staff development activities will become institutionalized. It also affords the school on-site trainers who can provide professional development to newcomers to the building. The entire staff benefits from having a "common language" and experiences.

Assess the context in which staff development is to occur:

- How much is already going on?
- With what will the intended staff development activity compete?
- What will be the financial and emotional cost associated with the effort?
- How many cohorts of people will it affect (students, teachers, administrators, parents, substitutes)?
- How complex will the implementation be?
- Does the venture have relevance for the staff?
- Has the staff been involved in the decision to consider the staff development activity?

The following example demonstrates how these guidelines can be combined to plan a school-level program.

Planning a Peer-Coaching Program

To implement a peer-coaching program or any other staff development program, the context must be assessed and the approach matched to key variables in this assessment. The following guidelines will help you create awareness, develop readiness, build commitment, plan, and implement a peer-coaching program in your school (Robbins, 1991b).

1. Set up a planning group to learn about peer coaching, assess your school environment and support for coaching, develop a program plan, and organize activities.
2. Assess the school environment to identify the factors working for and against a successful peer-coaching program.
3. Provide information about peer coaching, including the rationale, what peer coaching is and is not, the various forms that coaching can take, and so on.
4. Provide opportunities for teachers to raise questions and concerns and get answers to them.
5. Solicit input from teachers on what they want the peer-coaching program to be like.

6. Analyze the types and levels of support and resources available.

7. Examine other demands on teachers' time and energy.

8. Develop a plan for and provide training in peer coaching for teachers who volunteer to participate.

9. Examine the issue of time (for training, practice, follow-up, and networking).

10. Develop a plan for and provide follow-up with frequent review and refinement sessions.

11. Develop a plan for bringing new teachers into the program.

12. Go slowly.

The National Staff Development Council (NSDC) has published the NSDC Standards for Staff Development that address key context, process, and content standards, requisite for staff development success. These provide helpful tools when planning, implementing, evaluating, or maintaining staff development initiatives. They are available online (www.nsdc.org/bookstore.html) or by calling 800-727-7288.

Facilitating the Individual's Staff Development Experience

In working with thousands of individuals over several years, the authors have noted that participants welcome specific aspects of staff development experiences. Principals need to keep these tips in mind when facilitating staff development opportunities:

Choose trainers who "do their homework" in order to learn about participants with whom they will be working and federal, state, and local mandates affecting the training and the trainees. This information can then be used during a session to increase its relevance for participants.

Begin with time for participants to share their expectations about what they hope to get out of the session. Eliciting expectations enhances the consultant's ability to tailor examples, comments, and activities to participant needs. In this way, as adults, participants feel they have control, or at least influence, over what happens to them during a session.

Focus on ways to build meaning into a session. Stories or videoclips, followed by time for discussion of personal experiences and time to reflect, contribute to meaning. When a session has personal meaning for participants, they are more likely to buy into activities, and use them in their own context.

Invite participants to take responsibility for the pace of the workshop by providing "working" and "ready" cards. As a table group works together on a task, the working card is displayed. When the task is completed, the ready card is put up. This allows the consultant to pace the session according to participant needs. It also conveys the message that the workshop's success depends on both participant involvement and trainer planning and delivery.

Use participant's names. This makes individuals feel as if the consultant cares enough to personalize their experiences. Moreover, it indicates that the consultant has taken a personal interest in each individual from the first moment of contact. It shows, also, that every moment of the relationship is important and should not be taken for granted.

Provide participants with handouts that are hard copies of transparencies. This allows them to focus on what is being said, rather than focus on copying what is on the overhead. Because the mind can only pay conscious attention to one thing at a time, this enhances the participants' experiences. In addition, research suggests that 68% of the population learns best visually. Providing visual support also models effective practice and increases the possibility that teachers will provide this for students.

Provide Post-it™ notes. Many participants do not want to write on their handouts. Providing Post-it™ notes so that comments can be written on the Post-its™ and then placed on the handouts takes care of this problem. Some participants even use the Post-it™ notes to mark sections in their handout packets or make notes about which pages they wish to use immediately.

Deliver training content in a user-friendly way. Participants welcome overviews, agendas, and outcomes for a session. Instruction should reflect a healthy balance of research and practice. Frequent opportunities for movement should be provided, such as the "TalkWalk," mentioned in the next chapter on faculty meetings. There should be a variety of tasks that address the multiple intelligences and the needs of the auditory, visual, and tactile-kinesthetic learner in the session. Refreshments are always appreciated!

Search for and use humor. Cartoons, jokes, and sometimes "seizing the moment" add a special touch of warmth to a session. Consultants should be able to laugh at themselves. Humor often relaxes people. When the brain is in a more relaxed state, it is able to retain more.

Arrange furniture to reflect desired participant interactions. For example, consider positioning tables to facilitate participant discussion and table-group tasks, as well as access to the presenter's direct instruction. Invite participants to sit with a variety of people, but never insist. People should be invited to sit where they wish. Assigning seats takes control away from adults.

Establish norms regarding risk taking, participation, and accountability. Consultants should model risk taking and accountability, for example, by asking participants at the end of a session to review the expectations they generated, reflect on the session's content, and offer feedback. The trainer, in the beginning of the session, lets participants know that feedback will be solicited at the end of the session; hence the request for expectations is not an idle gesture. In this way, the person who conducts the workshop demonstrates a commitment to continual growth. The participants should be invited to set goals for themselves, take risks, participate as they feel comfortable, and assess their learnings. Many times participants are asked to brainstorm responses to "What have you learned?" and "What new questions do you have?" This data is used for program evaluation and future program planning. The adult participant recognizes, in this way, that input can influence a program. This contributes to a growing sense of efficacy.

The Big Picture

Principals play the key role in creating a context or culture in which adult learning flourishes (Champion, 2002). Validating this notion, Rick Du Four (2001) wrote, "I have come to understand the most significant contribution a principal can make to developing others is creating an appropriate context for adult learning. It is context—the programs, procedures, beliefs, expectations and habits that constitute the norm for a given school—that plays the biggest role in determining whether staff development efforts will have an impact on that school" (p. 14).

Principals who use the information within this chapter will increase the probability that the staff development program at a school will be responsive to both individual and organizational needs, will model effective practice, and will provide a variety of learning activities for the adults in the building who serve students. It is essential that the program be ongoing and provide for continuous improvement. Implicit in this orientation is the need to constantly assess how well the staff development program is meeting the goals for which it was ultimately intended: student and staff growth.

Reflections

This space provides for you a place to write in ideas that have been generated by this chapter, things you want to try, or adaptations of ideas presented herein.

1. Which of the guidelines for creating an atmosphere for positive staff development are most meaningful to you?
2. Create a plan for staff development with attention to the five stages (readiness, planning, training, implementation, and maintenance).

3. Review a staff development activity with which you have been involved. Evaluate it, using your learnings from this chapter.

4. What insights or questions do you have as a result of reflecting on the ideas presented in this chapter?

PART V

KEEPING THE PIPES FROM LEAKING: ADDING MEANING TO TRADITIONAL PRACTICE

15

Faculty Meetings:
A Tool for Capacity Building

Faculty meetings: 30-minute opportunities or obstacles.

A PRINCIPAL'S VOICE

Faculty meetings present opportunities to talk about curriculum, instruction, and assessment, increase our understanding of student development, strengthen staff cohesion, and build faculty morale and school culture. Although meetings have the potential to be used for these ends, too often they are not. As a result, they are sometimes perceived as a waste of time. A faculty member might be overheard saying after such a meeting, "We could have received the same information in a memo." In schools where faculty meetings have been transformed into learning opportunities, staff members look forward to these sessions. They know they can count on getting activities they can use immediately with students.

Faculty Meetings as Learning Opportunities

Faculty meetings should always be viewed as a learning opportunity. A principal should consider the meeting a success if teaching and learning were the central themes. Faculty members should walk out of these meetings feeling like they have actively participated in the meeting, had involvement in deciding the agenda, and most importantly, learned something. In a sense, these meetings represent a celebration, a gathering of teachers to reduce the isolation of the classroom, in which teachers share ideas about what works and what does not work.

Faculty meetings should not be used for "administrivia." Letting the staff know that you will not cover information during the meeting that could be mentioned in a memo can be comforting and helps build positive attitudes and perceptions about meetings. The trade-off is that teachers should read the memos. Many times, to encourage this, "gimmicks" have been built into the text of the memo. For example, a message might be written within the text regarding entering a drawing. The staff might need to estimate the number of reams of paper used by the school.

Prizes might be gifts donated by local businesses. Keeping creature comforts in mind—location of the meeting, how much sitting is involved, and the availability of refreshments—enhances the affective appeal of the meeting.

At one school, staff members routinely ask themselves at the end of the meeting, "What have we done for students today?" Asking this question keeps the mission of the school in the forefront of everyone's eyes.

The suggestions that follow represent practices many principals have used successfully.

The School Mission and Faculty Meetings

The principal should view the meetings as an opportunity to emphasize the school mission. Certainly, in the beginning of the year and with new faculty, this is especially important. By coming back to the mission periodically, the message is going out that the mission is not just an idea that looks good in the handbook. Examples of classroom activities that are taking place to support the mission further reinforce the interrelationship between daily classroom activities, schoolwide goals, and the mission statement. Reviewing the mission statement and the corresponding goals periodically provides the staff with the opportunity to tailor the guiding principles and documents of the school to current needs.

The following activity represents a mission-building strategy. It can also be used to refine a mission statement. Individual staff members are asked to reflect on the following:

- Describe the place you would like to go to work each day.
- Describe the place you would like to send your children to school.

Staff members are then asked to fuse these visions into one. Following this, individuals are asked to share at table groups and to develop a composite vision. Table groups then share these composites and ultimately create one that represents the collective vision. When this is recorded, it can become the basis of a school mission. Many schools have included parents and students in the mission-building process.

An alternative activity can help teachers focus on a vision of the future. Principals can encourage teachers to think about the world students will face in the future. The activity would begin with the principal briefly reviewing four or five trends that futurists have predicted. These might include the movement toward the global village, the aging population, the increasing mosaic of America, more leisure time, the widening gap between rich and poor, the technology explosion, or single parenting. The staff would also be encouraged to suggest a couple of trends. A discussion would then take place focusing on the following questions:

- How do I personally feel about these trends?
- Are we teaching to address these trends?
- Should we be considering alternative teaching, curriculum, and assessment strategies to address these trends?
- How are our nation's democratic principles affected by the trends?
- What are we doing on a schoolwide basis to address these trends?

The discussion can help to raise consciousness about the general outcomes of education as opposed to the microview of teaching objectives on which we so easily become focused during day-to-day classroom activities.

Increasing the Teachers' Roles in Faculty Meetings

As we work to foster greater teacher decision making in schools, faculty meetings become an important arena for teacher involvement. Teachers can collaborate in setting the agenda, co-planning the meetings, and presenting or facilitating (with or without the principal). Often, a teacher may desire to facilitate a meeting but would prefer to work with the principal or with another colleague. Presenting in front of the staff may not seem like a major occasion for a principal, but for a teacher who has not done so before, it can be both very stressful and rewarding. In many schools, the staff selects members to serve on a faculty advisory committee (FAC). The FAC works with the principal to develop the agenda and to plan, implement, and evaluate meeting effectiveness. The meeting agenda should be made public in advance, and requests for additional agenda items from staff should be solicited. On the meeting memo, space for additional written agenda items is provided. Meeting minutes can be recorded on butcher paper by faculty members so staff members can provide immediate feedback on the accuracy of the record of meeting proceedings. The recorder and facilitator roles can rotate on an ongoing basis. This level of involvement increases staff ownership and commitment to the school's activities.

Teachers and support staff may also play a major role in determining the focus of presentations during a given meeting. For example, the previously mentioned jigsaw activity (Chapter 3) could be used to share articles on a controversial issue or innovative teaching strategy. At one school, when interest in a new wave of technology grew, the teachers set up a series of presentations by colleagues who were using technology successfully in their classrooms. Displays of student work and how the teachers implemented some of their ideas made for a successful meeting, helped build staff pride, and made teachers aware of resources just beyond the doors of their classrooms.

Time should be allocated for interested teachers for discussing specific teaching or assessment strategies, fine-tuning their questioning skills, or diagnosing math skills. Often, teachers can select video presentations, guest speakers, or written materials that can be part of the faculty meeting. At some schools, teachers host monthly faculty meetings in their classrooms. This increases awareness of what is going on in individual classrooms across the school.

Some Successful Faculty Meeting Strategies

Success Stories

The following activity has been successfully used during faculty meetings and takes from 20 to 30 minutes, depending on the size of the group. It is a good idea to do this activity across grade levels or subject areas. Generally, a note to faculty is sent out in advance, so that teachers and support staff can plan what they want to share:

Success Stories

What works? Often we read about research studies that draw broad conclusions regarding how we should teach. These studies are very helpful. However, the studies frequently miss the day-to-day successes that teachers experience in our particular school.

Please share with your colleagues a success story from your class that you have experienced recently. Why were you satisfied with this experience? Can the experience apply beyond the context of a particular student or class? If the success story involves instructional resources or student work, please bring these items to the meeting.

A variation on this activity is to bring a frustration or problem to a meeting. Asking colleagues how to deal with a difficulty can be extremely rewarding. However, the staff must be supportive and willing to take risks to implement this activity. If this activity is used, be sure not to end on a frustrating note. Here is where humor comes in handy! For example, at one meeting, the FAC playfully handed out chocolate to support teacher efforts to problem solve. On a more serious note, the support of individual classroom teachers was the critical element for problem solving.

"Great Teachers" Visualization Exercise

This strategy is a powerful way to begin or continue a conversation about effective teaching practices.

Instructions:

Reflect for the next few minutes on the ONE teacher who made a positive difference in your life. Visualize the teacher's face, the entire person, the teacher with you and your classmates, and his or her room. As you picture this teacher and their surroundings, record on an index card the qualities this teacher possessed and practices this teacher implemented that made them most impactful in your life.

Meet with a colleague to compare your reflections. Then brainstorm a list of qualities and practices on a board or overhead based on the group reflections.

Questions for Group Reflections: On Great Teachers

1. The list you developed can be sorted using the categories "personal qualities" and "instructional practices." What other categories could be used to sort the list?
2. Are there teacher characteristics (e.g., qualities and practices) that represent a difference between what a "novice" teacher does versus an "experienced" teacher does?
3. Are some qualities and practices innate and others "coachable"?
4. Can an average teacher become a great teacher?
5. Are there fundamental qualities and practices that one must have to embrace the potential to become a great teacher?
6. Should we strive for greatness?
7. Are there some qualities and practices that are more important to students? Teachers? Parents? Administrators?
8. What additional questions should be asked?

Using Humor

Humor is a great tool for faculty meetings. In one school, a teacher approached a principal on the morning of a faculty meeting and mentioned that she would probably have to leave during the meeting for emergency root canal work. She was sorry that she would miss part of the meeting. To open the faculty meeting that day, the principal mentioned that one of the teachers had to decide which was worse, the faculty meeting or having to get a root canal. The teacher was such a masochist, the principal said, that she chose to accept a little of both! That opening got the meeting off to a good start. When necessary, such remarks also can come in handy at the end of a meeting. Often, an anecdote about a student can fit the occasion and emphasize an important theme. One teacher shared such a story by telling about a second-grade student who, while completing a math paper, counted on her fingers, recorded the answer, and then blew a kiss for every problem. When questioned about this technique, the student explained that her first-grade teacher told her, "When you get to second grade and do math, you can just kiss your fingers good-bye!" The story added humor to the meeting and reminded all of the importance of meaning in our actions.

Spreading the Word
About Effective In-School Practices

The principal can use faculty meetings to review some of the effective practices that are being implemented in the school. Citing specific examples of effective classroom practices spreads the word about instructional and curricular approaches that work and also serves as a source of recognition for those teachers whose practices have been noticed. If you are managing by wandering around, share highlights of your visits with an emphasis on effective practices at these meetings. This is an excellent way to remind teachers of the goals emphasized for the year or about the risk-taking behaviors being modeled by the staff. Let the staff know about positive comments made by parents about the school. Again, the meetings are a great opportunity to build staff morale and celebrate staff expertise.

Book or Article Talks

This strategy engages faculty members in reading books or articles and having professional dialogue about the content. The faculty also reflects upon strategies and techniques they might consider implementing in classrooms. For example, one faculty committed to reading *Classroom Instruction that Works* (Marzano et al., 2001). This book identifies nine instructional strategies that have a "high probability of enhancing student achievement for all students in all subject areas at all grade levels" (p. 6). Following the reading of each chapter, teachers tried specific strategies in their classrooms and reported back to their colleagues about the effects of that strategy on student learning. Eventually they began coplanning units of study, addressing key standards that employed the use of a variety of these strategies.

Supporting Vertical Articulation and
Interdisciplinary Curriculum and Instructional Practices

Faculty meetings are great opportunities to get elementary, middle, and high school teachers to meet across grade levels and across departments. Traditionally, the social studies, science, or foreign language departments meet separately, following a faculty meeting or on a different day. The principal can allocate time to facilitate departments meeting across disciplines to explore the possibilities for interdisciplinary curriculum work and to promote the sharing of effective teaching practices across disciplines and grade levels. Interestingly, when we discuss the interdisciplinary curriculum, we usually overlook the interdisciplinary instructional practices that should be considered. For example, if only one teacher is using cooperative learning, performance assessment, or reflective writing in a classroom, students may not see these practices as valuable throughout their other classes. The faculty meeting provides a special forum to foster the development of interdisciplinary planning for curriculum, instruction, and assessment. Approaches to differentiating learning experiences for students may also be shared. Interdisciplinary department meetings also give the staff an opportunity to pursue consistent strategies and activities to meet the school mission.

In the elementary school, faculty meetings offer good opportunities to break up into small groups across grade levels or departments (e.g., English as a Second Language [ESL]) to promote the vertical articulation of the curriculum. For example, groups of second- and third-grade teachers meeting together can reflect on the following questions: What are you finding out about the students we sent to you last year? What are their strengths and weaknesses? Standardized test results can also be reviewed in this way. What are the student strengths and weaknesses based on the test results? How can we work together across grade levels and disciplines to meet our school or district goals to help all students succeed?

The following faculty meeting guides have been used to pursue some of the goals mentioned previously while promoting articulation across grade levels.

Discussion Guide: Vertical Articulation of the Curriculum

Grade Levels _____ (two or more)

The following are intended as questions to stimulate discussion across grade levels. Please add to these as you see fit.

1. When your students leave your grade, what do you expect them to know? To do? (key concepts, content, and skills)

2. What would you like the incoming students to know? To do? (key concepts, content, and skills)

3. What are the congruencies and discrepancies in your view regarding the expectations?

4. Conclusions?

5. Next steps we plan to take . . .

At certain times during the year, staff members have found it helpful to meet to discuss standardized test results. The following guide has been used as a conversation starter.

Analyzing Standardized Achievement Tests Results

Grade Level _____   Subject Area _____

1. What patterns emerged as important for our grade level/subject area?

    Strengths:

    Weaknesses:

2. How can the results be helpful for the remainder of this year?

3. Do you have any recommendations for the previous grade level or the next grade level?

4. What are some of the major similarities and differences between the objectives of the standardized tests and our school curriculum? Differences between standardized tests and how assessment occurs in classrooms?

5. What are some of the major goals of our curriculum that cannot be assessed through standardized tests? How should we assess these goals?

6. Conclusions?

7. Next steps?

With software programs available to disaggregate data, many principals and teachers have found this information useful in schoolwide conversations about student learning and student needs.

The One-Legged or Standing Faculty Meeting for Short, Informative Sessions

Often when you have promised the staff that a short faculty meeting will take place to report on an immediate or emergency issue, the meeting tends to drag on. If you ask the staff to stand during the last 10 minutes of the meeting, you are symbolically illustrating that you are serious about holding a brief meeting. The staff member who wants to hold up the group with his or her own agenda will be very reluctant to do so when those who are able are standing and ready to go. Also, you can ask staff members to stand near the end of a regular meeting and promise them the meeting will end in 5 minutes. You will have to keep your promise! Furthermore, the staff will enjoy the opportunity to stretch!

TalkWalk for Energy, Exercise, and Dialogue

Teachers often come to meetings exhausted after a hard day's work. Imagine their surprise at an invitation to take a walk with one or two colleagues for 10-15 minutes! The TalkWalk (Caro & Robbins, 1991) engages the staff in professional dialogue while providing exercise, energy, a change of environment, and the opportunity to share expertise. Staff members tend to return from the walk in a more relaxed, reflective mood. They then articulate key points from their TalkWalk dialogue.

Encouraging Participation in Professional Growth Activities for Responsiveness and Meaning

The faculty meeting can also be used to share ideas about professional growth activities. Is there a new university program in the area? Is there a new e-learning opportunity? Is a well-known consultant presenting in the district or school within the next few weeks? Is grant money available for summer study? Are there professional growth experiences that teachers would like to see take place on site? Are teachers willing to share their professional growth experiences with other staff members? Do the ESL or Special Education departments desire to share strategies for the mainstreamed classrooms? The possibilities for professional development are endless. These possibilities can be highlighted on a professional development bulletin board kept in a prominent place. By making this an issue during faculty meetings, the principal and the staff are taking an important symbolic stand in support of professional growth.

Video-Stimulated Discussions— For Fun, Reflection, and Dialogue

Many staffs have begun a practice of bringing in a popular video and playing a portion of it to stimulate discussion. Examples range from *Robin Hood*, to begin a discussion on developing teams and, eventually, a collaborative workplace, to *Rain Man*, as a beginning for conversations about inclusion. Staff members rotate responsibility for bringing in videos. A variation of this approach is to use stories (either adult literature or children's) as a springboard for conversation.

Swap Meets—for Clean Rooms and Effective Use of Resources

To build a positive climate and to facilitate sharing, some faculty meetings periodically include a "swap meet." Swap meets provide the opportunity for teachers to exchange instructional or curricular resources. To illustrate, for the swap meet, teachers bring items they no longer use to exchange for items that other teachers bring. Sometimes these meets are preceded by classified ads in which teachers identify needs for resources in a "want ad" format. Requests range from coupons to books, plastic jars to magazines, or simply ideas—either written, recorded, or videotaped.

A Final Thought

In closing, it is important to reiterate that the faculty meeting is an opportunity for professional growth and the celebration of teaching as professionals gather together to share and learn. We often hear that teaching is the second most private act. The faculty meeting is the perfect forum for teachers to interact and break down the traditional barriers that serve as obstacles to discussing what goes on in our classrooms. Faculty meetings also provide the context to model those teaching behaviors we wish to see implemented in the classroom with students. Further, it is a powerful stage for building culture and schoolwide norms of practice.

Reflections

This space provides for you a place to write in ideas that have been generated by this chapter, things you want to try, or adaptations of ideas presented herein.

1. What is the level and type of staff involvement in your faculty meetings? Explain. What are some strategies to increase staff involvement?
2. Which idea from this chapter might you implement during the next faculty meeting?
3. What are some additional ideas that can be used to hold effective faculty meetings?
4. What is an initiative your school is currently implementing? How might faculty meetings support this?
5. What are some new thoughts that have occurred to you as a result of this chapter?

16

First Days of School

A time for renewal.

The first days of every school year are always both exciting and nervous times for students, parents, the newcomer to the principalship, veteran administrators, and teachers. Regardless of how many years one has spent in the profession, the new year is always a time of renewal and uncertainty. This is a time of renewal because it is a chance to try a fresh approach with new and returning students and teachers. It is a time of uncertainty because, whether one is a newcomer or a veteran, there are always questions: Will I succeed this year? What will be the new challenges? Often, principals try to speculate about what the challenges and issues will be for a new year. The best philosophy may be simply to say, "I don't know what the challenges or issues will be, but I'll try to be ready!"

The beginning of the year also has special significance because the brain remembers beginnings and endings. The first impression that a principal makes with the staff will be a lasting impression. Additionally, in the beginning of the year our senses are heightened, and the opportunity exists to face new and old challenges with a fresh perspective. On the other hand, too much change in the beginning of the year can be unnerving—especially if the changes come as a surprise to the staff. A blend of tradition and change may be the best approach if one has the chance to influence the beginning of the year.

Logistical Concerns

Distributing a schedule of preschool activities to teachers with a welcome-back letter a couple of weeks before school begins is a good way to let teachers know that all is moving along smoothly. The letter can help to encourage the staff to begin thinking about the new year and plan activities and actions that need to be taken care of before initial school meetings begin. In a year-round school, this will be necessary for each track. The letter also models valuing preparedness.

During the first days of the new school year, the principal needs to be very concerned about logistics, yet also ensure that human needs and curricula and instructional goals are not overlooked. The following "Beginning of the Year Checklist" addresses many of these concerns:

- Review district and school mission, curriculum goals, school and grade level testing data—alone, and then with key personnel
- Prepare the "Welcome Back" letter to staff, noting goals for the year
- Carefully review previous beginning of year memos and newsletters to staff, students, parents, and the community
- Examine faculty assignments, and *last minute* hiring issues
- Review master schedule, enrollment trends, and class lists with counselors and administrators
- Review the budgetary expectations for the year
- Meet with assistant principals, department chairs, grade level leaders concerning goals for the year and beginning of the year logistical issues
- Review with secretaries the "beginning of the year" tickler file
- Review orientation for new students with counselors and appropriate staff
- Review orientation for new teachers with key veteran faculty
- Meet with special services team, including counselors and teachers
- Remind secretaries of their role as ambassadors for the school
- Walk through the school with head custodian to make sure rooms have sufficient furniture for students and staff and that outlets, lights, windows, ceilings, walls, halls, and playgrounds are all meeting cleanliness and safety standards
- Ensure that restrooms have necessary supplies and are absolutely clean
- Review security, health and safety procedures, and critical phone numbers for fire, ambulance, police, and poison control
- Make sure procedures are in place for preventing intruders
- Meet with transportation and food service personnel
- Review the year's activities with athletic/activities director
- Review disciplinary procedures, especially new mandates, with assistant principals
- Carefully examine and test relevant computer hardware and software upgrades with technology personnel to minimize first day "glitches"
- Invite student government representatives to lunch
- Make sure substitute-teacher policies are in place
- Carefully organize beginning of year faculty meetings combining staff development and logistical concerns
- Meet with PTA representatives
- Make sure orientation signs for "first days" are completed. Include a banner in the front of the school with a slogan that students are familiar with from

television, such as *Good Things Are Happening* (from *Good Morning America*, ABC News, June 17, 2002)

- Schedule your time to be especially visible during the first few days of school
- Walk through the school on your own, "visioning" a typical day

One principal thought he was ready on the first day, except for one problem: the automated school bells had not been calibrated for the year. The custodian had forgotten about the bells, and the principal did not know how to set them. The principal quickly learned. What a way to start! Although operating the school bells should never be confused with educational leadership, the ability to calibrate bells in this case contributed to things running smoothly.

Before classes begin, teachers want to make sure they have resources and time to work in their classrooms. Scheduling a workshop in lieu of providing time to set up classrooms could be a "kiss of death" to the feeling tone in the school. There should be a balance in how the preschool time is organized with a sensitivity to teacher and classroom needs. Regarding instructional resources, each teacher should receive, without asking, essential classroom supplies and instructional resources. These items should include

Computer hardware and software	Crisis planning handbook
Curriculum guides	Teacher editions
Grading books	Planning books
Activities calendar	Copy of school's student planner
List of recent media acquisitions	Class lists and attendance forms
Chalk and markers	Pens, pencils, and erasers
Paper, tape, and stapler	Media request forms
Bulletin board material	Garbage cans

Having these items in classrooms when teachers arrive tells them that you care. If you have not used this procedure, develop a "beginning of the year supply list" with three or four veteran teachers and a secretary. Also, check with the library media center, and computer resource areas to make sure they have necessary resources and are ready for the first day of school. Teachers welcome lists of new library and media acquisitions.

Another logistical concern should be school maintenance. The principal should review the summer maintenance requests with the custodian and walk through the school several days before the year begins to make sure that the repairs have been completed and that the school is clean and safe. In elementary schools, the playground areas should be carefully checked for hazards. In the middle and high schools, checking locker conditions and common gathering areas is a must.

To remain on top of logistical concerns from year to year, keep a "beginning of the year" folder as part of your "tickler file" (see Chapter 17, section on tickler files).

Although the monthly tickler file will include important activities covered during each month, the beginning of the year file is especially important to help you begin successfully. Remember to update the file a few days after the school year starts. Soliciting staff input can be helpful in enhancing beginning of the year activities. The file is especially valuable to a principal who will be taking over a new school. Typical items that may be in the file include letters to parents, previous year's teaching schedules, programs from various school productions, minutes or agendas of faculty meetings, or reflections on how to improve Back to School Night.

Beginning of the Year Faculty Meetings Set a Tone

Faculty meetings are extremely important in the beginning of the year as colleagues, old and new, gather together, work collaboratively, and, it is hoped, grow professionally. These meetings present special opportunities for principals to strengthen staff cohesion and morale. Your first obligation during the meetings should be to remind staff members that you are there to serve them.

Consider a specific theme to set the tone for the year. For instance, if the theme is "The School as a Community of Learners," activities need to be structured to reflect that. One such activity is to remind teachers of the wealth of knowledge that exists among the staff. During a faculty meeting, teachers might be asked to add up their collective years of teaching at a table group and share. The table with the most number of years might be awarded a prize. Such activities remind one of the rich resources that exist just beyond one's classroom door. By seeking advice from colleagues, staff members are able to tap the wisdom of practice that exists in a school. Without doing so, one runs the risk of repeating an initial year of teaching several years in a row. Staff development should always be a significant part of faculty meetings. The beginning of the year is the perfect time to make this point. A principal should consider activities that help teachers think about the year and possibly create a vision of the kind of year they can have with their students and colleagues. Before beginning this visioning activity, review the school's philosophy or mission with the staff. Ask if they believe it needs revisiting or revising. Here is a variation on a "reverse visioning" activity used successfully in the beginning of the year from the book *If It Ain't Broke—Break It!* (Kriegel, 1991).

Reverse Visioning—A Variation

You are 85 years old . . .

1. What did you do with your life?
2. What were the significant milestones at 30, 40, . . . 80?
3. What qualities did you exhibit?
4. How do other people describe your life?
5. Do you have any regrets? If so, what are they?

6. What would you have done differently?

7. As you are sitting in your rocking chair, a former student comes to visit you on your 85th birthday. The student states that he or she remembers you very well. Ideally, what would you hope that the student would say about you?

Pair up with a new teacher or someone who is not on your grade level or specialist area and discuss your ideas.

After the exercise, teachers were asked to write on a small poster what they wanted the students to say about them. Teachers were given markers and poster paper to complete the activity.

These faculty meetings should be used also as a link with previous years. Review the school's traditions, successes, and what characterizes the culture of the school. This is not a time to review every topic in the faculty handbook. Certainly, new or very significant school changes should be mentioned, but teachers should read the handbooks on their own. This is the time, however, to remind staff members of the noble purpose of their profession and the years of dedication to students. Remember, what you pay attention to communicates what you value.

If yearly goals are developed, then a review of last year's recommendations and the refinement of that document needs to begin (see Chapter 8, "Building a Vision and a Mission Together"). These goals are important for teachers and students. The common goals can send a signal to students while they are in a class that the teachers are working together. For example, if fostering diverse student answers to questions is a school goal, emphasizing the goal in each discipline can be especially powerful in high schools as students move from class to class and realize that teachers are encouraging the same behaviors. This lets students know that teachers are communicating and working together.

Team-building activities should also be part of a school's opening. For example, the following activity helped the staff in one school become better acquainted and proved to be a pleasant icebreaker:

1. Teachers were divided into groups of four.

2. Each group member listed four statements about himself or herself—one statement was false.

3. Each person then read his or her list, and the other group members guessed which statement was false.

4. After all guessed, each person revealed which of the statements was false.

5. Points were awarded for accurate guessing and for "stumping" the group.

Another staff had a back-to-school breakfast. Following the meal, a scavenger hunt was scheduled so staff members could find additional resources. The winning team received gift certificates to a local teaching supply store.

Departmental and Grade-Level Meetings

These meetings should be prescheduled because the time for small groups to get together to plan the year is critical. Grade-level and departmental meetings should be held for reviewing and refining the curriculum and estimating time lines for completing work. This should include a review of the successes as well as hurdles of the previous year. The emphasis should not be to cover everything but to discuss key outcomes that should be stressed for the year. Also, this time should be used to review some of the major activities that are held during the year (e.g., Thanksgiving program, Spirit weeks, Martin Luther King commemoration, Earth Day activities) to adjust time accordingly. Ensuring that all members of the grade-level and department teams have sufficient supplies should also be a goal of these meetings. Veteran teachers should help newcomers review instructional resources and share their materials at this time.

Reviewing the vertical articulation of the curriculum should be an objective of these meetings (see Chapter 15, "Faculty Meetings"). Sequential grades should meet (e.g., Grades 3 and 4) to review the expectations for the present and following year. Too often, we forget to consider the next year and micromanage the curriculum for the next day. To facilitate a more far-reaching view of the curriculum, the third-grade teachers, for example, should ask the fourth-grade teachers, What do you expect fourth graders to be able to do when the year begins? This helps the staff to project for the next year, not the next day, and can have important implications for how one teaches. In middle and high schools, departmental members should be asking the same questions of one another to project for the future. Ideally, the teachers in exit grades in each school should talk about their expectations to all of the teachers in grades below them, as well as to receiving teachers in the grades above them. State standards, benchmarks, and frameworks are helpful tools to guide these discussions.

Discussing interdisciplinary curriculum and instructional strategies should, in addition, be considered at this time. Setting time aside early in the year can set the stage for various departments to meet together to discuss the possibilities of a parallel curriculum (e.g., teaching related topics at similar times) or actual interdisciplinary teaching (e.g., teaching common themes and concepts, developing interdisciplinary essential questions, working on projects and activities together, as well as team teaching). In elementary settings, grade-level meetings can also be devoted to these possibilities.

Orienting Teachers New to the School

Separate orientation sessions for new teachers and teachers new to the school should be set up. Usually 1 or 2 days before veteran school staff members return is sufficient time to hold the meetings. Whether a teacher is new to the profession or simply new to the school, this is an anxious time. A veteran teacher who may have been very successful in previous schools can find this time especially taxing as he or she will be experiencing some of the same frustrations as the total newcomer: Exactly how does that copier work? What are the rules for duplicating material? What is the schedule? Where are resources housed? How does the e-mail system work?

As with the general faculty meetings, the principal should view this time as an opportunity to set an example with the new staff by not only responding to their immediate needs but also emphasizing the school mission and the possibilities that exist for students when teachers are committed, have energy and enthusiasm, and care about kids. The principal should talk about the school culture and celebrate teaching. Also, the principal can use this time to stress that the school is a learning community and that the principal too is learning along with the teachers.

Devote very little time during the meetings to the faculty handbook—emphasize only those procedures that are essential. Send the message that you know the teachers are professionals and can read the manual on their own. Welcome questions about the handbook for the next meeting. As they will be anxious about curriculum material, make sure the material is available on the first meeting day with curriculum guides, teacher editions, and supplementary resources. A tour of the school and available instructional resources (both basic and enrichment) should also be a priority.

For the beginning teacher,

- Stress the importance of structuring the classroom early in the year.
- Suggest resources to create a positive class climate.
- Provide a variety of models for room arrangement.
- Encourage teachers to review basic school and classroom routines with their classes during the first few days of school. (This should help to save time and reduce possible student problems as the year progresses.)
- Offer time for teachers to check out resource materials.

Asking new and veteran teachers about the needs and questions they considered during their first year of service can be useful in determining elements for an orientation session. The following guidelines for assisting new teachers were developed by a combined group of new and veteran teachers in the school supervision graduate class at Eastern Washington University. *Guidelines for New Teachers* included

- Developing a new teacher packet with school philosophy and mission, schedules, staff data, routines, crisis plan, holiday policy, copier directions, hardware and software instruction, and community information
- Purposefully using a mentor/buddy program through the district and school, and initially assisting with curriculum, instruction, time management, and social issues
- Assigning equitable course loads and grade level responsibilities

- Sharing strategies to work with parents
- Scheduling luncheons with the principal every few weeks during the first year. Include one session devoted to explaining the school's jargon.
- Visiting classrooms, observing veteran colleagues, possibly with help of mentors
- Minimizing extra-curricular commitments during the first year
- Funding for professional development workshops related to the school's curriculum and instructional initiatives
- Allocating sufficient instructional resources and office supplies (e.g., curriculum guides, teacher editions, manipulates, etc.)
- Planning social events
- Team planning with department, grade level, and/or special service faculty
- Welcoming coffee with parent and community representatives

Instituting a buddy system for new teachers is a wonderful way to ease their transition into the school. Encouraging the veteran staff to show newcomers around and take them out to dinner or breakfast, at the school's expense, can go a long way in helping newcomers feel part of the group. By simply answering the various questions that newcomers have—and are reluctant to ask the principal—the buddies can give teachers a sense of security and help them get off to a successful start.

Teacher Time in the Classroom

Besides receiving their instructional supplies, teachers want to spend time in their classrooms. Teachers should have ample opportunity to do so. If you have several days scheduled of preschool meetings with teachers (this varies from school to school), try to make a symbolic statement by having one day or the greater part of a day without any meetings to show staff members that you respect their need to get into the classroom. Certainly, classroom time should be built in to every day before school. Moreover, many teachers will want to work in their classrooms the weekend before school opens. Make it easy for them. If building security is a problem, facilitate the process to keep classrooms open so teachers know you are serving them; the bureaucracy should not become an obstacle during this critical period.

Welcoming Students and Parents

If possible, hold an open house for new students and their parents the Friday afternoon before school opens. For middle and high schools, ask selected veteran students of the school to come to the open house to give the newcomers a tour of the school. Many middle and high schools have peer support groups supervised by counselors, activities directors, teachers, or administrators to organize social activities and/or academic strategy sessions for new students. Many programs extend throughout the school year. An open house is a good time to introduce assistant principals, counselors, secretaries, support staff, and custodians to the students and parents. This should be a light function, a social gathering, with refreshments. It should be scheduled for about an hour. The gathering can include ice cream for elementary students. A few students from the upper elementary school, middle school, or high school, depending on the setting, can serve as guides.

Ask the parent association to assist on the first day, orienting new parents, serving coffee, and so on. Encourage the association to have a welcome table for parents. Try to have parent volunteers to assist new families.

Be Out There on the First Days of School

Finally, on the first day of school, plan on being visible to teachers, students, and parents throughout the day. One principal wears a funny hat on the first day so people will gravitate toward him with any logistical questions. Again, the time needs to be built into your schedule well in advance. Circulate on the campus, in the hallways, and in the cafeteria. Also, try to visit as many classes as possible during the first couple of days to personally welcome students and wish them a successful year. Some principals have classes visit their office to emphasize school rules, review activities, answer questions, and generally get acquainted. Often, assemblies are held to go over school goals and rules. During the assembly, emphasize the school's commitment and personal concern for all students and the importance of community. Also, introduce the new teachers and honor the veteran staff. Remind students that academic success and caring about each other are mutually important school goals that both faculty and classified staff are committed to achieving with students. If possible, consider holding the assemblies on the second day, so teachers and students can start smoothly and begin their classroom routines. Most important, by being out there (e.g., in the cafeteria and corridor, on the field, by the buses) on the first days of school, the principal reaffirms that important events in the school happen in the classroom and on the campus and not in the administrative offices. In doing this, the principal can proactively troubleshoot logistical problems in order to see that the school gets off to a smooth start.

Reflections

This space provides for you a place to write in ideas that have been generated by this chapter, things you want to try, or adaptations of ideas presented herein.

1. Make a list of 5-10 priorities that a principal should act on before the school year begins.
2. Develop a 2-day orientation schedule for faculty.
3. Create an agenda for the first faculty meeting. Consider collaborating with staff members to plan it.
4. Share one or two fun activities that could be included during the faculty orientation period.
5. What were two or three particularly difficult situations for you as a first-year teacher? How could the effect of those situations been minimized?
6. What insights or new questions do you have as a result of reflecting on the ideas presented in this chapter?

17

Tips: Ideas That Work and Align With the School's Mission

Let's not reinvent the wheel.

We are often advised to work smarter, not harder. This chapter will help you follow this advice. There are many suggestions that we have made throughout the book that are really "tricks of the trade," so we are bringing some of these ideas together in this chapter for you as a "quick read." We will add new ideas (e.g., key questions to ask when interviewing prospective teachers) that can help you to enhance your performance. In addition to the tricks of the trade, we will include simple suggestions that can firm up the values that are important to your school. Each idea has gone through a kind of litmus test; that is, the idea is included because it has been used successfully and can add positively to the effectiveness of a principal and the culture of the school—ideas are not included because they are simply "cute."

Organizing Your Time

Using a tickler file. Probably one of the best organizing tools a principal can use is a tickler file that includes all of the important events, critical activities, memos, and time deadlines (end of semester or quarter, testing, grading periods, open house, parent conferences, etc.) for each month (you "tickle" the file monthly). Thus, when November is about a month away, the principal and secretary meet, review a list prepared by the secretary of items in the November file, and examine each previous November memo or important activity description. It is helpful to have separate "beginning" and "end of the year" files in addition to the August/September and May/June files. A very helpful addition to the file is a monthly section that includes your reflections on the events so errors are not repeated, successes are noted, and ideas for next year can be immediately added to the file. A tickler file is invaluable to a principal new to a school.

Tracking major projects—prioritizing. In addition to the tickler file, it is very helpful to have a card-monitoring system with your notes on the cards concerning major projects or key personnel. This can also be done electronically. The system enables you to quickly review and reflect on your priorities to always "keep the big picture in view." If done in hard copy, the cards are usually in a two- to four-page folder with viewing pockets for each card. These card systems are often advertised in business or commercial airline magazines. A system that holds about four pages is ideal. It is ideal because one can write down important ideas at any time. For example, a principal may have cards for next month's faculty meeting, the next parent bulletin, a specific school goal, the present science review, the holiday show, the professional growth workshop, key personnel, student concerns, and a daily "to do" card. The cards are reviewed and moved, sometimes weekly, at other times daily, depending on your priorities. Projecting toward the future, cards may include the names of possible teaching candidates, thoughts on scheduling, and goal suggestions for the next school year.

Blocking your personal schedule. We know that if principals are not careful about monitoring their time—and often interruptions are unavoidable—they will have little control over their schedule. A very helpful tip is to block in time well in advance if you want to be in certain places and engage in particular activities, such as exercise! We are not only talking about scheduled assemblies or formal observations. Principals should also block in morning walkabouts to classrooms and short periods to greet or say good-bye to students during the day if these activities are important. Principals must ask themselves, "What message(s) do I need to send to the staff, students, and parents through my behavior?" "What are my priorities?" "Am I spending time on these priorities?" As Kent Peterson, noted author and professor of educational administration at the University of Wisconsin–Madison, said, "What you pay attention to communicates what you value." It is especially vital that the school secretaries know the principal's priorities as secretaries can have tremendous influence on the schedule. Finally, principals often feel conflicted because they want to be available, but know that the question, "Do you have a minute?" usually means a half hour. One principal responded this way: "I have a minute if you can walk and talk with me on my way to my next appointment." This allows the principal to be responsive and to save precious time.

Making Record Keeping Easier

Pocket planner. Record keeping is a difficult job, given the fragmentation and variety that characterize the principal's role. To help keep things together, a pocket planner can be used. A pocket planner is a 3"x 5" index card system that one carries in the pocket. You can also do this through your personal digital assistant. It can be used to keep track of things accomplished that address goals or supervision data. For goals, for instance, one writes the goal at the top of the card:

Goal: To implement reading, writing, and thinking across the curriculum

Accomplishments:	Date of Completion:
Distributed article to staff	9-10-03
Faculty meeting discussion	9-18-03
Management by wandering-around visits	(ongoing)

Every time something is accomplished that addresses this goal, write it on the card. Then when reports are due, the data are all on the card. Similarly, the school vision can be written on a card, and indicators of that vision becoming reality can be noted and celebrated with the staff.

For supervision, write staff names down the left side of the card. Across the top write the months. Then every time a visit is made, jot down a note on your card:

Names	Sept.	Oct.	Nov.
Alvarez	9/13 walk through		
Bond			
Cathay	9/15 left a note		
Denny			
Elton			
Foster			
Gage	9/16 visit w/kids		
Hunt			

By keeping this record, you can make sure that your visits are distributed evenly among staff members. This can help, also, if you need documentation when working with a marginal teacher or other member of the staff. The walk-through technique, often called management by wandering around, can be used to learn how the first and last 10 minutes of classes are used and whether or not valued instructional, curricular, and assessment approaches are being practiced. Many principals use this time to interview students to learn of their perceptions of classroom experiences, and to examine the quality of student assignments.

Principals who use the pocket planner approach say that it is simple, convenient, efficient, and effective.

Additional Helpful Ideas to Stay On Task

Those memos and mail—touch once! A helpful management suggestion and first-rate time saver is to try to touch each item that comes across your desk only once (one major exception will be noted). How does this work? To begin with, make sure you have in and out boxes on your desk. Then get in the habit of thinking that there are only five possible actions that you can take with each in-box memo, and make a quick decision on each item. First, should someone else be dealing with this item? If yes, delegate and send it on to that person. Do not worry if you are not sure if it is his or her responsibility, you will surely get it back if it isn't! Second, does the memo require immediate action by you (often just a signature)? If yes, quickly write the appropriate comment for the colleague asking for the action. Third, is the memo something that does not require present action but may need to be referred to in the future? If yes, file the item for possible future reference. Fourth, does the item belong in the "circular" file? If yes, do not hesitate to throw it away, and keep a box next to your garbage can for nonconfidential items to be recycled. Fifth, does the memo require further review (e.g., reports, professional articles)? If yes, it will require a second touch. These items should be kept in a folder ("review") and reexamined when a block of time is available. Very few items should go into this folder.

Reflection log. Keep a log of your reflections. This provides an avenue for a "professional time out" and increases your capacity to be reflective and analytical. The art and practice of reflection allows one to view a situation from a different perspective, given the fact that time usually has elapsed between the occurrence of an event and when one makes the time to think about it. Often fresh insights emerge or one resolves to handle future, similar situations in a different way.

Using the computer. To begin with, do not assume that using a computer will save you time or paper. You may very well use more of both. But if you use the computer properly, you will likely be more creative and effective on the job. As software companies have become more familiar with schools and their needs, the programs for administrators on scheduling, attendance, student records (including discipline), programs to disaggregate test data, and report cards have significantly improved. However, it is a school's responsibility to examine the programs carefully and encourage the software companies to work closely with schools to work out program glitches. It is important also to avoid a situation in which only one computer "guru" in the school knows how a system works. If that is the case, the software program is not suited for the school. Additionally, there are excellent, very simple software programs for sending out announcements, fliers to parents, compliments to students, and, in general, just helping principals to communicate better.

A cautionary note: Principals spend their time with people. Because the computer is a fascinating and powerful tool, one can easily spend a lot of time in his or her office working with the computer. Even fancy memos, produced on the computer, are no substitute for personal interaction. Many principals dedicate time at the end of the day, after staff members have left, to spend time on the computer.

The look book. An excellent way to communicate daily morning announcements is to use a look book for all teachers to quickly read. It works equally well in elementary, middle, or high schools. The book can be placed in strategic spots in large schools to help save paper and reduce loudspeaker interruptions in the school building. In the look book, the teachers view important information for that day. For example,

1. The report card comments were thoughtful, objective, and informative. Your hard work is much appreciated.
2. Assembly at 10:10 instead of 10:15 because we are recognizing 5 students for their environmental work.
3. Reading Committee meeting at 12:05.
4. Math Department meeting during 8th period.
5. Reminder: Student council representatives will be visiting 7th-grade classes to generate interest in the charity drive.
6. Today is Mr. Abram's birthday; we can't give his exact birth year because records were not kept in those days!

The book keeps everyone informed, enhances the idea of community, and when humor is added, can create a friendly and positive tone to begin the day. The principal should write in the look book before leaving on the previous afternoon. The look book has a couple of extra benefits: It serves as a detailed record of what took place each day at school, and it breaks down the isolation that sometimes occurs in schools by bringing everyone to a central area to read the daily comments. It really works!

A variation of the look book is used at P.S./I.S. 123 in The Bronx, New York. Virginia Connelly, principal, uses a large flip chart on which to post daily announcements, recognitions, and communications. The flip chart is placed in the office where most staff members check in daily.

Interviewing Teacher Candidates

One of our most important job responsibilities is to hire the best teaching candidates available. Remember, the candidate is also looking you over so it is important to ask thoughtful, insightful questions that get to the heart of the matter and reflect the values you wish to emphasize. The candidate may decide to select your school over others based on his or her feelings about the quality of the interview. The following are some helpful questions (this is not an exhaustive list) and ideas that might yield important information about teacher candidates:

- In your opinion, how do children learn best?
- What do you remember about your best teacher?
- What would a visitor to your classroom hear, see, and experience?
- If I were to speak to a friend who knows you well, what might the friend say to describe you?
- When not in school, what do you enjoy doing?
- What are your greatest professional strengths? or After reading your recommendations, I'm curious about what you think a supervisor would say about your teaching.
- If you could return to school or work with an expert mentor, what would you like to study? How would you like to grow?
- Why, in your opinion, do some children have an easier time learning than others?
- What are your beliefs about classroom management?
- How should the "high flyer" student be taught? The student having difficulty?
- How do you go about differentiating instruction?
- How do you feel about professional development?
- What other career would you pursue if you were not teaching?
- If you could choose your No. 1 ideal position in our school, what would it be? What would your second choice be? Why?
- What new ideas and teaching strategies do you think you can bring to this school?
- What excites you about education?
- Why should we hire you over other candidates?
- It's important that you don't leave this interview thinking, "I wish I had mentioned that!" So, is there anything that you would like to tell me or that I should know about that we have not already discussed?

A helpful addition to an interview may be to request that a classroom photo album be brought to the interview by the candidate. Looking at the faces of students or the walls of the classroom can tell us much about a candidate. Many systems also show a video lesson and ask a teacher to analyze it. A teacher portfolio (writing samples are especially helpful) or video of a lesson is invaluable. If the candidate is short listed, can you take the time to see the candidate teach? Multiple data sources provide for sound decisions.

Retaining New Faculty

After a teacher is hired, it is important that we do our utmost to support and retain this person. Statistics indicate that without this support one third to one half of new teachers leave the profession within their first three years of service, citing a lack of institutional support as a key reason. Support strategies might include the provision of a quality mentor who teaches the same subject or grade level; meetings among new teachers with a facilitator to problem solve, share successful practices and resources; and scheduled new teacher time with the principal. (See Chapter 16, "First Days of School," for more information on assisting new teachers.)

Providing Experiences to Celebrate the School's Culture

The following activities, events, projects, strategies, or professional development recommendations have all been successfully implemented. A few of the ideas may be right for your school or, we hope, may spark an idea that will strengthen the values essential to your school.

"See them teach before they leave." When teachers are permanently leaving a school, especially the retiring veteran, ask the departing teachers if it would be okay for other teachers to watch them teach during the final month of the school year. Use the slogan "See them teach before they leave" (in the look book) for a couple of days to encourage teacher visits. The principal should offer to cover some of the classes while staff members visit their departing colleagues. This type of project could become a catalyst for increasing classroom visits among teachers during the school year. At one school that observed this tradition, the departing teacher was presented with a plaque with the doorknob from her classroom mounted on it. Under the knob were the words, "Thank you for opening your door and sharing well kept secrets. You saved the library of knowledge from burning."

Worthwhile faculty meetings. Although Chapter 15 covers faculty meetings, it is important to stress that the meetings should not be used for communicating information that could just as easily be conveyed in other ways. For example, teachers quite rightly feel cheated if they have to remain at a meeting in which a list is being read to them. Faculty meetings should be for staff development, such as providing tips for working with non-English speakers or students who have been placed in inclusion settings, sharing ideas from professional articles, discussing classroom successes and seeking collegial advice to deal with frustrations, learning about new teaching strategies, analyzing data from test scores, or working on departmental, grade-level, or schoolwide curriculum issues. If a school schedules regular faculty meetings and there is very little substance to cover for a particular meeting, it would be wise to cancel the meeting every once in a while so that teachers can use the time to complete important class work. One principal did this, referring to the action as giving the staff "the gift of time" for the afternoon. "Whenever teachers encounter content that can be used to inform daily practice in the classroom at faculty meetings, they begin to actually look forward to them," one principal noted.

Phoning the good news. How often do we call parents to give the good news? Unfortunately, our reflex goes like this: Billy has messed up again; is it time to call his parents? It is rarely: Johnny was very helpful with that new student, should I call his parents? We need to call home and send letters home when good news takes place. In some schools, students call from the principal's office to give the good news themselves. One particular principal even uses a cellular phone while walking around the school and calls parents about a positive observation with the child present. This has served to positively influence parental attitudes toward the school.

The principal as reader and teacher. Students love to have the principal visit class to read a story or a poem. The holiday season is a perfect time for this type of activity. The school librarian can be very helpful in selecting a variety of stories for each grade level to be read by the principal. About 15-20 minutes of time in each class works. Two or three classes a day for several weeks will do the trick. One principal who is a Vietnam veteran teaches when secondary students are working on this part of the curriculum. It is very important for students to see the principal in a role other than the traditional one—the disciplinarian or person "in the office."

Principal for a Day. A contest can be held in which individual students send the principal letters stating why they should be chosen from among their classmates to "take over for a day." The principal would become the student when the exchange takes place. To get several students involved, the position can change each hour or class period. Principals have also exchanged jobs with business leaders for a day as a community project.

The principal's scrapbook. School principals receive notes, pictures, art work, poems, photographs, and so on from students throughout the year. Posting these items as a principal's scrapbook is a rewarding exercise. Students are drawn to this interesting three-dimensional scrapbook as it "grows out" on a bulletin board near the principal's office. It becomes a folk history of the principal's school year.

Principal walkabouts—and follow-up. Before school, in the morning, in the afternoon, or after school, two or three weekly, 1-hour walkabouts into classrooms is a wonderful way of demonstrating that the principal knows where the true center of the school is. If time permits, complimentary follow-up notes should be sent to teachers, letting them know that you noticed their effective questions, the way they showed extra concern for a particular student, or that creative bulletin board display. This is an excellent time to pay attention to those aspects of the school culture that you value and want to promote. One principal carries a pad of Post-its™ and writes notes to give to others on these walks.

Providing buddies or mentors for teachers new to a school. How many times have we all said, "If only I knew that when I entered the school?" A buddy or mentor system for new teachers is an excellent way of giving the newcomer a head start regarding those questions that are not answered in the teacher's manual or during the faculty orientation meetings. A small stipend could be set aside for buddies or mentors to take the newcomers out for dinner or breakfast.

Building traditions to celebrate important values. October 24, United Nations Day, is an excellent opportunity for any school to unify around themes such as respecting all humanity, global unity, strength in diversity, exploring other cultures, or the work of the United Nations. A school should celebrate and commemorate the importance of respecting one another regardless of race, ethnicity, religion, or gender. Having the faculty working together on an activity such as United Nations Day reminds everyone of one of the most important reasons for schools: learning to get along with one another. There are, of course, other special days that can equally serve this type of theme, such as Earth Day or Martin Luther King Jr. Day. These days also give a school an opportunity to celebrate a theme that should go to the heart of schooling. A variety of activities stressing particular themes should occur throughout the day or possibly week of the special occasion. Student projects, films, and outside speakers should all be involved in the activities. School principals should do whatever they can to support faculty committees organizing these special events. Faculty, students, and parents all take an interest in the important values that are brought forth on these days and, one hopes, throughout the school year.

Student tutors and peer counseling. High school students enjoy tutoring younger students, and elementary school students welcome help offered by older students. A relationship between a high school and middle or elementary school to develop a student-tutoring program is an extremely worthwhile activity. It is especially helpful for elementary students who need special attention and for high school students who can use a boost with their self-confidence. For all involved, this process builds important social and emotional skills. Often, these programs can be set up following the regular school day. Many secondary schools offer course credit for this type of work.

Peer counseling is also a very worthwhile activity for middle and high schools when organized by school guidance counselors who can provide meaningful orientation sessions and monitor the peer counseling during the year. The peer counselors work with fellow classmates who may need someone to talk with because of a personal difficulty or just someone who can help them get into gear regarding their studies. Peer counselors have even worked with upper elementary school students, especially in conflict resolution on the playground. School principals should view these student-to-student programs as important opportunities to assist students in their social and emotional growth. Some high schools have peers operate a mock court system. Such judicial systems have greatly reduced a variety of crimes at the school site and in the immediate community. They have fostered the development and understanding of important principles as well.

School recognition assemblies. These assemblies should be scheduled to recognize students for positive accomplishment during a 6-to-8-week period. Teachers submit student names for recognition by the principal for a variety of accomplishments: improved academic performance, an outstanding oral report, helping with a charity drive, persistence, making excellent contributions to class discussions, improved English for the nonnative speaker, and so on. The assembly gives the principal an opportunity to emphasize important themes (behavioral or academic), wish happy birthday to students and staff, and welcome newcomers or say good-bye to students leaving the school. A student musical interlude or class play may be a part of the assembly program.

Practical Guidelines for Preparing Printed Materials for Internal and External School Community Members*

The following guidelines are offered for developing letters, memos, daily announcements, newsletters, posters, handbooks, planning documents, reports, policy manuals, school profiles, yearbooks, student newspapers, calendars, brochures, menus, and electronic memos:

- deciding on a clear purpose or objective for the document, always considering the mission of the school. Ask yourself, What does this memo/article have to do with student learning and quality teaching?
- keeping the document concise and to the point
- targeting a specific audience
- considering issues of appearance related to format, graphics, font, white space headings, and balance. Decide whether the document is attractive and "eye-catching"
- using clear, understandable, comfortable, and familiar language. Avoid jargon!
- considering how each newsletter article is organized, including sequencing and placement of articles and graphics
- making sure the document is timely and up to date
- weighing budgetary issues, relating to quality of paper, number of copies made, quality of print, method of distribution, and color copying
- keeping articles unbiased and avoiding language that might be interpreted as sexist, racist, or otherwise insensitive
- considering other stakeholders who should receive the printed material in addition to the targeted audience
- ensuring the material reaches the targeted audience
- keeping the information relevant to your school/community

- considering the 30 second, 3 minute, and 30 minute "rule" when publishing a newsletter. Audiences that have 30 seconds, 3 minutes, or 30 minutes must all feel the newsletter is worthwhile. Thus headings and subheadings are critical

- seeking feedback to evaluate the success of the document. Consider how to obtain reliable and helpful feedback concerning the document. If two-way communication is a goal, how is it being reached?

- remembering that all documents that emerge from the school are a reflection of the administration, and the school

- proofreading, proofreading, and proofreading

*The above guidelines were developed by school leadership graduate students in a School-Community Relations course at Eastern Washington University, following an examination of several hundred documents distributed by their public and private schools.

Using Tips in Your Setting

The preceding ideas are all tried-and-true strategies used by principals and other school personnel to improve their effectiveness or positively affect the culture of the school. Although only some of the ideas may work in your school, all of the ideas are intended to identify themes or strategies that might lead principals and their professional colleagues to come up with successful activities for their schools. Perhaps one of the most powerful ways to continue this tradition is by organizing support groups of principals (no larger than 10 members) to meet regularly, problem solve, and share successful practices.

Reflections

This space provides for you a place to write in ideas that have been generated by this chapter, things you want to try, or adaptations of ideas presented herein.

1. What are some tips that you can offer to your colleagues?
2. What kind of events, activities, or strategies might be added to those mentioned in the chapter to positively affect the values of a school?
3. What insights or new questions do you have as a result of reflecting on the ideas in this chapter?

(More tips: We encourage our readers to send in their tips for us to use for subsequent editions of this book. Send your tips to Pam Robbins, 21 North Newport Drive, Napa, CA, 94559, or 1251 Windsor Lane, Mt. Crawford, VA, 22841.)

PART VI

UNDERSTANDING YOUR CONSTITUENCIES

18

Working With Parents and Partnering With the Greater Community

When it comes to schools, everyone is an expert!

Effectively Communicating With Parents

A strong parent-school partnership is a valuable resource. This chapter examines facets of this relationship and relationships with the greater community and offers several tools to enhance these relationships. It is clearly the responsibility of all school personnel and especially principals to communicate effectively with parents. Thus schools need to take the initiative in this area. In the past, school leaders and teachers were reactive with parents, or viewed the relationship as a back-burner priority. This should not be the case. As one assistant principal noted, "Principals must be P.R. persons today. You have to welcome parents and be much more accommodating to a very demanding public. Parents need to be courted. Also, they want their kids to come to school with green hair!"

Schools need to be proactive when communicating with parents regarding all school issues, from a new program to an individual child's progress report. For example, unsatisfactory grades on a report card should not come as a surprise to parents. Parents should be notified if their child is having difficulty well before the report card is distributed. School principals need to build this idea into the system and communicate ways this can be done.

When schools have good news to report, parents should hear about it. There is no better public relations effort than reporting good news. For example, an elementary school principal may hold recognition assemblies about every 6 to 8 weeks to positively reinforce students for a variety of accomplishments. These may include helping a new child in school, a first-rate math test score, having a painting sent to a museum, or improved behavior. Following up the assembly with notes to parents that compliment students and explain how the students were recognized sends a clear message concerning what is important in that school. Recognition assemblies, in this way, not only serve as public relations tools but communicate cultural values to parents as well. Another effective strategy to report news to parents is through the student-led conference. These conferences, appropriate from kindergarten to the 12th grade, can be arranged as special events or as part of scheduled parent-teacher conference days. Student-led conferences give parents an opportunity to observe and hear their children report and reflect on their progress. Whether teachers help students prepare working or showcase portfolios, or specific samples of student work, students, by engaging in a dialogue with their parents and by showcasing their work, have an opportunity to demonstrate what they have learned. These conferences are a powerful tool, transcending, by far, the minimal effect provided by traditional report cards.

When considering how parents view schools, it is interesting to note that as an institution, a school is one of the few professional organizations with which all feel some familiarity. We all attended school. The mysteries of medicine, for example, may cause parents to hesitate about questioning a particular diagnosis of their child. This is not the case when schools are concerned. Parents are likely to be much more assertive about questioning "the school system." One's own experiences in school, good and bad, have left many parents with firm ideas on how to approach schools and how schools should be run. For some parents, school was a very unpleasant experience, and the school principal may remind them of memories better forgotten. Thus a smile, handshake, and warm welcome can be important icebreakers for those who feel less comfortable in schools.

The role that parents play in schools varies greatly and depends on factors such as whether the school is private, public, elementary, middle, or high; the nature of the parent community; the administrative approach with parents; current issues; teacher comfort with parental involvement; and the degree of parent input formally built into the system for educational and political reasons. Thus parents may play roles ranging from the more traditional role of attending school only on open school night and during parent conferences, to volunteering several days a week as a class tutor, to serving on school boards and making general policy decisions, to becoming a member of a site-based management team involved in the everyday running of the school. Schools have the responsibility of informing parents about the various roles they can play.

Again, principals should be proactive with parents and not assume that they are an adversarial group. The overwhelming majority of parents will support the school as long as the school is communicating with them and has kept them aware of important issues. When there are interest groups that have a personal agenda that may interfere with the best interests of the students, it is very helpful to have a majority of parents familiar with the issues. When conflicts occur, a principal should look at the conflict or problem as a challenge and an opportunity to work out a solution. When working out solutions, it is important always to take the higher ground, not viewing the conflict as a personal battle. This, of course, is easier said than done.

When parents raise questions regarding general school issues or policies, the school philosophy or mission statement should play a major part in helping the principals and teachers remain focused regarding the direction of the school. This is why it is advisable to involve parents in mission building to create understanding and ownership. Certainly, change should be considered if the change will lead to progress, but school leaders constantly must consider the school mission when working with groups that are asking for change. A key question to ask is, Is the proposed change consistent with the school mission?

Additionally, it is important for the principal to actively listen to all ideas and factions. This does not mean that the principal is not aligned with a particular point of view—one should have strong feelings on significant issues—but the appearance of an inflexible position quickly tells parents that you are uninterested and not listening. It is important also for principals to meet, possibly monthly, with the president or head of the parent association. Particular parents, however, should not be seen as the principal's favorite or the decision makers for other parents.

Here is an interesting view from a principal on remaining neutral with parents:

What I try to do is stay right on the fringes of all groups so that they're comfortable with me and me with them. But, I don't want to drink beer with them, or whittle at the courthouse, or hunt and fish or haul wood. I just want to be close enough to them so I can sit and be comfortable, and them with me. But, that's it. (A Principal's Voice)

Building Bridges With the Parent Community

To build up parent interest in a school, an open house before school officially opens or early in the year can be held for parents (and students) to meet the administration and teachers. This kind of positive interaction can help to build the bridges that will come in handy when communication on important issues is necessary.

Holding monthly parent coffees is an excellent proactive forum to discuss school issues. Although you cannot eliminate griping by some parents at these meetings, the forum can be used to present important school issues with the administration taking initiative. The following format has been used successfully to carry out monthly coffees: (a) general announcements updating parents on school events and student successes; (b) a presentation of interest to parents (e.g., on the new school reading program, how to deal with a student's fears, trends in education, etc.); (c) occasionally, breaking up into small groups to talk about the presentation issues; and (d) open comments and announcements by parents. Holding these meetings in the morning or evening with a 1-hour time limit lets the community know that the sessions will be both meaningful and doable, given a parent's busy schedule. Furthermore, it emphasizes the value placed on communication in a clear, concise way.

This format works because many parents attend coffees if they think a topic of substance is on the agenda. By setting a positive tone with planned presentations of interest to parents, the meetings proceed in a supportive climate. The climate of these morning or evening coffees can be an essential element in maintaining positive home-school relations throughout the year. It is important to stress that all parents should be welcome at the coffees. The more the general public knows about what is actually taking place in the school, the less chance there will be for rumors or inaccurate information to be spread around.

Additionally, these coffees can serve as important opportunities—within a structured environment—to gain parent input on a hot issue. For example, coffees can be used to exchange ideas on the adoption of a new science program, pilot testing based on state standards, or the institution of major changes in a disciplinary or homework policy. Principals can open these coffees to parent ideas, letting them know that the ideas will be brought back to the professional committees to consider. Often, parents make excellent suggestions that can become part of the new policy or curriculum change.

Although it is more convenient for school personnel and many parents to hold the coffee on site, principals should consider parents' homes and community centers as other venues for coffees. For some constituencies, a community center may seem less threatening and an indication that the school is reaching out to the community. This may be particularly true in some low-income settings. Parent reading groups, sponsored by the school, are another effective way to build bridges with the parent community. A school principal, assistant principal, counselor, librarian, or teacher can help sponsor the reading group. In one school system, the following books were used during a two-year period with various elementary and secondary school parent groups: *A Tribe Apart* by Patricia Hersch, *Emotional Intelligence* by Daniel Goleman, *Reviving Ophelia* by Mary Pipher, *Raising Cain* by Michael Thompson and Dan Kindlon , and *Letting Go: A Parent's Guide to Understanding the College Years* by Karen Levin Coburn and Madge Treeger. *Letting Go* was the only book selected for a very specific group: parents of high school seniors, who were, literally, experience the anxiety of "letting go."

Excerpts from the following letter to parents introducing the reading group for *A Tribe Apart* may help to demonstrate the potential of this parent-school activity:

Dear Reading Group Parents,

We were quite pleased with the number of parents who expressed an interest in joining a high school reading group during our recent coffees. We've received the first order of 28 copies of *A Tribe Apart*, by Patricia Hersch. To pay for the book, please make a check out for _____ to (school name), or bring exact change, to the high school office.

After reflecting on the book, and trying to pace our discussions, we'll divide the readings into three parts to follow the natural sections of the book as outlined by the author. Thus, for the November session, please read Part I, "Stepping Inside," pages 3-120 (mostly about life in schools); for the December session, read Part II, "Making Contact," pages 121-228 (about adolescent life outside of school); and for February read Part III, "Making Sense," pages 229-375 (mostly about how adolescents try to make sense of who they are and where they are going). [Exact dates and times are provided for each meeting]

A Tribe Apart follows eight teenagers through three years of their lives. The teenagers are Chris, Jessica, Jonathon, Joan, Ann, Charles, Courtney, and Brendon. You will know them well before you finish the book! A good theme and question for us to consider during the first session in November would be: Is teen culture really different for the present generation of adolescents, when compared to twenty years ago? Of course, many other questions will emerge from our discussion. Please bring questions to the reading group!

The fun and goals of the reading group should include intellectual stimulation, strengthening the relationships among the adults in the reading group, and engaging in a lively discussion. As with all reading groups, it will be important for us to be supportive of the comments made by others, stay relevant regarding the text, and develop questions and responses based primarily on our interpretations of the book. Additionally, the group will give all of us an opportunity to work on our listening skills as we gain insights from other group members. The PTA will be providing refreshments for each session.

Finally, we look forward to taking this journey with all of you these next few months. We suspect that we will all grow from the text and the ideas that we will share with one another.

Sincerely,

The traditional open school or open house nights and parent conference days provide unique opportunities for schools to show what they are all about. Creative variations during these traditional activities can have very positive long-range results in the parent community. For example, teachers should be encouraged to show parents videos of students working and student-teacher interaction in their classes. Parents appreciate the effort made by teachers who prepare videos, and they love to see their children in action. As noted earlier, student-led conferences are very effective. The use of student portfolios displaying the work and progress of each student significantly affects parents. One parent, after viewing her child's portfolio, remarked, "I wasn't aware that my child was capable of that work." Furthermore, the walls of a school should be lined with student work every day, and especially on these special days. Student work should be the heart of these events. Open School Night, if organized to start with presentations by the administration and parent association, provides a special opportunity for principals to reassert the vision of the school and publicly thank and recognize the important role that teachers and parents play in the lives of children. One principal made suggestions to faculty members concerning the group meetings with parents on "Back to School Night" (usually held within two or three weeks after the opening of the school year), and concerning the individual meetings with parents later in the year. Both sets of guidelines follow.

"Back to School Night Guidelines for Teachers"

- Welcome parents at the classroom door.
- Clearly display, or verbally note, the room number, your name, and class (sometimes parents are lost and in the wrong room!).
- Review syllabus expectations of the class, sharing samples of books, and instructional resources to clarify points.
- Review major class activity, testing, and homework expectations, possibly showing samples of exemplary work.
- Let parents know that you are accessible to their children.
- Let parents know how you can be reached, and that they are welcome to get in touch with you.
- Tell parents that if their child is experiencing difficulty they will be notified (e.g., progress reports), and that positive news will also be reported.
- If time, consider having parents write a short note to their child to be read privately by their child the following day.
- Finish with positive comments.

The following suggestions for teachers apply for the individual parent-teacher conferences, usually held a couple months after the school year begins.

"Guidelines for Individual Conferences with Parents"

- Pleasantly greet parents and thank the parents for taking the time to meet with you.
- Some parents know their children are doing poorly and are quite uneasy about the conference. It is especially important to comfort these parents and let them know that "we are in this together."

- Be specific about strengths and weaknesses, possibly including samples of the child's work to emphasize a point. Again, consider student led conferences as an option for the evening.

- Ask parents for helpful information about their child that might be of assistance in your particular class.

- Discuss specific strategies, for their child, to achieve success in your class.

- Ask parents for help, and review activities that they can do at home with their child to strengthen the home-school partnership.

- Avoid educational jargon when talking about the curriculum, instructional strategies, or concerns about a child.

- Before closing, ask parents if there is anything else that they would like to know, or share, about their child.

- Keep the meetings on time, so waiting parents do not have to wait longer than expected.

- Try to finish on a positive note: Thank parents for coming, remind parents that you enjoy working with their child, let them know that you are accessible, and how you can be contacted.

(Principals should make sure that refreshments are available during conferences in central locations, or in each classroom.)

A school might consider a Saturday morning workshop sponsored by the administration and teachers for parents to provide information on an important topic or topics. Topics might be faculty or parent generated and include helping children with homework, the role of technology in education, discussing learning styles, or suggestions to instill greater responsibility at home. In settings where parents' own experiences with school were so negative that they feared school, the school has extended an outreach program. In Hawaii, for instance, school personnel took blankets to the local park and set up learning stations for parents.

Comparing Parent Roles:
Elementary Versus High School

It is interesting to compare how parents of elementary and high school students view their roles as advocates of their children. In working with elementary school parents, the immediacy of academic "success" usually is not a major issue. The elementary school principal can emphasize the importance of developmental stages and help parents to recognize that it will take time for the children to master certain concepts and skills. Parent workshops and the intervention of effective guidance counselors are much appreciated by most parents of young children as they are highly motivated to find out what is developmentally appropriate for their children. On the other hand, principals must be ready for the minority of elementary school parents who feel that they need to intervene early in their child's school "career" to make sure they are early readers and get into the "best" schools and classes right from preschool or kindergarten. When working with these parents, it is important to review developmental literature and stress the importance of minimizing pressure and frustrations for young children so they have the opportunity to develop cognitively, socially, physically, and emotionally and possess a positive feeling about their initial school experience. At the same time, it is important to be sensitive to the parents' feelings about these issues and celebrate their support.

To recommend patience to parents of adolescents in a high school setting may be unrealistic. When an adolescent is a junior or senior, time and the immediate consequences of good or bad grades are a greater reality. Immediate decisions must be made about continuing high school, going to college, enlisting in the armed forces, getting a job, or seeking vocational training. Thus, in a high school setting, most parents and their children are much more interested in product than in process. This emphasis on product may be unfortunate when considering the long-range goals of education, but it is reality because of the need to make important decisions about a teenager's future. Also, high school students, for obvious reasons, will play a much greater part in determining their future than will elementary students, yet they still benefit from the insights of others. Moreover, the relationship between the teenager and their parents will have a great bearing on the role the parent will play in the school regarding the child's education. If there are problems at home, you can almost guarantee that the problems will emerge in school or that the parents' relationship with the school either will be strained or nonexistent. It is very important that a school does not give up working with a parent who may appear helpless in dealing with a teenager. On the other hand, if the school is having difficulty relating to a teenager, the school should seek assistance from the teenager's parents when a strong, positive relationship exists. Often, the school counselor can play an invaluable role in giving the parent strategies and bringing the student and parent together.

Additional Ways to Bring
Parents and Community Members Into School

Involving parents in school-related activities can build bridges with the parent community and help the school in areas in which resources may be scarce. To illustrate, parents can serve as volunteers to help with tutoring, with field trips, in the cafeteria, or with transportation problems (be sure to check on vehicle insurance). Volunteer tutoring is especially helpful. Using retired community members for tutoring can be a wonderful experience for both the student and the retiree. It is important, though, that when tutoring takes place, volunteers are aware of the importance of confidentiality and working hand in hand with the classroom teacher. The school, at the appropriate time, should make sure that parents and other community volunteers receive necessary training in instructional and curricular strategies and are recognized for their work. For example, workshops could be held reviewing the primary objectives of the reading or math programs, examples of confidentiality, and basic dos and don'ts about working with children to support their self-esteem. In one school, parents and community members joined together to create assistive technology devices, such as communication boards, to support special education students participating in inclusion programs.

A parent or community resource file can be set up by each school to note parents and community members who have a particular expertise or hobby that they can share with the school. Having adults from the community visit classrooms to tell about their careers or hobbies brings the real world to the classroom and lets students know that there is a clear link between what they are doing and what is taking place in the world of work. Furthermore, it fosters great public relations, and the children, parents, community members, and school all benefit from the experience. One school invites students to shadow parents at work and then participate in a forum in which critical skills are discussed.

Also, booster clubs have been an important traditional way for parents to become involved in schools. Frequently, these clubs help with sports activities, but these organizations can also help to purchase technology for a school, raise funds to improve playground equipment, or help to repaint the walls of a school. The variety of possibilities are limited only by one's imagination.

Many parents do not reach out to a school because they do not know how they might help. Some schools facilitate the reach-out effort by sending home a list of suggestions. Suggestions range from supporting the school on campus to assisting students by sponsoring a homework group. Working parents may appreciate that even by saving labels from cans—something they can do with limited time—they can help. A school starting a new science program asked parents for jars, lids, and bottles to build up the science resource room supplies.

In summary, effective communication with parents is a primary responsibility of each school. Why? Because it is very difficult to succeed with children if relations with parents are unsatisfactory. We need to create a partnership. So often, a school looks to what parents can do for the school. We must also examine what the school can do for parents and the community. By taking a proactive stance, schools send the message that "we care, we want to work with children, and we welcome parent and community input." In the end, the school principal is in the most effective position to lead the way in taking the initiative with teachers, parents, and the larger community. Building this bridge can enhance learning opportunities for parents, community members, teachers, students, and the principal and thus enrich the overall school climate.

Broadening School Support

Although developing relationships with parents is essential, schools need to reach out to the broader community as well. This provides opportunities to counter the traditional skepticism about the effectiveness of schools in communities ("Schools just ain't what they use to be!"). Also, it addresses the need to get the public to support schools and enables the school to maximize the use of existing and potential human and financial resources.

In pursuit of building broader support, schools need to communicate with a wider circle of people. This may represent reaching out to an audience with whom they have not had contact and beginning a conversation. One principal suggested, "Schools need to meet folks on their turf." For example, the reach-out effort may extend to the beauty parlor or barber shop, senior citizen center, local business associations, the chamber of commerce, and churches, mosques, or synagogues. This type of effort can generate human resources and financial support for the schools.

Both younger and older students can visit nursing homes, sing for the adults, provide companionship for walks, and play board games with elders. Senior citizens or disabled veterans served by community organizations can be invited to schools for special programs at the holiday season or even special programs just for them. When appropriate, staff development opportunities in a school can include participants from the business community who can benefit from the experience (e.g., learning style workshop). And, as noted earlier, people in a nursing home or retirement community can tutor children. For these senior citizens, this experience can be most rewarding and meaningful. For students, these experiences build important values about reaching out and serving others.

Reaching Out and Working With the Media

Newspapers, television, and the radio are always competing for an audience. They compete with other newspapers or stations and with one another for stories that attract the largest audience. Unfortunately, conventional wisdom and marketing strategies indicate that the news vacuum is often filled with stories that are negative: "If it bleeds, it leads." The public sometimes complains that the media are only interested in selling bad news. Yet we know that news organizations do extensive surveying for marketing purposes. If good news sold, then good news is what would be presented most often. How can schools overcome this conventional logic concerning news stories? Well, they cannot overcome it completely, but interestingly, some schools have succeeded incredibly well in getting their story across. For example, one school district in Washington State conducted a news audit and found out that during a 180-day school year, 105 articles were printed about the district in local papers—only 3 articles were negative! How did this occur? What can a school district do to minimize the negative news and get the true message out about school success? Larger districts do this by hiring a public information specialist (that "PR" person!) responsible for collating and distributing news about the schools for dissemination to various media. Smaller school systems must rely on superintendents, principals, and classroom teachers to work with the media. Regardless of whether you are a principal in a big city system or in a small town, the following guidelines can help you reach out to spread the message of success:

1. *Focus on the school vision and mission.* Every television appearance, radio interview, and newspaper article that you are involved in should focus on teaching and learning and the health and welfare of the students. Always consider the school mission and your responsibility to students, teachers, and the community. Of course, there will be many situations that do not directly relate to these issues, but school leaders need to bring the subject of the media event back to these issues. A trick of the trade is to quietly ask oneself before an interview: How can I focus on teaching and learning during this media opportunity? Remember, each time an administrator speaks with the media it is an opportunity to step forward, be an advocate, and state what is best about the school. Even when a violent incident occurs, drawing media to the school, the direction of the interview from the school standpoint should be toward the health and welfare of the students and getting back to teaching and learning.

2. *Build a reputation based on honesty and trust.* Successful public information officers will tell you that it is vital to build an honest and trusting relationship with the media. This is especially true when there is bad news to report—and the bad news should be reported just as we report the good. The community is entitled to know what takes place in the tax-supported public schools. Sadly, there are times when an administrator, teacher, or classified worker engages in inappropriate or criminal behavior. Trying to hide a major incident will backfire on the school district. After receiving legal advice, schools must be up front about incidents that may hurt the image of the school. However, if a trusting relationship between a reporter and school district has been nurtured, even the most difficult situations can be ameliorated, at times. For example, in one school district an embarrassing incident concerning a staff member was going to be reported in the local newspaper. Because of the trusting relationship between a reporter and school administrator, the school was told when an article about the incident would be in the paper, and whether the incident was going to be in the widely circulated main section of the newspaper or in the "zone" (local) section. This forewarning helped the school prepare for the "fallout." Trust is also maintained with a little common sense. For example, never ask to see a story in advance, and send a brief "thank you" note when a positive story is published.

If a school leader is unhappy with a story because of inaccurate or biased reporting, he or she should avoid contacting the news service when angry. When calm, one should send a letter presenting one's point of view. And, if possible, contact the reporter who actually reported the story. If you initially contact the editor, the message of "going to the boss" may embarrass the reporter. The consequences can hurt the school district. Of course, contacting the editor should be an option if inaccuracy or bias continues.

3. *Recognize that each story needs an angle.* Consider that the average 30-minute television news show may select from hundreds of stories for the evening broadcast. Maybe 10 stories will be selected as "news," with only about 20 minutes of actual broadcasting time. Why should the station show a story about a school? What makes your story news? Whether we like it or not, it is only news if the media says so! So the story needs to be unique or have an angle that will get the viewer to stick with the story instead of flipping to another station. A story about school service might pique a station's interest. For example, the ecology club in one school created a trail with Braille signs for visually impaired hikers. A newspaper and local television station picked up the story. The story was inspirational and sent a strong signal to the community about the school's devotion to service and its ecological mission.

Interestingly, because of standards, high stakes testing, and accountability issues, school test results are big news. Public interest on a national, state, and local level means that test scores often are listed in newspapers as columns of statistics with a school's score, compared to others in the district or state. When school leaders are asked to comment on these data it is important to keep a perspective. Thus, if interviewed about a school's test results, one might consider avoiding the appearance of being overly thrilled or overly disappointed, depending on a school's scores. (Don't set yourself up for the surprises that next year's scores may hold!) Further, one might let reporters know that high stakes testing is only one of many ways to assess students and that some students simply do not test well.

4. *Seize opportunities to showcase the students.* In small and midsize cities newspapers and television networks will often showcase stories about students receiving awards or special recognition. This is especially true when a major state or national honor is achieved. In small towns, local newspapers will publish honor roll information, and zone editions of some major papers will publish local school information about awards, the work of clubs, special class activities, and big school events. A key to all of these opportunities is that they are about local kids, with local names that stakeholders will know. If a newspaper lists the names of 300 high-school students that made the honor roll or a photo of the city-wide chorus made up of 4 middle-school groups, there is a good chance that all of the parents or guardians of the children mentioned would buy papers.

5. *Serve as an educational resource.* Although reporters are college educated, it is unlikely that they are familiar with all of the issues facing schools. A commandment of working with nonschool personnel is *avoid jargon;* yet it is sometimes difficult to do so completely. A familiar and simple comparison can help a reporter or the public understand an important educational issue. To illustrate, Meek (1999) offers the following advice: ". . . if you try to explain 'alternative assessments,' you are likely to use education jargon that is not clear to the public. If you must explain, use examples people are familiar with. To explain portfolios and exhibitions, you

should use examples such as an artist's portfolio as a collection of work over time or a basketball game as an exhibition in which performance is judged, the same as a science fair" (p. 129).

Additionally, you may be asked about issues related to testing, data driven assessment, students with disabilities, the Elementary and Secondary Education Act, and so on. A reporter may not have a comprehensive understanding of an issue and will want to check with a trusted educator they know. Help out! Tell the reporter what they need to know. If the information is not at your fingertips, let the reporter know that you will check it out and call back. Likely, the favor will pay off in the future.

6. *Be accessible and visible.* As with other principalship roles, accessibility is critical. When the media calls, try to get back to them as soon as possible. Obviously, if there is a serious issue, it may be necessary to check with the superintendent and in larger districts with the public information specialist before returning a call or accepting an interview. When positive or negative issues arise, the community expects the principal to be there. Events like *Principal for the Day* are excellent opportunities for the principal to be visible. In one high school, this event was featured on the front page of the school newspaper, giving the principal an opportunity to be seen in a very positive manner.

7. *Approach news proactively—good or bad.* Districts should keep a steady stream of school news flowing to the media. As noted above, there will be negative stories that need to be shared. Keep the media informed consistently about district and school events; the number of positive stories will greatly outnumber the negative. Moreover, schools must advocate for students at every opportunity and get the message out. The best way to do this is by raising the consciousness of all staff about the importance of sharing school successes beyond the classroom walls, and by developing a system in which interesting stories are routinely sent to the principal and district public information specialist. These administrators can select the stories that will likely receive recognition, and make decisions concerning which media source would best suit the school's needs.

8. *Respect deadlines.* Because newspapers, television, and the radio are different media, they handle deadlines differently. Check with newspaper reporters and editors and radio and television producers to find out about local deadlines. For example, ask, What kind of advance notice is necessary for a human-interest story? If you request a photographer, will that change the deadline? For a crisis or emergency situation, schools need to know print and broadcast deadlines. For example, television producers often meet about 10 a.m. with the anchors and reporters to decide on the evening stories. Anyone who has been in a television studio before an evening news show or in a newspaper's news room knows that the deadline pressure is extraordinary; schools do not need to complicate the situation.

9. *Writing effective news releases.* Newspapers thrive on good, crisp writing. They expect those who wish to have stories published do the same. A news release should be written in the active voice with a strong first paragraph, arousing the

interest of editors and reporters. Furthermore, the news release should be no longer than one page, with a notation of "more" at the bottom of the page if additional
information is included. The traditional who, what, where, when, how, and why
questions need to be answered in the news release. In addition, the news release
must include a date line (noting the date the story is released by the school), contact
line (noting the contact person at the school) and release line (noting when the story
should be released to the public). Calling the newspaper to find out if the release
was received is perfectly acceptable. Normally, newspapers prefer about a 5-day
notice for news releases. Warner (2000) makes the following wonderful suggestions concerning news releases: "One way to get the reporter's attention is to print
a special news release envelope that identifies it as such. To further catch the reporter's eye, you might consider using a neon-colored envelope that stands out in a
stack of mail" (p. 91). Using district and school stationery to identify your releases
and sending out a routine release form (e.g., *Activity TIPS for the Week*) for regular
school athletic, social, and parent events keeps the media current about school activities.

   10. *Get to know the key media players.* Part of building a professional relationship
with the media is simply getting to know the key players. For example, find out if
there are particular newspaper, television, and radio reporters who cover the education beat. Identify the influential editors and producers. Keep this information
easily accessible in a Rolodex or personal digital assistant for future use. Meet these
important contacts for lunch, invite them on a tour of your school, and prepare a
"press kit" for them with essential and lively information about your school (include sample news release forms in the kit). Also, it is essential that all media are
treated equally, especially since reporters are with competing newspapers and
radio and television stations. Equal treatment includes returning calls promptly
and recognizing deadlines. If the relationships are trusting and strong, ask for advice regarding the best way to handle a story.

   11. *Partnerships with the media.* Members of the media should be actively
courted for school-community partnerships. Career Days, journalism classes,
video production classes, and social studies and English classes, all present opportunities to actively involve the media. Classes can visit newspaper offices, radio,
and television studios for worthwhile field trips. School-to-work courses and media internships are excellent credit earning possibilities for high school students.
Also, the media should be routinely invited to unique class events, showcase assemblies, science and math exhibitions, fundraisers, and other major academic and
non-academic programs and sporting events.

   12. *Prepare for interviews.* A public information officer once advised one of the
authors to remember the following admonition when giving an interview: "Don't
say dumb things and don't do dumb stuff!" Of course, this basic admonition is ignored too often. Nonetheless, there are a few general points that can help a principal prepare for an interview. First, decide upon the critical points of your message
and state the message by *sticking to the facts* during the interview. Second, remem-

ber that short 10 to 20 second sound bites are what the public remembers. Thus, brevity! Third, since the brain remembers best beginnings and endings, state your point firmly at the beginning and repeat it at the end of the interview. Fourth, when television interviews are taped, the dead time will likely be edited, so patiently collect your thoughts before answering. Fifth, school leaders represent what is best in society. If a reporter gets argumentative, stay calm and ethically above the fray. Sixth, at the end of the interview, express your thanks for the opportunity to talk about the school.

13. *Recognize that there are no "off-the-record" comments.* Reporters are trained to supply the public with news. When school leaders try to confidentially share a little news with a reporter, sometimes hoping to avoid an unfortunate consequence, the school leader forces the reporter into an ethical dilemma. It is unfair to do this to a reporter. Thus, principals should only make comments that are "for the record." In fact, even during a newspaper interview, it is a good idea to record the interview so both sides can recognize that the whole story is for the record.

14. *Contact foreign language newspapers and television and radio stations.* A very powerful message is sent to all of the school communities when an effort is made to contact foreign language newspapers and television and radio stations about school events. Through the foreign language media, the school can notify the non-English speaking community that translators are needed or will be available especially for events like *Back to School Night*. This action sincerely tells the non-English speaking community that the school is reaching out. It may also be possible to initiate a liaison relationship to share information between the English media and foreign language media.

15. *Respect the legal and moral privacy of your students.* Recently, one of the authors noticed a front-page newspaper photo of a student in a school lunchroom being admonished by a police officer for poor attendance. The story's purpose was to highlight budget cuts that would curtail the services that city police could offer to schools. However, the photo was disturbing because anyone who read the paper would know about the child's attendance "issues"—and yes, the child's name was written below the photo. The budgetary cuts, purportedly the purpose of the article, could easily have been stressed with a positive photo of students and the police officer. The child's rights (e.g., privacy of attendance records) may very well have been violated, under the 1974 Family Educational Rights and Privacy Act (Public Law 93-380).

16. *Keep the superintendent informed.* Skip Bonuccelli, a very successful public information specialist with the Central Valley School District in Spokane, WA, has the following advice for all school principals: "Remember, little kids love surprises, superintendents do not!" As with all important school issues, the superintendent or an appropriate assistant superintendent must be kept informed. There are very few administrative gaffes that annoy a superintendent more than finding out for the first time about a major school district story via the evening news or in the morning paper. Actually, this type of communication oversight is really more than

just about keeping a superintendent informed. One would hope that with years of educational experience, the superintendent would be consulted as a rich source of information on how to handle a problem *before* it becomes news.

Community-Based Organizations[1]

In urban and rural areas, community-based organizations (CBOs) may provide the greatest direct support to schools, other than the direct help of parents. This is especially true in areas with large numbers of at-risk youngsters. Often, the organizations provide support that cannot be offered at home. CBOs provide direct or indirect assistance to schools, individual students, parents, and teachers. The organizations usually work in collaboration with a school to enhance educational opportunities and provide the kind of individual or family aid that can make the difference between dropping out of school and making it. CBOs provide support to help with such questions as, Where do I go for a job? Where can I get adequate day care? Where can I find food or shelter? or How can I get health care?

Both public and private agencies are involved in community-based support efforts. Community agencies are reaching into schools and schools are learning how to reach out to the community. This is reflected in the growth of full-service schools and community school partnerships. Jane Quinn (2002), assistant executive director of the Children's Aid Society of New York, emphasizes that as a result of these partnerships, "The principals in these schools no longer have to double as educational leaders and social workers because our agency provides social services (as well as medical, dental, and mental-health services; before- and after-school enrichment; summer programs; and parental involvement opportunities)" (p. 40). Quinn emphasizes that *joint planning* will be a key to successful partnerships in the future.

Harkavy and Blank (2002), of the Coalition of Community Schools, state their views on the effectiveness of full-service community schools based on a vision of partnership representing the ideas of 170 organizations: "Community schools are public schools that are open to students, families, and community members before, during, and after school, and throughout the year." "These schools, as family-support centers help with parent involvement, child rearing, employment, housing, and other services . . . . Community schools use the community as a resource to engage students in learning and service, and help them become problem solvers in their communities. Volunteers come to community schools to support young people's academic, interpersonal, and career success" (pp. 38, 52). Beyond the focus of high-stakes testing, Harkavy and Blank maintain that successful community schools will foster "after-school enrichment opportunities, programs in such areas as violence prevention, service learning, family literacy, mentoring, mental health, and others, and services that go beyond a narrow focus on core academics" (p. 52).

Community-based support efforts may include

- Health clinics, including dental facilities
- Hospitals
- Neighborhood associations
- Religious organizations
- Women's centers
- Community colleges and universities
- Youth centers
- Art organizations
- Museums
- YMCAs and YWCAs
- Merchant associations
- Drug and alcohol rehabilitation centers
- Sports associations
- Girl Scouts and Boy Scouts
- Zoos
- Teachers' unions
- Parks and recreation departments
- U.S. Forest Service and National Park Service
- U.S. Postal Service
- U.S. Armed Forces
- Police, fire, and emergency service personnel
- Newspapers, television networks, and radio stations

Often, major city school districts or local, state, and federal agencies will list the CBOs in a particular area that provide resources to schools. For example, the New York City Department of Education maintains an Office of Community Relations that partnerships with numerous organizations. Organizations are linked on the O.C.R. Web site: www.nycenet.edu/ocr. These organizations often receive financial support primarily from the United Way or the Department of Education.

The services in the New York area are broad and attempt to meet educational, family, and community needs. Services available for students and adults include assistance for students at risk of dropping out of school; academic support for first-time youthful offenders; support for academically talented youths in need of college scholarships; training for substance abuse prevention; education for adults and their pre-kindergarten children; service to combat alcohol and drug abuse for elementary school children; nutrition awareness for school staff; homework assistance for at-risk youths; employment preparation; special employment preparation for disabled students; providing child care so parents can attend school conferences; programs on effective parenting skills, coping with domestic violence, stress reduction, and crisis intervention; and education in conflict resolution for children, parents, and staff.

Seeking School Support Through Educational Grants

In addition to CBOs, another source of assistance for individual schools can be public or private grants. Millions of dollars in grants are available to schools from public and private sources for worthy and innovative school programs. These grants may be from federal, state, or community agencies; from private industries or foundations; or from different educational associations. Often, a grant is targeted for a specific community or general region in which an industry operates. The hope is that the grant will eventually "pay off" for the community or possibly the corporation. One source of information about grants is the weekly report *Educational Grants Alert* published by Capital Publications, Inc. A typical issue will list grants from federal agencies (e.g., Labor or Commerce Departments, Health and Human Services) and many industrial or private industries and foundations (e.g., Scott Paper, the Bill and Melinda Gates Foundation, Danforth Foundation, the Phillips Petroleum). Grants can range from a few hundred dollars to millions of dollars and may be available for early childhood learning, academic achievement, innovative educational reforms, environmental issues, consensus building, substance abuse education, teen pregnancy prevention and assistance, after-school and summer activities for inner-city youths, professional teacher reform, Native American education, and math, science, and technology projects. Interestingly, with the move toward site-based management, grant proposals often need to be approved by district personnel, principals, teachers, and union and parent representatives.

Unfortunately, the needs of many students today extend far beyond the resources that schools have traditionally offered. Creative school leadership, in which principals reach out to the community, can bring a variety of assets to students. Resources can range from programs that enrich academic and extracurricular activities to essential survival services for those students in need.

Collectively, through relationships with parents and the broader community, including public and private agencies, the school can provide a variety of services to enhance student life in and out of school.

Note

1. We would like to thank Richard Shustrin from the New York City school system for his assistance with this section.

Reflections

This space provides for you a place to write in ideas that have been generated by this chapter, things you want to try, or adaptations of ideas presented herein.

1. Thinking about the school in which you work, in what ways might parents be involved?

2. Does your school look to parents for support and provide support for parents?

3. What are some possible risks when parents play an active role in schools? What are some possible benefits?

4. What community-based organizations play an important role in your school? What organizations would you like to see play a larger role in your school? How can this be achieved?

5. What insights or new questions do you have as a result of reflecting on ideas presented in this chapter?

19

Those Wonderful Kids

Our school goes home at night.

A PRINCIPAL'S VOICE

It is not the building or instructional resources that make a school; it is the students, teachers, and parents. A school is made up of people. When the doors close, we only have a building, an empty shell without a soul. The soul of the school is the kids.

In this chapter, we will try something a bit unusual. It is often through anecdotes about children that we get our greatest insights regarding their needs and how they think. Humorous anecdotes are especially interesting and often poignant. We find relief in the comical stories of children as they remind us of our special connection to kids and the joys of innocence. Thus a portion of the chapter will be spent on anecdotes about students from elementary school through high school. We will then discuss ways to structure student success by encouraging greater student responsibility. Important components of the Individuals With Disabilities Education Act will then be examined. Next, this chapter offers key considerations for developing an effective school discipline plan, including addressing the issue of bullying. The chapter will close with reflective thoughts about the horrific events of September 11, 2001, and how schools have responded in the aftermath of the tragedy.

The Challenge of Excellence and Equality

Success in North American schools and other progressive nations present a much greater challenge because the intent is to reach for both student excellence and equality. As we move further away from ability grouping all of our children and providing the least restrictive environment for children with disabilities, our democratic ideals can become a reality in the classroom. The success of the cooperative learning movement is attributable to an emphasis on academic and social skills as well as on the value of equality for all. The phrase "late bloomer" is often used in

American schools because a student in high school or even college may be succeeding for the first time. Many nations track students early for high schools, colleges, and careers; in this context, the late bloomer does not have a chance. Reaching for both excellence and equality is a tall order and, in many circles, quite controversial. But it is a noble goal and one that very few nations seek to attain.

Let us talk about kids for a few minutes. First of all, to consider kids, it is important to get into their shoes. A good way is to try to recall your own school experience. What do you remember about school? Do you recall a specific class? An incident in the hallway? What special events do you remember? Which teacher had the greatest effect on you? Why? As a school principal, are you promoting the kinds of experiences for students in school that reflect your own positive memories of school?

As ideas flash through your mind, consider what you remember about your school principals. We all remember our interactions as students with principals. How many of us, when growing up, never saw the principal except on the stage during school assemblies or in his or her office because of a disciplinary infraction? One of the authors recalls playing with drumsticks on the school stairs as an eighth grader. All of a sudden, two legs appeared on the stairs. They belonged to the principal. Fortunately, the principal's reprimand (for pounding out a popular tune on the stairs) was in a soft tone—he had obviously decided that this was not a major infraction. More than 30 years later, the feeling of that incident remains!

Those Kids and Their Stories

A principal recalls many memories of students. At high school graduation, pride flows when the student speeches surpass those of celebrities and politicians who are asked to address the senior class. The humor of simulated U.S. presidential debates by students in middle or high school always brings a smile to the principal's face. In one example, the principal recalled the vehicles with their tops down bringing the "candidates" to the debate accompanied by "secret service" personnel with secure earphones (Sony Walkmans). The goal of both excellence and equality emerges when a teacher, assessing students for entrance to calculus class, mentions to the principal that a student new to the school who did not have the grades and did poorly in the assessment test asked some great questions during the test. The teacher indicates the student should be given a shot at taking calculus. The student eventually received a "B" in the course. High expectations pay off! Another memory is crystallized when recalling the high school student whose captivating violin solo led to a standing ovation during a school assembly. The student's reputation among the faculty as indolent and unmotivated needed to be revisited after the memorable performance.

The elementary school stories often tend to be comical, yet valuable.

During the morning of the first day of school, one principal walked into every classroom to greet students. He mentioned to the students how lucky they were to have Ms. Smith as their second-grade teacher and that this would be a special year for them with this special teacher. A little girl smiled and raised her hand. The principal confidently called on her. She said, "You said the same thing last year."

In the beginning of the year, one child new to the school saw the principal a few days after school began as he was walking downtown. The child looked at the principal with an odd expression on his face and then smiled and said, "Do you know who you are? You're the principal!"

A first grader walked up to his teacher a few days before the school year ended and said, "You know, in the beginning of the year I didn't like you. But now I like you better than I like my dog!"

In kindergarten class, a teacher told students that 10 bears were going on a picnic. They had only eight cups. Would that be enough cups? All the students, except one child, said no. When the single child was called on to explain his answer, he said that eight would be enough because "they could share." In another kindergarten class, a teacher asked the students to draw a picture of a birthday party. One child approached the teacher with a picture of a house, flowers, trees, and a picket fence. After looking at the picture, the teacher immediately thought to herself, this child is a product of poverty and has never experienced a birthday party. I was foolish to assign this project. Still the teacher asked the child, "Where is the birthday party?" The student, after hearing the teacher's question, fashioned a facial expression that could only mean one thing: The teacher must be an idiot! The student proudly pointed to his picture and announced, "The birthday party is out back!"

While saying good-bye to students by the school buses one day, another principal asked Nicholas, a second grader, "Did you learn a lot in school today?" He said no. (The principal was immediately disappointed.) Then Nicholas added, "You don't learn a lot in one day. You learn a lot in a whole year."

A library teacher shared a story in which she was explaining to the children that previously, it was legal to separate Blacks and Whites in some parts of the United States. She asked the children to state the word that indicates a separation between races. The children could not come up with the word. So she gave them a clue and said that the word starts with the letter *s*. A student raised her hand and said that the *s* word for separating the races is the word *stupid*!

The Right to
Be a Child and to Make Mistakes

Janucz Korczak is one of the best known European educators from the first half of the century. He was a Polish doctor, teacher, and great advocate of children's rights. Tragically, he was killed with his students in Nazi concentration camps. Korczak was so famous the Nazis offered to let him escape the camps, but he chose to remain with his students, knowing that they would be arrested and later murdered. This story is told of him:

In 1919 Korczak was giving a series of lectures at the Institute of Special Pedagogy in Warsaw. His first lecture was titled, "The Heart of the Child." He asked the assembled group to accompany him with a child he was holding by the hand to the x-ray room of the children's hospital. The child was placed behind a fluoroscope and the lights in the room were dimmed. Everyone assembled could see only one light. It was the light of the child's heartbeat. Korczak then stated: "Look, and remember in the future, sometime, when you are tired or angry, when children become unbearable and distract you from your thoughts . . . remember what a child's heart looks like." (quotation from Kulawiec in Brendtro & Hinders, 1990, p. 239)

Korczak also wrote a Bill of Rights for children, which included the admonition that "children have a right to make mistakes." This is a key point to keep in mind when encouraging students to take risks as they answer questions or respond in class. In the end, if school does not provide an environment where it is safe to make mistakes and learn from them, where might this occur?

For students to grow intellectually, they must be encouraged to become risk takers and make mistakes. Therefore, we must help children to overcome their concern about failing in front of classmates or their teachers. If failure can be viewed as a source for learning, rather than a defeat, it takes on a positive air. This cannot be accomplished without caring. We have to nurture students so they are not afraid of trying to experiment, even though they may not succeed. Trial and error are part of learning. The risk for society is that a fear of failure may inhibit a child's desire to take on new challenges or creative enterprises. Many important intellectual leaps for our society have come about as the result of risk-taking, intuitive, and creative behaviors.

Maximizing Opportunities for Students With Disabilities

Introduction

Special education programs have mushroomed since the original PL 94-142 legislation in 1975, which mandated Individual Education Programs (IEP), free and appropriate education for students with disabilities in the Least Restrictive Environment (LRE), and due process rights. Today, approximately 5.4 million students received special education services. According to the U.S. Department of Education, in 1998, about 72% of disabled students received most or all of their education in regular classes. Approximately 25% of special education students are in self-contained classes, with approximately 3% in special schools or facilities (Ornstein & Levine, 2003). In a recent study, parents of special education students indicated that teachers care about their children and were able to properly work with their children. Yet parents maintained that school districts do not really provide the maximum assistance possible. Ann Duffett, reporting on the study sponsored by the advocacy group Public Agenda, found that more than 80% of the 510 parents surveyed thought teachers cared about their children with disabilities, and almost 70% of the parents indicated that they were satisfied with a teacher's knowledge of their child's disability. However, 55% of the parents said they "must work to find out what help is available and 16%—about one in six—said they have considered suing or threatening to sue a school district over an issue related to a child's education" (Associated Press, 2002).

The 1997 IDEA Legislation

"Perhaps the most significant change in the new Individual with Disabilities Education Act (IDEA, 1997) is the clarification of special education as a service and not a place" (NAESP, *Implementing IDEA: A Guide for Principals*, 2001). Federal law mandates that all students, regardless of their degree of disability, must receive a free and appropriate public education. The 1997 IDEA legislation, stipulating that special education is a service, sent a clear message that special education students should not be isolated. Consequently, another key feature of the 1997 law was the mandate that the IEP must relate more clearly to the general curriculum. Thus school principals are expected to support the notion that the needs of all students must be met.

The educational standards movement, designed to maintain high expectations for all students, has significant implications for students with disabilities. For example, special education students must be offered the same opportunities to engage in the full school program, including appropriate extracurricula activities. If a school has an extracurricular art club, special education students must be given the opportunity to participate in the club and have their work displayed just like other students. Schools must provide transportation for extracurricular activities for students with disabilities, ages 3 to 21, without extra cost to parents.

Concerning disciplinary issues, the 1997 law (PL 105-17) stated that students with disabilities should receive explicit instructions and services to help them follow school rules and socialize effectively with other children. Also, the law stated that students with disabilities who bring weapons or illegal drugs to school could be removed from a school by a district hearing officer for up to 45 days without the authority of a court.

Individual Education Programs

The Individual Education Program (IEP) is at the heart of the movement to serve students with disabilities. IEP's must be developed before permanent placement is decided upon. The 1997 legislation mandated that at least one regular education teacher must attend IEP meetings, if appropriate. Thus IEP teams consist of a regular education teacher; parents; a special education teacher or a special education provider; a public agency representative who is familiar with the needed services; an individual who can interpret the evaluation data and recommend specific instructional practices; and, at the discretion of the parents or public agency, a person with specialized expertise on the student's needs. When appropriate, a child may also participate on the team. IEP team meetings must be scheduled at a time convenient for parents.

Important components of an IEP include

- A statement of the child's current educational performance level.
- An explanation of how the disability affects progress in the regular curriculum.
- A statement of measurable annual goals, with short-term objectives.
- A statement of related services, instructional aids, and modifications to be provided.
- An explanation relating to why the child may not participate in certain activities with nondisabled children.
- An explanation of state assessments in which the child may not participate.
- The projected date when services will begin, with information on frequency, location, and duration of services.
- An indication of how annual goals will be measured.
- A statement of how parents will be informed about their child's progress concerning annual goals. (NAESP, *Implementing IDEA, A Guide for Principals,* (2001), p. 69)

The Principal's Role

Principals can set an ethical tone for a school by embracing the spirit and law of the IDEA legislation. For example, principals are not required to attend IEP meetings, as a general rule, but their attendance at meetings can send a strong message of support for special needs students. Principals can also address the needs of special education faculty, and the parents, by providing time for staff to meet and plan lessons for special education students. Arranging teacher schedules to accommodate parent meetings also can be very helpful. In addition, principals can help facilitate relevant staff development for special education, regular, and paraprofessional staff.

Recognizing the accomplishments of special education students, displaying their work, and paying attention to the students in one-on-one situations will send a strong and positive message to students, staff, parents, and the community. Principals can help to "cut through the red tape" to ensure that proper assistive technology devices are available and that regular instructional resources are modified. Spending time with parents of disabled students, and giving them an opportunity to share their hopes, can help build trust and confidence in the school's program.

Equity Issues and Students with Disabilities

Ornstein and Levine (2003) note that "Data on special-education placement show that students from some racial minority groups are much more likely to be designated for mental retardation programs than are non-Hispanic white students" (p. 390). This news is disturbing. Fair testing, with extensive documentation and a variety of culturally sensitive assessment tools, is necessary. States, therefore, are required to gather data to ensure that school districts are not identifying and placing minority students and limited-English-proficiency students disproportionately in special education classes. School principals must examine disaggregated data to ensure that race and ethnicity are not student placement factors.

Section 504 of the Rehabilitation Act of 1973

". . . Section 504 prevents discrimination against students with any disabilities in all programs and activities receiving federal financial assistance. Examples of Section 504 handicapped conditions not covered by the 13 categories specified in the IDEA legislation include disabilities such as HIV, asthma, allergies, attention deficit disorders, behavioral difficulties, and temporary medical problems" (Alvy & Robbins, 1998). Other common disabilities covered by Section 504 include alcohol or drug abuse (but not illegal drugs), hepatitis, and environmental disabilities. Student accidents that require home schooling for a temporary period are also covered under Section 504.

Although Section 504 assistance does not provide the extra funding or extra services that IDEA legislation requires, it does offer a broad range of services to level the playing field for students who are experiencing difficulty in school. Although an IEP is not mandated for a Section 504 child, a specific plan to help the child is required. Furthermore, parents must be notified regarding identification of needs, evaluation, placement, and significant changes made in the child's program. Again, if our mission is to meet the needs of all students in the school, Section 504 special needs students also must receive the attention of school principals to ensure that proper services are provided.

Structuring Student Success

When thinking about the avenues to follow to encourage student success, schools should encourage behaviors that include a degree of responsibility (and that degree will fluctuate with age and maturity) within a nurturing environment. The environment, as much as possible, must address student behavior in a positive manner so students feel a commitment to the order and structure necessary in schools.

Involving students in worthwhile community or school projects that contribute to improving the quality of one's life or the school environment can teach responsibility and be the most valuable activity that students experience in school.

Activities that focus on the less fortunate—helping the elderly, tutoring other students—and other concerns, such as cleaning up the environment, can help students to feel better about themselves and take pride in the school that encourages these outreach activities. At some middle and high schools, students, along with teachers, serve poor children in the neighborhood every week. They distribute snacks to the children, teach them health habits, tell stories, watch videos, and enjoy one another's company.

Peer counseling in high schools and tutoring by high school students is a wonderful way to teach responsibility and give students an opportunity to feel good about themselves. Tutoring can give students who may not be popular in other arenas (e.g., sports, music) a chance to feel good about themselves and recognize their talents. The tutoring can be one-on-one or with a class. When high schools can coordinate tutoring programs with middle or elementary schools, it is very satisfying to see high school students assisting a teacher by working with a few students or serving as a "buddy" to an elementary school student.

Elementary school principals should strongly consider instituting formal student government activities or informal representative assemblies, just as they occur in middle and high schools. Of course, the level of activity or structure will not be as sophisticated as the model for older students, but similar principles and activities can occur. These include such events as charity drives, cleaning up the school, fund-raisers to increase school resources, and presentations in which students make suggestions to improve the school. The student organization can study some of the principles of American government or American history to apply to their activities. The school principal and teacher advisors can meet with the students periodically during lunch to support the students and teachers organizing the activity. The National Association of Elementary School Principals and the National Association of Secondary School Principals distribute literature to support elementary, middle, and high school student government activities.

Discipline Guidelines

Another aspect of structuring student success rests in a sound discipline program, often one that reflects the input of students. Such programs enable students to be clear about expectations and allow them the information they need to be successful in school. Specific school rules must, of course, align with federal, state, district, or local school board policies. School law and the legal system often are in flux, yet general guidelines concerning the extent of the school's responsibility with regard to discipline and student rights must be followed by school principals. Taking a school law class and following legal updates in principalship journals is a must. For example, school principals must be familiar with laws related to due process, random drug testing, search and seizure, truancy, disruptive students in special education, zero tolerance, censorship, and bullying prevention related to violence, intimidation, and sexual harassment. Access to a lawyer with school law training has become an imperative for today's schools.

When developing disciplinary guidelines for a school, consider the following:

1. State the guidelines positively and with clarity. A list of don'ts sets a negative tone.
2. Except when absolutely necessary (see Guideline 3), avoid guidelines that are too specific; consider general principles that would include specific offenses.
3. Guidelines that should be absolutely specific should include the right to undisturbed teaching and learning; total intolerance for weapons, physical violence, and drugs; hurtful, sexual, sexist, or racist language; bullying behavior; academic dishonesty; and vandalism.
4. If you are not sure that a particular guideline is the responsibility of the school, consider leaving the guideline out (e.g., students are not permitted to smoke within three blocks of the school).
5. Safety should be a prime consideration when developing guidelines; a school must first be safe.
6. If students can be involved in developing guidelines, their commitment will increase—however, remember that student responsibilities go along with student rights.
7. All guidelines should have a rational basis; "It has always been a rule" is not good enough.
8. School rules should align with the school mission.
9. School rules must reflect district, state, and federal legal statutes.

The following is an example of one elementary school's rules:

Students care and come to school prepared to learn and to do their best.
In order to do this we

- Are polite and helpful
- Take care of our school
- Respect others—teachers, aides, students, secretaries
- Care about ourselves and take responsibility for our behavior
- Practice good health habits
- Enjoy games in the proper areas
- Are responsible for our belongings

Students are "Safe, Smart, Clean, and Friendly"

The following section of the *American Embassy School Board Policy Manual* was written by administrators, teachers, board members, and members of the high school student association. The document is based on the premise that although students have many rights, these rights are meaningless unless each individual accepts the responsibilities that accompany rights.

Students' Rights and Responsibilities

The American Embassy School [AES] endorses the belief that education should be directed to the strengthening of respect for human rights and the fulfillment of students' responsibilities. All students shall be informed of their rights and responsibilities.

AES is a community of learners, and in any effective community, rights and responsibilities balance one another. Consequently, at AES, student rights and responsibilities are interdependent. The rights are dependent upon each member of the student body exercising the responsibilities of respect for the educational process, consideration for others, honesty, and accepting the consequences of one's actions.

In order for students to be able to conform to the community's standards of conduct, rights, responsibilities, and expectations must be articulated. At the same time, it is impossible to describe and specify all situations, hence common sense and trust must be used. Indeed, an atmosphere of mutual trust, synonymous with the sense of community for which we strive, is best achieved by establishing a few clearly described universal expectations rather than a host of rules which anticipate misconduct.

Students' Rights

1. Students are entitled to all the rights set forth in this policy, without distinction of any kind, such as race, color, sex, language, religion, political or other opinion, national or social origin, property, birth, or other status.
2. Students have the right to pursue education in a climate of mutual trust, respect, and interpersonal concern where openness and integrity prevail.
3. Students have the right to a meaningful education which will prepare them to be confident and independent learners in the lifelong search for understanding.
4. Students have the right to a curriculum which is relevant to the world in which they live and a right to provide input into determining that curriculum.
5. Students have a right to safety of both person and property, including the right to safe and clean school facilities.

6. Students have the right to freedom of thought, conscience, and religion.

7. Students have the right to protection from arbitrary interference with privacy, family, home, and correspondence.

8. Students have the right to freedom of opinion and expression. This right includes the freedom to hold opinions without interference and to seek, receive, and impart information and ideas, unless this would violate the rights of others.

9. Students have the right to express an opinion and have that opinion considered in any matter affecting a student or students.

10. Every student has the right not to be a witness against himself or herself.

11. In any action against a student that could result in expulsion, the student has the right to obtain assistance for his or her defense and should be informed of that right.

12. Students have the right to freedom of peaceful assembly and association, unless this would violate the rights of others.

13. Students have the right to choose freely whether to belong to an association.

14. Students have the right to confidentiality of individual student academic records.

15. Students have the right to confidentiality of counseling sessions and records.

16. Students have the right to inspect and review all academic records directly related to the student.

17. Students may seek a correction or deletion where a record is felt to be inaccurate, misleading, or otherwise in violation of the privacy or other rights of the student.

18. Students have the right to seek representation on the Board of Governors and may attend any committee meeting when dealing with matters directly related to students.

19. Students have the right to have their views solicited and considered by teachers, administrators, and the Board of Governors when dealing with matters directly related to students.

Students' Responsibilities

Students safeguard their rights by taking full responsibility for their actions. Students are responsible for their own behavior. They must care for the individual rights of others and help to provide a safe and positive school environment within which to learn. Specifically, students have the responsibility to:

1. Conduct themselves with honesty and integrity

2. Exercise self-discipline

3. Be courteous, communicate respectfully to other members of the school community, and treat with respect the views of others

4. Respect the educational process and learning environment by refraining from any classroom behavior which diminishes the rights and opportunities of others to receive an education

5. Act in a manner which safeguards the health and well-being of others

6. Respect the property of fellow students and the property of the school

7. Dress in a neat attire which takes into account cultural sensitivities

Effective Classroom Management: Handling Disciplinary Problems

The very best disciplinary guidelines may reduce, but will not prevent, disruptive behavior. Handling disruptive behavior is certainly one of the most difficult and potentially controversial aspects of a principal's job. Helping students behave properly is one of the most important aspects of our job. Setting limits and showing a caring attitude when disciplinary problems occur can be a very important lesson for all students. Major responsibilities for principals, then, include helping teachers develop effective classroom management plans and consistent schoolwide plans as well as working directly with the more difficult disciplinary problems. Often, middle and high schools assign an assistant principal to be responsible for discipline. However, principals need to let these administrative colleagues know that the principal should be kept informed and consulted when difficult situations occur. Ultimately, the principal is responsible for disciplinary decisions taken by the assistant principal.

Before discussing discipline management plans, it is important to define *effective classroom management:* Effective classroom management is *the conscious use of proactive strategies and procedures to help students behave in a way that provides maximum learning opportunities for each student in the class*. Through such a management system, students are encouraged to develop skills for self-discipline. Based on this definition, attention should be devoted to behavior management at both an individual and schoolwide level. Thus there should be an overall school procedure for handling disruptive behavior and specific recommendations to teachers on how to resolve problems with individual students. Both situations, however, must always be viewed as "embedded in a social system; it [a disciplinary problem] is never an isolated event" (Ross, 1981, p. 211). This is a critical point because principals and teachers must act on the assumption that every student is a witness to the decision. In this setting, fairness and a justifiable rationale are essential.

The social context is especially important when examining Curwin and Mendler's (1988) "80-15-5 Principle" describing the typical classroom. Curwin and Mendler maintain that 80% of the students infrequently break school rules and come to school prepared to learn, 15% break rules somewhat frequently and show inconsistent motivational tendencies, whereas 5% are frequent rule breakers and come to school with almost no motivation or direction in their lives. The social context is critical here as the teacher has the seemingly insurmountable task of keeping the 80% motivated while using appropriate disciplinary strategies to control the 15% and firmly deter the 5%. Curwin and Mendler believe that the key is helping the 15% to improve their behavior without antagonizing the other students.

When developing a disciplinary plan, it is, of course, a good idea to examine what research has told us about what effective teachers do to maintain discipline in a caring environment. Curwin and Mendler (1988) reviewed the research of Emmer, Evertson, and Anderson to stress "that effective teachers teach classroom rules and procedures, monitor compliance with the rules, follow through with consequences quickly and consistently, establish a system of student responsibility and accountability for work, communicate information clearly, and organize instructional activities" (p. 13). Ross (1981) also stresses the importance of clear rules but adds that praise (e.g., catch the child being good) and ignoring undesirable behavior when possible have proven to be effective management techniques.

The "catching the child being good" strategy is the cornerstone of Lee Canter's (1989) Assertive Discipline Plan. Canter (1989) observed "that, above all, the master teachers were assertive; that is, they taught students how to behave. They established clear rules for the classroom, they communicated those rules to the students, and they taught the students how to follow them." Canter recommends a three-step discipline cycle that includes teaching specific desired class behaviors, positive repetition and reinforcement of desired behaviors, and the use of negative consequences if repeated attempts to promote positive behavior have failed. He stresses that "as a general rule, a teacher shouldn't administer a disciplinary consequence to a student until the teacher has reinforced at least two students for the appropriate behavior" (Canter, 1989, p. 59). The strategy of catching the child being good raises, also, the important issue of intrinsic versus extrinsic motivation. If, while catching the child being good, the teacher uses too many extrinsic rewards, students may become dependent on external reinforcement and teacher behaviors that diminish the value of being good simply because it is the right thing to do. Too often in school we resort to instant extrinsic rewards and reinforcement (e.g., stickers, exaggerated praise) to promote desired behaviors. As Kohn (1996) reminds us, "The promise of a reward is sometimes not just ineffective but counterproductive, that is, worse than doing nothing at all" (p. 33). We need to adopt long-term strategies to foster intrinsic behaviors that encourage the joy of learning, or the personal satisfaction of reading a book or helping a classmate who is having difficulty with a math problem.

Based on suggestions by Curwin and Mendler (1988) and shared experiences of many educators, the following steps are recommended for principals and teachers when consequences need to be administered to an individual student:

1. In a balanced tone, let the student know what he or she did wrong.
2. Ask the student to explain why the behavior is unacceptable. If his or her answer is inadequate, explain why the behavior is unacceptable.
3. Discuss the consequence and how it will be administered. Begin with the least threatening intervention and, when possible, give the student a choice of consequences.
4. If necessary, describe and model the desired behavior.
5. Ask the student if he or she has anything else to share with you.
6. Finish the meeting by emphasizing that although you are displeased with the unacceptable behavior, you separate that behavior from your positive feelings about the student.
7. If the inappropriate behavior continues, reflect on the environment in which the behavior occurred. Should changes take place?
8. Communicating with the parent should be considered depending on the frequency or degree of the misbehavior.

When viewing the big picture, principals should remind teachers, and especially new teachers, that everyone experiences disciplinary problems—and one should not take the problems personally. Also, teachers should keep administrators informed when problems occur frequently. Such happenings usually indicate that the student feels troubled. This warrants further study. It is the sign of a good administrator when a teacher can discuss a disciplinary problem with the administrator without worrying that the administrator will think less of the teacher because of the problem. Although at times it may be frustrating or inconvenient, a principal must be there for teachers.

Reducing Bullying Behavior

"Bullying is frequently mentioned as a possible contributor to school violence . . . [and] bullying is one of the most common forms of victimization at school" (Harris, Petrie, & Willoughby, 2002, p. 3). Although it would be an overstatement to assert that all incidents of extreme school violence, including school shootings, are a result of bullying behavior, clearly bullying has contributed to some of the most tragic events. Bullying should be stopped, and not just because it may lead to the "worst case scenario" of a school shooting. Bullying is unacceptable because it is wrong to verbally or physically intimidate or harass others. And obviously, students cannot learn successfully when fear is a part of their lives. Also, those who exhibit bullying behavior at school often "experience a greater degree of depression than is found among adults who did not bully others at school." Moreover, bullies are more likely to receive future criminal convictions (Harris et al., p. 6).

School principals must communicate to the school community that bullying is unacceptable. Sadly, the victims of bullies do not feel that school officials care and bullied students are unlikely to tell about their victimization for fear of reprisals. To support these students and schools, states and school districts are establishing antibullying policies. For example, Washington State's new law describes bullying as, "Harassment, intimidation or bullying . . . when the intentional written, verbal or physical act (a) physically harms a student or damages a student's property; (b) has the effect of substantially interfering with a student's education; (c) is so severe, persistent, or pervasive that it creates an intimidating or threatening educational environment; (d) has the effect of substantially disrupting the orderly operation of the school" (Substitute House Bill 1444, State of Washington, 2002). Washington State has also mandated as part of the bill a section that provides immunity to school employees, students, or volunteers who willingly report incidents of harassment, intimidation and bullying. Furthermore, staff workshops and other professional development programs that stress positive character traits and values as part of an antibullying policy are mandated by state legislation.

Goleman (1995) notes that bullies often lack empathy, are unable to interpret social cues, and misread neutral expressions as hostile actions against them. Elias (2002) indicates that if bullies are going to change their behavior they must learn to internalize and practice appropriate skills. One program described by Elias that is used to minimize inappropriate behavior is called the "Keep Calm Force." Elementary school students who display appropriate behavior are selected for the Keep Calm Force and help to maintain good behavior on the playground wearing their Keep Calm Force T-shirts. When they observe dissension or fighting the students walk over to the conflict and point to their T-shirts. Among the Keep Calm Force students are former "troublemakers." Also, students who no longer qualify for the Keep Calm Force (possibly because of bullying behavior), are reminded that they are Keep Calm Force alumni—good behavior is part of their history!

Based on the recommendations of Harris et al. (2002), our own experiences, and the suggestions of other educators, the following recommendations are suggested to reduce bullying behavior in schools:

- If possible, organize large schools into smaller "units, families, or houses" to reduce the feeling of alienation some students may experience in a large school.

- Initiate programs that connect an adult with every student in the school, and that connect students with peers. Mentoring programs and peer intervention programs should both be instituted, so that every student has someone to talk with and receive effective intervention strategies from, when difficulties occur.

- Use community resources to help students prone to bullying, especially those students from families unable to provide positive support.

- Survey students concerning their perceptions about bullying and share results with staff, parents, and community members.

- Ensure that students who are victims of violence recognize that the administration, counselors, classroom teachers, and community resources are there to support them.

- Use student leadership organizations or other appropriate avenues to get the message out that a dialogue concerning antibullying prevention and intervention strategies is a major school priority.

- Recognize that bullying behavior is everyone's responsibility and that overt acts of bullying (e.g., violence) are not the only concern; verbal harassment and intimidation must also be addressed.

- Supervise areas where bullying behavior may occur carefully. These areas include hallways, lockers, cafeterias, restrooms, playgrounds, buses, areas immediately surrounding the school, and even classrooms.

- Initiate staff development programs that emphasize character and values, and work with the faculty to model and support a positive school climate and a culture that promotes antibullying behaviors.

- Keep students informed concerning the school's antibullying policy and consequences relating to suspension and expulsion for students who defy the policy.

- Initiate programs to assist students who bully others by providing social, emotional, personal, and academic skill support to cope appropriately in a school environment.

Student and Teacher Resiliency

As the tragic events of September 11, 2001 were evolving, we learned a great deal about heroes. "On September 11th, more than 8,000 children—from day care to high school seniors, from fully mobile to multiple-handicapped—were safely evacuated from the vicinity of Ground Zero in lower Manhattan. Not a single child was harmed or lost in all of the chaos. The principals, teachers, staff, and parents were heroes in every sense of the word" (Lehmuller and Switzer, 2002, p. 54). Paul Houston (2002), executive director of the American Association of School Administrators, reflected, "Perhaps the most powerful lesson for me was to find that all I had learned about heroes was wrong. Most of us were raised to think of heroes as those extraordinary people in history books who do extraordinary things. What we learned on September 11th was that we are genetically programmed to act heroically. Heroes are ordinary people who do extraordinary things and they are all around us. It is in each of us to act heroically when called upon. What a wonderful lesson for our children" (p. 46).

School principals all around the country were "tested" concerning their leadership skills on September 11 and following days. On September 11 teachers, students, and parents wondered if their schools would be closed or if lockdown procedures would be implemented. Following September 11, teachers looked to principals to determine whether they should "stick to their routine" or teach about death, grief and anxiety, tolerance, current events, the tenets of American democracy, or the geography of Afghanistan.

A consistent theme in all of the nation's schools was a desire to express appreciation to New York and Washington firefighters, police officers, and emergency service workers, and to the heroic civilian and military men and women who were attacked at the World Trade Center and the Pentagon. Students created banners, drew pictures, collected money and wrote thousands of letters to express their feelings. Like thousands of other classrooms across the nation, Shannon Collinge's class of second graders in Spokane, Washington, received the following thank you from the Uniformed Firefighters Association of New York:

Thank you for the drawings and letters from the children in your class. Please convey to them our gratitude for the concern and compassion they have shown us in this difficult time.

We have received an outpouring of kindness from the children of America in such letters as those you sent and we have taken the letters and drawings to fire stations all over the city so that they can be displayed where firefighters can see them. We also placed as many pictures as would fit in the front window of our building so that other New Yorkers could see them as they pass by.

Again, please let the children know how much their kindness means to us.

Sincerely,
Uniformed Firefighters Association
Widows and Children's Fund

Richard L. Curwin (2002), in an inspiring article, *Finding Jewels in the Rubble*, noted that "Character is not determined by what happens to us, but rather by how we deal with what happens to us" (p. 80). Curwin gathered information from schools all across the nation to find out how they were coping with, and responding to, the events of September 11 as part of their school programs. Altruism, building community, accepting others, and finding a common ground were some of the themes emphasized by schools. Positive action was taken, such as, visiting nursing homes, collecting food for the homeless, considering the negative effects of cliques and bullying, and refining the art of compromise. As noted earlier, we have redefined heroes and heroism as a result of September 11th. Curwin suggests,

Schools can take the opportunity to explore the notion of heroism, pointing to new role models for students to emulate as alternatives to sports figures and movie stars. More important, students can begin to explore their own heroic qualities and choices and discover how they can be heroes in their own school communities by, for example,

- Stopping fights
- Reporting dangerous behavior
- Standing up to bullies and defending their victims
- Watching the school neighborhood for suspicious outsiders

Even low-achieving students and those with behavior problems can find heroic qualities within themselves. They may not be top students or great athletes, but they can defend the defenseless. Gang members can help eliminate drug sales around the school perimeter and patrol for dangerous strangers. Why not reward those who demonstrate these qualities with New York Fire Department hats? Everyone has the potential to be a hero in small, meaningful ways." (Curwin, p. 81)

Collecting Information About Students:
Comparing the Elementary and Secondary School Models

When working with students who have disciplinary, academic, or social problems, it is interesting to consider the differences in collecting information between the elementary and secondary levels. The elementary school model, in most situations, easily lends itself to this process because, in most cases, the regular classroom teacher can supply almost all the pertinent information to a principal, guidance counselor, or other member of a pupil service team. The teacher who spends several hours a day with the child is able to observe the various dimensions of the child's personality, not only with regard to academic strengths and weaknesses but also concerning social and emotional needs. In secondary school, it is often necessary to have a meeting with four to seven teachers to gain an accurate view of a student's performance. Just arranging this forum can be very difficult.

One should not assume, however, that the extended time spent with an elementary school child is always an advantage. If a teacher has difficulty with a particular child or if their personalities clash, it can be an unfortunate situation for everyone concerned—especially the child. That teacher may very well develop and provide a biased view, detrimental to the child. In fact, an argument can be made that the variety of teachers who assess a secondary student can be an advantage, because the number of teachers involved provides a kind of "reliability factor" concerning the child's performance. If several teachers draw similar conclusions about a student's performance, their assessment is probably accurate. When facing a difficult decision concerning a child, many principals have often wished that both the elementary and secondary models were within reach; clearly, both models provide advantages.

Final Thoughts on "Those Kids"

When considering our quest for excellence and equality, it might help to consider the ideas of Howard Gardner (1995) who reminds us to recognize that students may display "intelligence" in different areas. Gardner asks us to consider eight separate areas of possible intelligence, including the verbal/linguistic, mathematical/logical, musical, bodily/kinesthetic, visual/spatial, naturalist, interpersonal, and intrapersonal areas. When we recognize that students' talents may vary and when we show our respect for various talents whether they be linguistic or musical, we are telling students that we admire them for their strengths and are not simply looking to find their weaknesses. The popular disciplinary refrain to "catch the kids being good" should go beyond discipline and into the multidimensional intelligence areas—"catch their strengths" and help students build from areas of strength.

Students remember not only the rules but how they are treated and what others think of them. School leaders cannot afford to miss opportunities to support students and celebrate their strengths. Terry Deal reflects that industries can recycle poor products, but a "lost child is a lost treasure." Caine and Caine (1991) remind us that creating a positive climate in school can directly affect how students think and function. They stress that under threat, the brain actually "downshifts" and does not perform at its maximum capacity. Thus communicating often with students, setting a supportive tone in class, and sending positive nonverbal signals are as critical as the rules. Finally, learning what responsibility is all about is a lifelong challenge. If schools can foster responsibility through positive guidelines and valuable activities, then the possibility of developing the tools for lifelong learning can become a reality.

Reflections

This space provides for you a place to write in ideas that have been generated by this chapter, things you want to try, or adaptations of ideas presented herein.

1. What do you remember about your school principals?
2. What humorous anecdotes can you recall about students in your school that tell a larger story?
3. What are some guidelines that should be included in a student disciplinary code?
4. What are some of the effective strategies used in your school to assist students with disabilities? Which strategies need to be improved?
5. Review the recommendations in this chapter described to reduce bullying behavior. What else would you suggest to solve this problem?
6. What insights or new questions do you have as a result of reflecting on the ideas presented in this chapter?

PART VII

PROFESSIONAL AND PERSONAL ISSUES

20

The Newcomer
to the Principalship

There were some days, you know, I can't describe this feeling. It's like when you're a kid and you're about to go up [to bat], and there are three guys on base, and it was the bottom of the ninth, and there were two out, and you were up, and there were two strikes on you. Your stomach has this feeling like, boy, I got to do it! There were some days I had that feeling all day long in my stomach. And that is a bad feeling.

COMMENT FROM A FIRST-YEAR PRINCIPAL

First-time principals face dual problems: the difficulties encountered by newcomers to any organization and the daily challenges facing all principals. However, because of the importance of the principalship, schools obviously cannot afford to suspend operations while new principals are learning the ropes. Thus it is crucial to identify the problems that are especially challenging for new principals and offer practical suggestions to assist new and prospective principals. Many of the ideas discussed herein will be useful to experienced principals who move to different schools as well as for superintendents and veteran principals serving as mentors for new principals.

Problems That Challenge New Principals

The literature on the principalship indicates there are several areas of difficulty that seem to frequently surface with new principals (Alvy, 1983). In the following paragraphs, these difficulties are described, not to scare off prospective principals or newcomers but to reduce their anxiety about what they might face. For newcomers, the information may be especially welcome and stress reducing as they will notice they are not alone regarding the problems they are experiencing. This chapter will then move forward with suggestions to acquaint prospective as well as new principals and offer some practical suggestions to get started on the job.

The limitations of preservice training. When moving into the principal's role, new-comers usually find that the preservice training could not possibly duplicate all of the challenges that one immediately faces on the job. For example, there are many unique situations in each school, regarding staff relations, student needs, and the physical plant, so that on-the-job trial and error is simply a necessity. For some, it has been helpful to experience the realistic and practical training provided through a vice principalship, administrative internship, or administrative assistantship. Preservice courses generally do not address how to use the latest administrative software, or design a temporary schedule to implement the statewide testing of all middle school students, or operate a fire drill system. Yet these frequently are the responsibilities of a principal. Universities and principals' centers are working to improve their ability to provide more realistic experiences (e.g., case study analy-sis, simulations) so prospective principals are more familiar with some of the chal-lenges they will face. Increasingly, school districts and universities are pursuing mentoring programs to link up prospective or new principals with seasoned veter-ans or retired principals to help newcomers face the job challenges. An effective mentoring program benefits the protege and mentor. The protege gains an ally and sounding board while the mentor may find the relationship renewing, enabling the veteran principal to gain new meaning from his or her leadership career.

It's lonely at the top. New principals are not only on unfamiliar ground but will find that by virtue of their positions at the top of the management hierarchy in their schools, they do not have professional peers with similar responsibilities in their immediate environments. Quite simply, there may be no one else around who can relate to the problems being faced. Elementary principals may find themselves even lonelier because many elementary schools have only one administrator in the building. Role models and on-site assistance may be desired but not possible. "I felt like I was alone. I couldn't go across roles and confide with somebody" (A Princi-pal's Voice). The absence of readily available role models and adequate sources of assistance may present particular problems to women new to the principalship. Be-cause of gender role stereotyping in our society, there are fewer women in adminis-trative posts, and the male-dominated old boys' network is still difficult to break.

> As the only woman principal in this district last year, when I would go to a principals' meeting, all the dirty jokes would end when I walked into a room. And you know that's sex stereotyping. And . . . I would kind of laugh about it, and knew I was accepted at Christmas time when one of the administration members told me a dirty joke, knew that I was "part of the clan." (A Principal's Voice)

Ironically, although the principal may be lonely with regard to having a profes-sional peer on the same organizational level, a principal is anything but alone dur-ing the school day. The principal is constantly interacting with teachers, students, secretaries, parents, salespeople, student teachers, and any strangers who happen to walk into the school. Thus, for someone who enjoys human interaction, the principalship can be very rewarding and an opportunity to meet interesting people from various walks of life. Yet opportunities to sit down at the lunch table with other principals may occur only at districtwide meetings or at annual state or national association meetings.

Time management—finding time to visit classes. It is an understatement to say new principals quickly learn that there are frequent and various demands on their time. For many newcomers, time management becomes their most significant problem. Unfortunately, the first casualty of a new principalship may be the instructional responsibility of taking the time to visit classes (Alvy, 1983). If one's early actions are a predictor of future actions, it may be difficult for newcomers to reverse patterns that develop early in their principalship. Managing one's time, then, becomes a challenge to be addressed from the first day on the job.

New principals may also feel resentment about the amount of time required of them. Why do I have to return to school in the evening? Should I take the phone off the hook during dinner? What happened to my summer holiday? "I've been surprised at the amount of time, and weekends, that this particular superintendent has asked me to give. . . . It surprises me and that's the one thing about the job that bothers me" (A Principal's Voice).

Staff relations and introducing change. There is always some nervousness when a principal is new to a school—especially when a first-timer takes over responsibilities. The nervousness, of course, is mutual. Newcomers usually find that staff resistance to change is one of the major obstacles they face. The resistance may be even more pronounced with the more experienced teacher veterans who may comment, "We tried this two principals ago." Implementing change may be especially hard for the principal who is hired in-house. Relationships with long-time friends may have to change. In this context, the teacher evaluation process can be a particularly difficult hurdle to overcome.

Satisfying the various constituencies. Teachers, students, superintendents, unions, school boards, parent associations, specific parent interest groups, businesses, and other community groups often have conflicting interests. Just trying to find out what these individuals and groups desire is a considerable task for the new principal. Principals may be tempted to state simply, "My responsibility is to follow the directives of the superintendent who is acting on the authority of the board in the best interest of the students." But reality tells us that interest groups will not be satisfied with this bureaucratic response. Various constituencies will disagree on the purpose of schooling. Group conflict and the consequences are a given. The principal must manage the fallout of conflict.

Unrealistic expectations—making immediate instructional changes. When hired for the principalship, one usually can take pride in knowing that he or she was selected for the job over some pretty stiff competition. Also, with all of the literature on the principal as instructional leader, often the newcomer hopes to make a quick and significant curriculum change or implement an instructional innovation. However, these ideas usually will need time to be nurtured as staff members adjust to the newcomer and the newcomer learns about the culture of the school. Thus implementing immediate curricular or instructional changes will probably have to wait until the principal has the opportunity to assess the context and build trust with staff members. For a change to be institutionalized, one should know the organization well—the mission, teachers, parents, students, and resources—so the change can become a part of the way "business is conducted" at the school. This is, however, usually a disappointment for the first-timer who is ready to jump in and immediately have an impact on the organization (Jentz, Cheever, & Fisher, 1980). One veteran principal advises newcomers to be patient with the staff: "Trust took almost five years to build. But we created a world together."

Meeting individual student needs. Principals and teachers want to address the needs of each student. However, it is the teacher in the classroom who experiences the day-to-day challenges of moving the whole class forward while addressing the needs of each child. For most teachers, decisions for the whole group usually outweigh a strategy for one child, if the strategy slows down the group. Effective principals remind teachers of the importance of meeting individual needs and work with teachers to provide instructional resources, additional help, or information on innovative practices. Disaggregating testing data is a helpful strategy that principals should initiate to provide teachers with information for targeting specific concerns. Many new principals see the school as a whole—instead of individual children who are not making it. But, the principal is responsible for all children. Obviously, for these new principals, this is a considerable frustration. Immediate solutions are often difficult to find for struggling students.

It's difficult to become an instant sage. A new principal in his mid-30s had a veteran teacher, close to retirement, enter the office one afternoon after school to ask the principal for advice about what to do on retirement. The newcomer was struck by this image of the older, white-haired teacher coming to this newcomer for advice. If anything, it was the new principal who should be going to the veteran teacher for advice. However, as the weeks progressed, many others asked critical questions that required the principal to respond. The newcomer realized that many people just expect the principal to know. If they only knew the truth!

A Profile of the New Principal

The following characterization may serve as a helpful summary of the above remarks about difficulties facing newcomers to the principalship.

After a few days as a principal, the newcomer realizes the preservice training program has not sufficiently prepared him or her for the job. The new principal is having trouble with experienced staff who are resisting "necessary changes" and former teaching colleagues who refuse to take the beginner seriously. The principal is not sure how to respond to teachers regarding students who are experiencing academic difficulties. The newcomer is surprised at the variety of responsibilities but is eager to accept all challenges.

As the year progresses, the new principal is somewhat disheartened because numerous details and ambivalence concerning evaluation stand in the way of spending more time as an instructional leader in classrooms observing student work and assisting teachers. Yet the beginner is still unsure—and a little fearful—about delegating responsibilities to free himself or herself to provide more time for instructional leadership. The new principal also is learning the values of significant others in the school, district, and community, and is accepting selected values. Finally, the beginner encounters difficulty receiving satisfactory assistance to cope with job realities.

Helping Prospective and
New Principals Make the Grade

Identifying the problems of new principals is, of course, a first step in helping newcomers make the grade. We know what their particular concerns are. From there, we need to consider how we can help individuals acquire the socialization skills necessary for the principalship and then offer practical suggestions on how to succeed during those critical first years.

Socialization for the Principalship

A major aspect of socializing for a job is developing the kind of positive mindset that will best enable one to function effectively in the new position. As you reflect on the ideas below, try to step out of the arena for a moment and consider how these suggestions may affect your decisions and performance.

The leader as learner—a habit of mind. The leader-as-learner concept (Bennis & Nanus, 1985) is a blessing to new principals. Why? Because the concept implies that the leader who is willing to learn has an excellent chance to succeed. Thus, when you are asking questions and soliciting ideas about how the school works, you are not revealing a weakness or ignorance but a strength, the desire to learn. You are letting others know, right from the start, that they are important, and without their information, you could not do the job. This is a refreshing attitude to see in a leader; most professional colleagues will appreciate the newcomer who wants to know how things really work. The key, though, is to keep this characteristic throughout your career.

Reflecting on your professional background. Sarason (1982) reminds us that as teachers, we often remember the supervision and evaluation process with some disdain. Do we carry this hostility for the process with us when we become principals? When becoming a principal, individuals need to examine their professional (and personal) experiences with supervision and evaluation to reflect on which of those experiences may enhance or inhibit possibilities for success. With regard to teaching experiences, prospective principals need to consider their feelings about classroom isolation; how they felt when supervisors entered their classrooms; relationships with teachers and supervisors, students and parents; and the professional climate in their schools. For example, what kind of supervisory role models has one worked with? In addition to teaching experiences, new principals need to evaluate the type of university training received and how previous administrative positions may affect their performance. For instance, if one has served for several years as an athletic director, will he or she be able to make budgetary decisions fairly when the athletic budget may need slicing to provide more funds for a new program for a major group of non-English speakers entering the school district?

Developing a broad view. When teaching in a classroom or taking responsibility for a particular program, one does not have to consider the broad scope of responsibilities and multiple consequences of decisions that a principal experiences. To illustrate, imagine a cone-shaped funnel. The teacher can look toward the narrowing end of the funnel while the principal must look at the funnel becoming broader with increased responsibilities.

> There is a tendency, and I went through it myself, for teachers to feel that administrators forget that they were teachers once too. I don't think that's the case. I think that once you start operating from a different frame in the system, your outlook changes from single program to total program, and that causes some real problems. (A Principal's Voice)

Thus, for the principal, it is critical to look at the big picture. What is the mission of the school? What are the important goals of the school? Are we meeting the needs of all students with disabilities? Is our school providing a caring environment for students, teachers, parents, and the community? It will certainly take the newcomer time to figure out how to decide collaboratively with the staff where the school should go and intends to go. When one sees the big picture, then it becomes easier to figure out which battles are worth fighting. For example, is it really important that a particular bulletin board was not changed on the due date? Shouldn't the real question be, How is that teacher doing in the classroom? The following statement from a new principal is insightful: "Step back, look at the whole program, and then step in again."

Exercising patience and flexibility—yet holding on to your convictions. In relationships, leaders of an organization often have to deal with impatient individuals who want to see things change, yesterday. For example, the principal must remain calm and patient when that irate parent shows up or a teacher is upset because there are not enough textbooks or the school air conditioning system has broken down. Listening patiently is very important. However, when incorrect information is presented, it is equally important to give your point of view politely. For example, an angry parent says, "That teacher just doesn't care for my child." The principal's response: "I'm sorry you feel that way, Mr. Smith, but if the teacher did not care about your child, or any other child in this school, he would not be working here. We just don't operate that way."

Additionally, remaining flexible and actively listening is critical during discussions if one is going to remain open to various points of view. Yet, when all is said and done, it is very important to state your convictions. People need to know where the principal stands on issues.

> But, the one thing about change is that you're supposed to do it over a long period of time, and I've got to learn that. You are supposed to go in and be very low key the first year, and then the second year you're supposed to do that, and then the third year you're supposed to hit. Well, that's just not my personality. And people have to learn that that's not going to happen. If I know something has to be done to change academic achievement of kids, or their mental health, I'm not willing to wait one, two, or three years. I simply will not settle for that. (A Principal's Voice)

Coping with the loneliness and time factors. As stated previously, two problems that many newcomers face are loneliness and time difficulties associated with the position (i.e., both fragmented time and long hours). Interestingly, these two factors are connected in that there are extensive periods after school, in the evenings, or on the weekends when principals are alone at the office or working on the job at home. This, of course, is quite normal for many in professional work. However, because the principal's job can be so fragmented during the day, it may be that it is only during these "lonely" times when true reflection concerning the job can take place. And it is during these times that one must recall the important work that is taking place each day and consider ways to improve one's performance. Thus the prospective or new principal needs to recognize that loneliness and time constraints may be problems, but the problems also may present opportunities to improve one's effectiveness.

Practical Suggestions for Newcomers

"The buck stops here . . . for everything." Harry Truman was right. Thus it is important from day one on the job that the new principal accepts responsibility for

whatever takes place in the school. Regarding the school operation, it is especially important to take responsibility for the items that may appear to be petty but are very significant for the teachers in the beginning of the year. For example, make sure that there are enough desks in each room, drinking fountains are working properly, toilets are flushing properly, and the lights are working in each class-room—Has that broken lock been fixed on the teacher's desk? These may seem like petty items when discussing instructional leadership, but it is very difficult to educate children if classroom lighting is inadequate.

Although whatever takes place in the school may, in the end, land on the principal's doorstep, it is important that one does not misinterpret "the buck stops here" to mean you cannot delegate and trust others with responsibility. If anything, it means surrounding yourself with the best possible teachers and support staff so all of the activities in a school that you cannot become involved in have the best people operating in those areas.

Seek out people—especially the experienced staff and secretary. If the three rules of real estate investing are location, location, location, then the three rules of the principalship are communicate, communicate, communicate. In the principalship, you are investing in people. It is critical for the new principal to seek out the experienced staff (especially the school secretary) to get their opinions about what works and what does not work in the school. They know the history of the school. By seeking these people out and carefully listening to what they have to say, there is an excellent chance that they will give you honest views of how things really are.

You might try to seek out veterans and some newer teachers to get a variety of views before the school year begins. One principal spent time before school with a long-time veteran and asked, "What, in your opinion, separates this school from others?" The veteran stated, "Our teachers are always accessible to students." The new principal used that information as a positive theme with students, teachers, and parents whenever he wanted to describe the school culture. Send a letter to all staff members during the summer, letting them know that you look forward to meeting with them. At the first faculty meeting, let the staff members know that you are eager to learn and you would appreciate having them visit with you. These early meetings will also be your first opportunities to build up the trust to work productively in the future.

As the year progresses, continue to take the initiative regarding relationships with faculty, students, and parents. As you develop relationships, try as much as possible to meet "on their turf." The principal's office is daunting for many, and until others see you as approachable, it may not be the best place to meet. Teachers appreciate the principal who says, "Let's meet in your room."

Be visible. Visibility, from day one, is crucial. Your secretary needs to know that you believe the most important events in the school take place outside of your office. Research indicates that finding time to visit classrooms is especially difficult for new principals. By visiting the classrooms, library, cafeteria, labs, gymnasium, art studios, and music rooms, you are sending a strong message to the staff and students that what they are doing is important to you and the school.

Keep in mind that your visibility may very well be a new approach for staff members; make sure you let them know during the preschool faculty meetings that you believe that what takes place "out there" are the important events of the school, so you intend to be visible. Some of the staff may be skeptical about your motives at first, but most will soon appreciate your effort. As a consequence, visits later in the year to classes for teacher observations and interactions with students will, for most, be less stressful because everyone will know who the principal is.

Control your time. We have provided many suggestions in this book regarding time management strategies. However, a few points should be emphasized for newcomers. Although it is very difficult, try to take control of a significant part of your schedule. Block out time on your schedule for events that signify your commitment to the educational goals of the school. If the effort is not made, others will quickly fill up all of your time. During the year, constantly think about the school priorities and see if your schedule reflects those priorities. There will certainly be days and even weeks when you will not be able to meet your objectives, but keep on coming back to them. The teachers and your secretary should know your basic philosophy about time use. This will help ensure that teachers will usually be able to see you at times that are convenient for them. The secretary needs to know that teachers should never feel shut out when they want to see the principal. If the principal is unavailable at a particular time, then the secretary should set up an appointment for the next available time. In a less formal way, when teachers know that you are going to make the rounds during the day, they will often hold a miniconference with you.

Additionally, it is crucial to learn to say no to people and projects and to take a backseat on some committees and community requests for your time. For example, if the Cub Scouts ask you to speak at their annual awards ceremony, you should probably say yes, but that does not mean you should also say yes to the request that you join them on the overnight campout in April.

Make sure that you leave time for your own lunch and for leisure activities. Your productivity and spirit will suffer, and resentment may surface if the job becomes all-consuming.

> There have been some things that just wear on me personally. Part of that is the time factor that you're expected to spend, and expected by others, and you inflict on yourself. You just have to spend that amount of time. But I don't think it surprises me. It kind of eats away on me because I'm not real comfortable with it. (A Principal's Voice)

Model the desire to grow professionally. In the long run, this may be the area in which you make your most significant contribution in serving students and teachers. Begin modeling a desire to grow professionally as a principal. Share professional articles and recommend journals and Web sites to the staff. Let them know about professional growth opportunities. Share with them your professional growth objectives during your first year. For example, as a new principal, you should try to get involved with a mentor, either in the district, through a local university, or possibly through a state principals' center. Subscribe to professional journals and try to attend state and national association meetings. Share your experiences with the staff. When you have the time, continue to read about the principalship. It can be very therapeutic—and you will find out that you are not alone!

Final Reflections on the Newcomer Experience

Coping with the daily events of a school and all the constituencies that go along with a school can be very overwhelming for a new principal. Yet there is no greater feeling than to be part of a school community and to know that you made a difference in the success of that community. The newcomer to the principalship, during his or her first year, can make a contribution to a school community every bit as significant as the 10-year veteran of the principalship.

Often, new principals are told that they will experience a honeymoon period in which they will be forgiven for their early mistakes. However, it may be foolish to hope for such a present. It is more important for the newcomer to assume that many mistakes will be made, and not only during the first years. But if the principal is a learner, he or she will grow professionally through each mistake. If the teachers, students, and parents perceive that the newcomer is growing, trust will slowly build; they all want to be proud of their principal. Then, as a community of learners, the principal, teachers, and students can grow together.

Reflections

This space provides for you a place write in ideas that have been generated by this chapter, things you want to try, or adaptations of ideas presented herein.

1. What were some of the major difficulties you faced (or are facing) during your first year as a principal?
2. What characteristics would be suitable for a principal mentor? On what areas of study would you like to focus, given the opportunity to work with a mentor?
3. Do you agree with the characterization of the principalship as a lonely position?

4. To add to the advice offered in this chapter, what suggestions do you have for aspiring or new principals?

5. What insights or new questions do you have as a result of reflecting on the ideas presented in this chapter?

21

Taking Care of Yourself

Educators would do well to ponder Elizabeth Cady Stanton's injunction that self-development is a higher duty than self-sacrifice.

BARTH (1990, p. 47)

Principals must take care of themselves in order to care for others. Setting an example as a leader does not end with the leadership, instructional, and management roles of a principal. Does the staff get a chance to see you relaxed during the day, enjoying the job, and slowing down the pace when necessary? What about how your private life may influence your job performance? In all walks of life, if you come to work unhappy or stressed out, it takes a tremendous amount of energy and psychological manipulation to reverse your disposition in order to function effectively for others and yourself. Moreover, if you want your staff to take time off and enjoy vacations and professional growth opportunities, then you owe it to yourself to enjoy vacations and growth opportunities. If the school leader is not refreshed when the year begins, then the school year is off to an ominous start.

The Selfish Nature of Martyrdom

School leaders, because of pressure and long hours, can easily begin to see themselves as martyrs and burn out in their quest for martyrdom. Much has been written about the effect of burnout on principals and about good people leaving the profession because of too much stress. We have to learn to take care of ourselves. It seems that everyone wants a piece of the principal's time. But if the slices are too small, no one can derive the benefits.

One principal shared the following personal experience:

I was very proud of myself because I did not take time for lunch during my first 6 years in the principalship. How foolish! I thought I was setting an example for the staff of how to effectively use time by meeting with teachers during my lunch hour. Often, I would eat my sandwich during a meeting demonstrating how hard I was working. My favorite line was "Do you mind if I eat during our meeting?" Undoubtedly, I enjoyed the martyrdom. Two years ago, I started taking 30-40 minutes a day for lunch to have real time away from my office. And do you know, the school did not burn down! In fact, I doubt if anyone noticed that I was out. I think the staff probably felt more at ease with my decision. Moreover, skipping lunch was not a healthy example for the teachers. Following lunch I was relaxed and refreshed. I was ready to work in the afternoon. (A Principal's Voice)

What Is Burnout?

"If in the beginning your job seems perfect, the solution to all your problems, you have high hopes and expectations, and would rather work than do anything else, be wary. You're a candidate for the most insidious and tragic kind of job stress—burnout, a state of physical, emotional, and mental exhaustion caused by unrealistically high aspirations and illusory and impossible goals" (Miller & Smith 1997).

Taking Control of
Your Schedule to Care for Yourself

Unless we proactively organize our schedule with a lunch hour, leisure time, exercise, and other activities that refresh us, it will not happen. Thus, as you plan your schedule, build in leisure time. Place it on your schedule just as you place a school meeting on the calendar. The idea, obviously, is not to place these activities during the school day at prime times but, rather, to allocate time for daily personal activities at the beginning or end of the day to recharge your batteries. For example, if you need to leave at 5:00 p.m., it should be noted on your appointment calendar so you do not miss that jog, basketball game, or tennis match.

Interestingly, the professional development time that you might take to read a journal to "stay on top of the field" is the first thing to go when unimportant but pressing items arise in the schedule. Yet, if we are to grow and our staff are to grow, we need to recognize that reading a professional journal in our office is as important as any other aspect of the job. Professional reading time should be identified on the calendar and used accordingly. This can also be a time to inform our practice. One principal routinely writes down on index cards quotations from articles she reads. She uses these to open faculty meetings with an approach called "Quote of the Day." Individuals read a quotation they are handed and can swap quotations with others! Also, we need to allocate time to reflect, write, and read about the principalship and follow other professional interests—and there should be other interests. These interests need to become part of our professional and personal schedules. Taking time out for yourself gives you an opportunity to think about your own experiences and your interaction with the staff. You can gain a greater understanding of the faculty by taking the time to reflect on why a teacher acted in a particular way or made a comment that seemed inappropriate. This can help a principal to respond appropriately when addressing the needs of colleagues. Reflection often affords a principal a valuable new perspective.

A Personal Mission Statement

An interesting and productive activity would be to develop a personal mission statement based on your professional and personal goals to transcend the day-to-day responsibilities and keep your long-term vision in mind (Covey, 1989). As you develop the mission statement, consider the following questions:

- When you retire from education, how do you want to be remembered?
- What do you want teachers, parents, and most of all, students to say about you?
- What will be your legacy as a principal?
- What kind of a friend are you?
- How productive are you outside of your professional work?
- What should be written on your tombstone?

Such questions cause one to connect daily activities with a meaningful, long-range vision. After your mission statement is developed, post it in a place where you can glance at it during the week.

Gaining Perspective by
Spending Time With Students

When a principal feels stressed, the "batteries can be recharged" by taking time to visit with a class or spending a few minutes with students on the playground, in the halls, or in a courtyard. Students appreciate spending time with the principal, and this helps to spread the message that the principal is more than the office figure or school disciplinarian. Having students see you as a "real person" helps in the process of building relationships with all students. Principals should consider taking occasional field trips with classes. The trip gives the principal an opportunity to spend quality time with students, teachers, and parents. One principal rides the bus with students once a month. Another greets students at the bus when they arrive every morning. Still another participates regularly in book club discussions with different classes. These acts not only build relationships but also inform the principal about the pulse of the school.

Body and Mind, Healthy and Ill Together[1]

If you do not feel well, it is hard to help others while on the job. From a practical viewpoint, the better you feel, the better you will perform. Your personal level of health and well-being must be maintained if you are to perform effectively on or off the job. This concept of well-being is dependent on attention to four areas: physical, physiological, emotional, and psychological. Although these are four separate experiences, their functions are interrelated. For example, when you are stressed, often you do not sleep well or eat properly. You may indulge in too many sweets, which can adversely affect your blood sugar level and put your system out of balance. A quick examination of these four interrelated categories can help you to see the importance of paying attention to your personal well-being.

Physical Awareness

We all like to have greater energy. A primary way to gain greater energy is to make sure that, through exercise, we have the strength to make it through each day. It is interesting that we all recognize, from a commonsense view, how increased energy and endurance can sustain us with a greater degree of alertness through the day. Yet we still fail to take the necessary steps, before or after work, to fine-tune our bodies to perform at a higher physical level while on the job.

The physical aspect of well-being can be maintained through systematic exercise to improve our cardiovascular fitness. Also, systematic exercise releases endorphins in our body that can have a soothing, pleasurable effect on our mind and relieve stress. And, of course, from a physical standpoint, exercise, energy, and longevity are inextricably linked for most people.

Unfortunately, when time gets tight on the job, exercise is often the first thing to go. Planning your own prescheduled exercise program or joining an exercise group or club that meets at a specific time may be a good start. Needless to say, the exercise program should go on to your schedule, and you should not be shy about saying that you need to leave work at a certain time to make your appointment. Because of the facilities often available in schools, you may be able to get your exercise on-site if you do not feel that you need a different environment to relax. Another possible solution is to try and commit to an exercise program or sports activity with a friend. This serves two purposes. First, the friend will expect you to show up! Second, having a friend to talk with can help to get your mind off of work, if necessary, and reduce stress.

Physiological Awareness

The old adage "You are what you eat" holds some truth. Although nutritionists and physicians may disagree on some specifics as to what is good to eat and what is not, there are certain principles that apply to most people. For example, moderation of consumption is better than excess. Overindulgence in food or inappropriate foods can lead to adverse consequences for your body and mind. Excessive food intake at meals can lead to marked swings in blood sugar levels. This physiological occurrence can lead to unwanted alterations of brain function, adversely affect attention and creativity, and contribute to lethargy. Unfortunately, overindulgence or erratic eating habits are most common when we are under stress.

Even when one strives to maintain a balanced diet, often the rapid pace of the day makes a principal skip meals or choose inappropriate foods. Principals should prepare for this eventuality by planning and having some healthy food that is quickly accessible and provides for both energy and brain power. Also, complex carbohydrates such as fruits and vegetables are a good source of healthy food. Low-fat foods are helpful. For example, there are many low-fat breakfast foods and snacks on the market (e.g., bagels, granola bars, low-fat crackers). Keep these items readily available in your desk or refrigerator. Too often, it is a temptation to have a candy bar and indulge in the wrong snack when under stress or when a busy schedule may lead to omitting a meal.

Emotional Awareness

As discussed in Chapter 4, the leader's emotions influence emotions of constituents. In fact, it has been said that the heart gives out an electromagnetic field that is sensible within three feet! Keep in mind that emotionally intelligent leaders exceed their goals by at least 20% (Goleman, 1995).

Psychological Awareness

Psychological rest or peace of mind takes place when your behaviors match your values and beliefs. There is more to life than the job. If you have peace of mind, that feeling can positively affect the level of energy that you give to your job or personal life. Unfortunately, principals may often experience psychological discomfort by doing things that they do not enjoy (e.g., completing reams of paperwork, responding very politely or patiently when one would like to take a more aggressive stance). You need to anticipate that this will happen and have a plan for this. In a proactive way, anticipate that stress will enter your life and plan how you will cope. Different people will handle stress in different ways. Some take comfort by spending time with family or friends; others go for a walk, exercise, read a book, travel, or pursue a hobby such as art or music. Having an outlet is very important because it gives us an alternative to reduce stress and brings a richness to our lives, enabling us to be more well rounded and aware of other ways of doing things.

Finally, it cannot be emphasized too often that it is very difficult to make an effective contribution to an organization if one is functioning below par because of physical, physiological, emotional, or psychological reasons. Principals owe it to themselves, their families, their colleagues, and their profession to do what they can to maintain a high level of physical, psysiological, emotional, and psychological well-being.

Maintaining Institutional and Individual Balance

Principals also need to be careful about letting the institutional and bureaucratic values smother them; one's individuality can be lost with the pressures to conform. It is hard to feel good about yourself if you know that your individual convictions are always being sacrificed to preserve the status quo. But it is very difficult to overcome the socialized pressures within the system. Interestingly, principals to a great extent have been socialized as "school folks" sometimes their whole life—responding to bells, following a certain calendar, and always relating to students, teachers, and administrators.

The classical business and sociological theorists Barnard (1938, pp. 8-21) and Merton (1957, pp. 195-201) agreed that over time, bureaucracies depersonalize or stifle individuals to satisfy bureaucratic needs. Merton, for example, maintained that bureaucratic controls such as career promotions and salary increments force individuals to adapt their behavior to official regulations. Furthermore, individuals can become so engrossed in bureaucratic roles that they may disregard their responsibility to assist clientele to preserve the common interests of bureaucratic colleagues. For schools, this can mean neglecting the needs of children or blocking necessary change to satisfy the professional or support staff.

These valuable insights clearly indicate that a strong possibility exists for principals to become the organization. Principals become increasingly socialized as the years of service increase. Moreover, one is less likely to promote change in the organization if maintaining the bureaucratic status quo becomes one's mission and personality. Reflective activities can help principals maintain their individuality and keep the organizational or institutional bureaucracy in perspective. Activities such as reading, writing, and exercising while away from the job can help to reduce the bureaucratic ties to the organization and help the practitioner hold on to his or her individuality.

"Taking Care of Yourself"

Marcy Holland, a graduate student at Eastern Washington University focusing her research on teacher burnout, found the following useful advice from the Web site of the Georgia Association of Educators (www.gae.org/teacher/te_burnout.html):

"Understand that the only people without stress are in the cemetery! It is not so much the stress in our lives that hurts us but how we respond to it." The Georgia Association of Educators offered many techniques to avoid burnout, among them:

- Exercise
- Don't schedule all of your leisure time
- Get plenty of sleep
- Pursue a project or hobby
- Find a friend
- Don't procrastinate
- Don't feel that you must do everything
- Keep a "things to do" list
- Recognize and accept your limitations
- Learn to tolerate and forgive
- Learn to plan
- Be a positive person
- Learn to play

Consider how you will integrate these techniques into your calendar. Both you and the organization will benefit!

Note

1. We would like to thank Dr. David Jay Caro, from San Mateo General Hospital, for his assistance with this section of the chapter.

Reflections

This space provides for you a place to write in ideas that have been generated by this chapter, things you want to try, or adaptations of ideas presented herein.

1. Have you learned how to say no in order to provide yourself with quality time away from the job? Think of three school situations and practice how you would say no in each situation.
2. How do you feel about reading a professional journal while in your office? How do you think the staff would react to seeing you read a journal during the day?
3. How much have you become "the organization"?
4. What are you doing or might you do to take care of yourself?
5. What insights or new questions do you have as a result of reflecting on the ideas presented in this chapter?

22

Keeping the
Professional Candle Lit

Through learning we re-create ourselves.

SENGE (1990, p. 14)

How does a practitioner remain on the cutting edge of their profession? Before accepting the principalship, he or she is often taking courses and learning as much as possible about the job. Unfortunately, once in the position, the practitioner is so busy that it is difficult to keep the professional candle lit. Again, taking a proactive approach is the only way to stay on top of the field regarding leadership and educational literature. No one else is going to take care of ensuring your professional growth. It's easy for those professional journals to stack up. And, it's difficult to commit time away from the school site for professional growth experiences. This chapter will provide suggestions for taking a proactive approach to keeping the professional candle lit.

Institutionalizing
Professional Growth Activities

The key to remaining proactive is to institutionalize specific activities through memberships, conferences, writing, relationships, and the creative use of time. As has been emphasized throughout this book, the personal example set by the principal can be a strong motivator for the staff. Teachers will notice if you are current in your field and if you can be counted on to keep them current. Moreover, by staying abreast of the field through professional activities and professional relationships, routines are broken, which helps to keep the practitioner stimulated, thus reducing the possibility of burnout.

There are many activities that can be institutionalized and will require your professional dedication and attention. It is just a matter of choosing what is best for you. Probably the most important action the practitioner can take is to become actively involved in one or two professional organizations. Active involvement means attending the state and, if possible, national conferences of the organization and reading the journals sponsored by the organizations. The logical organizations for principals are the National Association of Secondary School Principals and the National Association of Elementary School Principals (both organizations address the needs of middle school principals). The Association for Supervision and Curriculum Development (ASCD) and the National Staff Development Council are also key national organizations for principals. All four organizations and state affiliates hold annual conferences that are sure to keep practitioners on the cutting edge in the field. Each one publishes excellent journals and newsletters.

The national associations also sponsor leadership academies in the form of 1- or 2-day workshops throughout the school year and longer workshops during the summer. Many states have principals' centers, often affiliated with universities. The opportunity to network with colleagues through the associations, workshops, principals' centers, and universities should not be missed. In fact, the loneliness of the principalship as a day-to-day feature of the job almost makes the networking through the various organizations imperative.

The opportunity to meet with other principals is especially important for the newcomer who needs affirmation that he or she is on the right track. Moreover, developing a mentor relationship through the organization can be an asset for newcomers and veteran principals. Becoming a member of specific associations will assure that time will be set aside to meet with colleagues and keep up on issues in the field.

The principal should institutionalize subscriptions to several journals for himself or herself and the school. The national principal associations all publish journals for elementary, middle, and high school principals. *Educational Leadership* (ASCD), the *Phi Delta Kappan,* and the *Journal of Staff Development* would be excellent additional choices. *Teacher* and *Instructor* would be good hands-on choices for elementary school principals. *Education Week* is a good source for current events in education, especially as related to national and state political agendas.

To keep the professional candle lit for teachers, each school should be getting journals in the various disciplines. Publications for elementary, middle, and high schools are produced by all the major organizations such as the National Council for Social Studies, the National Council of Teachers of English, and the National Council of Teachers of Mathematics. Each department should keep up to date. In elementary schools, the *Arithmetic Teacher* or the *Reading Teacher,* for example, should be subscribed to and distributed to the staff or kept in a professional library. All organizations such as these maintain active Web sites that carry important information about available resources.

As principals are in key leadership positions, they have much in common with those leading noneducational organizations. Thus it can be very helpful to subscribe to a professional journal outside of the educational field. For example, *Harvard Business Review* has excellent articles on leadership that not only give ideas that principals can use but also let principals know what is taking place "out there."

This can be very helpful information when making curriculum decisions to prepare students for the world of work.

Beyond journals, the practitioner should maintain a professional library with modern classics in the educational field (to revisit) and current books of interest on leadership and educational issues. A good selection would include books on educational philosophy, curriculum, the life of principals and teachers, and leadership books from the business and education world. (It goes without saying that books other than those that are education related are certainly welcome.) Important educators of the last century are always interesting to study; this enables one to compare comtemporary writers with classical ones (e.g., Dewey, Tyler, Hutchins, Cremin).

Listening to books on tape when driving to and from work or jogging can also be professionally productive. These tapes can be ordered from professional conferences, from association catalogs, or purchased from bookstores. Watching professional videos has become a very popular activity with colleagues in school or in the comfort of one's home. Principals can play the key role in ensuring that schools receive professional audio- and videotapes for all school professionals.

Visiting other schools can also be very rewarding. Drucker (1992) refers to this as managing by wandering around—outside. Spending a day in another school with another principal in the district can certainly help one to pick up a couple of tips on how others do the job. In fact, the opportunity to visit a school outside of your district or in another state may be more advantageous because one is likely to see activities and curriculum projects a bit differently from those in the home district. The experience may even lead to a strong professional friendship.

Reflection as a Tool

The importance of reflection has been stressed throughout the book. Keeping a personal journal certainly can help one to reflect about the job and any other aspect of one's life. Often, the experience of seeing one's ideas in writing helps to affirm convictions and brings greater insight to a particular problem. As the journal grows, one can reflect on past experiences—so that is how I handled this problem last time! Reflection is a great asset and can help one to avoid making the same mistake. To illustrate, in July of 1993, golf great Jack Nicklaus played the Senior Open Golf Tournament. As he led the tournament till the 12th hole, he recalled playing on the same course and approaching the 12th hole more than 30 years ago. He reflected back to that earlier tournament. He vowed not to make the same mistake that he had made in 1960. He won the Senior Open by one stroke!

Writing can extend beyond the journal to professional articles authored alone or with colleagues. Writing with another principal, consultant, or university professor may be the best route for the practitioner because it becomes very easy to drop a project when you are working alone and busy with the day-to-day responsibilities of the principalship. It is very helpful to have someone driving you on. (The computer will hold your ideas until you are ready to return to them!) Involvement in action research projects with teachers in your school also can be very rewarding. Presenting the results of the research project as a workshop during a state or national conference can be an important extension of the effort.

Holding a miniconference in a school or on a university campus could be a great way to stimulate a staff. The faculty could get together to recommend speakers to the administration. Administrators and faculty members could present at the conference, possibly during a staff development or inservice day or afternoon. This highlights the importance of keeping learning as a valued centerpiece of the school.

A Principal's Portfolio

Whether a principal is remaining in a school for several years or preparing to move on, developing and updating a principal's portfolio is a valuable resource to keep a record of and reflect on one's growth during a particular school year and over one's career. The portfolio could open with a personal mission statement, professional goals, and schoolwide goals and objectives. The orientation of the portfolio should be to demonstrate growth within a particular area or areas. At times, principals may elect to identify themes for their portfolios: enhancing student work, building positive parent-community-school relationships, staff development, teacher supervision and evaluation, professional presentations, or reflections. This portfolio can serve as a valuable resource when applying for new positions.

Artifacts may include photographs of the faculty, students, and classroom activities; important staff development ideas; journal entries; speeches; staff evaluations; newspaper articles about the school; successful grant applications; important memos; faculty meeting agendas; letters or notes from students, parents, community members, and faculty; a video of school activities and the activity calendar of the school year; notes for possible journal articles; student work; information on awards given to students or faculty; information on workshops or conferences attended; presentations made to the school community or at professional meetings; organizations that one belongs to; and family photos.

Other Growth Opportunities

A strategy for assuring one is current is to examine the Interstate School Leaders Licensure Consortium Standards (ISLLC). These are highlighted in the preface of this book. One can reflect upon these and assess personal strengths and areas for professional growth.

Involvement in a support group on a topic of interest can also be rewarding. The support group may sponsor topics such as global education, the at-risk student, closing the achievement gap, differentiated instruction, working with special needs students, brain research, or effective instructional practices. The group may meet at lunch or even during dinner at various homes during the year. In one school district, K-12 administrators and department heads get together for dinner and conversation prior to board meetings. They read and discussed *Classroom Instruction That Works* (Marzano et al., 2001) chapter by chapter. This was so rewarding that they elected to read a second book, *Shaking Up the Schoolhouse* (Schlechty, 2001).

Seeking out people with similar and alternative views to join a group can be very stimulating. Many schools are instituting Socratic seminars for teachers and administrators to discuss various issues, usually unrelated to school. These seminars may occur after school and on a variety of topics. The bottom line is that colleagues get together to discuss a short story, poem, work of art, film, or anything else that may stimulate the group.

Working to develop an inviting professional resource area in the school can be a significant professional boost for administrators and teachers. This should be an area to exchange professional articles, books, and ideas. Principals should encourage teachers to pass on professional articles to colleagues and the principal to help him or her stay on top of particular issues and, probably more important, remain informed regarding what teachers think is important. Having an area in the school for professional reading just might make it easier for administrators and teachers to spend time there during a school day—actually building the time into their weekly schedules. The actual physical structure for professional reflection can symbolize the importance of remaining on the cutting edge.

Finally, remaining intellectually stimulated throughout one's career is a tall order. Yet doing so benefits the principal and the organization. For instance, underlining important quotations while reading a journal, and sharing these at faculty meetings, followed with a discussion, can show that the leader is academically up to date and can provide valuable resources to staff members in a time efficient way. We need to create our own opportunities for professional growth through institutionalizing interaction, reflections, and readings. It is through these encounters that we remain alert and ready to approach the next challenge. Focusing on our own professional development builds an incredible resource bank from which to draw. By nurturing our own growth, we are able to enhance our ability to serve, and help others grow.

Reflections

This space provides for you a place to write in ideas that have been generated by this chapter, things you want to try, or adaptations of ideas presented herein.

1. Are you keeping your professional candle lit? Discuss this with a colleague.

2. Which two or three professional development activities discussed in this chapter can you use?

3. What are some additional ways you can keep the professional candle lit?

4. What insights or new questions do you have as a result of reflecting on the ideas presented in this chapter?

23

Reflections on the Principalship

The power of personal example is the essence of true leadership.

STEPHEN COVEY (1989)

A school is much more than a physical structure; it is a community made up of adults and children engaged in a journey that will lead to greater understanding for all. To help students, a principal serves teachers by empowering them to be the best they can be. As servant leaders, school principals find that their professional vocation is, in many ways, a calling. When principals meet that calling and serve teachers, students, and parents effectively, students have a greater opportunity to enhance their skills in a climate that promotes growth, understanding, and a love of learning.

Serving the School Community

As a school leader, a principal's foremost asset may be his or her ability to *lead by example.* How principals conduct themselves on the job—what they pay attention to—says more about ethical practice and their leadership ability than any specific decision, regardless of how important. Nair (1997), commenting on the life of Gandhi, notes that, "Leadership is not a technique, but a way of life." Leading by example must be sincere; if a principal is uncomfortable with small children or teenagers, the nonverbal cues will quickly be picked up by the students. Moreover, if the personal example lacks consistency, others will soon comment about the lack of sincerity on the part of the principal. Thus, when reflecting on the principalship and considering experience and sound theory, the authors believe that the following behaviors and characteristics, if modeled consistently, can go a long way in helping a principal best serve a school.

Principals thrive on the ethical responsibility to help teachers grow. As suggested above, principals serve teachers by empowering them to be the best they can be. James MacGregor Burns (1978), in his classic study on transformational leadership, noted that, "Transforming leadership ultimately becomes *moral* in that it raises the level of human conduct and ethical aspirations of both leader and led, and thus it has a transforming effect on both" (p. 20). Principals who enthusiastically accept the responsibility of helping others grow foster the aspirations of teachers by distributing leadership throughout the system. Promoting teacher growth also includes helping colleagues become autonomous decision makers who engage students successfully when the classroom door is closed. These teachers are confident in their decisions, partially because they are part of a school culture that thrives on collaboration, peer coaching, mentoring of new teachers, and teacher-generated professional development opportunities.

Principals respect and dignify others. The importance of positive human interaction has been a main feature of this book; therefore, it should not surprise the reader that leading by example must include *respecting and dignifying each individual* connected with the school. Students must see the principal as someone who believes in them and respects them for what they are and what they can become. Teachers must see in the principal someone who has great respect for the teachers' professional role and what they can bring to students. Dignifying the classroom teacher is of paramount importance and should be modeled often by the principal during public and private occasions. Parents should see the principal as someone who listens to them and displays concern and interest when they are with students.

Principals lead through learning. There is no setting in which this concept of the leader as learner is more applicable. This leadership role can be achieved by promoting several ideas. For example, when working with teachers in a supervisory role, principals must create an atmosphere that fosters mutual trust and growth. Trust is a requisite characteristic if one is to take chances in a professional relationship. Teachers must feel that they can trust the principal if risk taking is to occur during a class lesson. Furthermore, principals and teachers need to believe that they will grow from the relationship if they are to talk honestly during conferences about their profession and discuss what they think they are doing right and ways they can improve.

Additionally, as a leader of learners, the principal needs to provide the structure and forum to ensure that a dialogue concerning curriculum, teaching, assessment, and student learning takes place throughout the school. The principal needs to participate in this dialogue as an equal member, sharing articles, structuring faculty meetings to facilitate conversation, promoting staff development in and out of the school, creating areas in the school for professional discussion, promoting classroom visitations by colleagues, and recognizing those teachers who are growing professionally. The dialogue that develops can create lasting relationships and a synergy that demonstrates the strength and potential of the group.

Principals promote and embrace the success of others. As ideas are generated, *the school principal must give credit to teachers and others* whose ideas and dedication improve the school program. Stephen Covey (1989) calls this strategy "the abundance principle" in which credit for successful actions is spread around as much as possible. Furthermore, principals need to hire the best personnel available and show a willingness to give them the freedom to use their talents to maximize student learning and address the never-ending challenges that face schools.

Giving credit to others, inspiring colleagues to take on difficult tasks, and taking satisfaction when the accomplishments of associates bring them into the limelight may be difficult for some, but it is a necessary requirement for successful leadership. Thus Drucker (1992) emphasizes,

> But precisely because an effective leader knows that he, and no one else, is ultimately responsible, he is not afraid of strength in associates and subordinates . . . an effective leader wants strong associates; he encourages them, pushes them, indeed glories in them. Because he holds himself ultimately responsible for the mistakes of his associates and subordinates, he also sees the triumphs of his associates and subordinates as his triumphs, rather than as threats. . . . An effective leader knows, of course, that there is a risk; able people tend to be ambitious. But he realizes that it is a much smaller risk than to be served by mediocrity. (pp. 121-122)

Encouraging others to be strong associates and distributing leadership can be frustrating for principals who have been raised on the formula of "the principal as the sole instructional leader" or the one who must say "the buck stops here." Yet these are the days of shared governance. Is shared governance consistent with "the buck stops here"? Some make a distinction between shared decision making, in which the principal takes input but ultimately decides and takes responsibility, versus shared governance, in which decision makers exchange ideas and share accountability. We have learned that the factory worker may know more about how the company works than the executive on the top floor. Barth's insight regarding this dilemma may be helpful: "It's far more powerful to join with others to do what needs to be done" (quoted in Sparks, 1993, p. 20). School principals are joining with others to try to make schools work better. But principals know and accept that for the most part, *teachers, students, parents, and the community continue to expect the principal to take ultimate responsibility.*

Effective principals recognize active listening as an essential communication skill. The image of the leader who dominates a group discussion is inappropriate in a setting that thrives on teamwork and developing ideas through mutual understanding. Many school leaders who achieved their success because of their decisiveness and public speaking ability may have a difficult time becoming good listeners and reflective thinkers. Yet creative ideas and solutions often occur after listening, reflecting, and working in groups.

Real listening with patience and attention is critical if one is truly trying to support and foster growth in others. Showing concern for students, teachers, and parents means hearing them out. Listening shows support and may go a long way in meeting the needs of colleagues or others in the school community. Often, individuals do not come right out and say what it is that is bothering them. In fact, Soder

(2001) warns leaders "that many people will be likely to tell you what they think you want to hear, and the likelihood poses dangers for the leader" (p. 33). Active listening, then, means trying to find out the subtle messages—what is really being said? At that point, it is possible to begin meeting the needs of others. To illustrate, when conferencing with teachers, principals will find that as the trust relationship begins to grow, teaching colleagues will take small "leaps of faith" to explore how sincere the principal is about trust and working with them. Unless a principal is listening carefully to the teacher, the principal may very well and quite inadvertently miss the leap on the part of the teacher.

Principals address their own needs. The school principal should also remember that it is important to *recognize one's own basic needs.* That is, one's private life, responsibility to family, and need for leisure and recreation should not be sacrificed. A workaholic is not a better principal than someone who knows how to manage his or her time and who takes the time for family and friends. A principal's life outside of school must receive the time and energy necessary for success so a positive attitude on the job results.

Principals accept success and frustrations. As part of our basic humanity, it is important also to *take in stride both the successes and frustrations of the job.* One should not be too enthralled with the positive press—when it happens. On the other hand, do not get too upset with the negative reviews. Reflection is a characteristic needed in both situations. What happened? What can I learn from this experience? Find the humorous side when possible. Bringing in humor often helps to relieve tension, reduce one's feelings of self-importance, and place an issue in a more realistic perspective.

Effective principals take the high road. When the negative reviews appear or when individuals complain, one should behave in an ethical manner. Regardless of tactics used by others, *the school leader should always represent the best in society.* Character is very important when crises occur. In fact, character is the key in a crisis, and character is often judged not by what one says but by how one acts. Persons who whisper but act righteously are heard loud and clear. Stay above the fray and avoid the shouting match. As one principal said, "What you do speaks so loudly I can't hear what you say!"

Where Do We Go From Here?

Of course, there are no formulas for successful leadership that can be universally applied. An individual who exhibits or models some of the above characteristics may still fail if he or she is unable to analyze situations appropriately. The challenge is to find out what works in a particular setting. Newell (1978) stressed that "effective leadership is possible only through an analysis of the situational elements in a particular system" (p. 242). Each school is different; therefore, each leadership situation is different. In the end, the effective leader, collaborating and building relationships with teachers, parents, and students, must discover how to meet the needs of students in a specific setting. And the discovery will show that no secret formula exists; the setting will dictate the approach.

Because there are no secret formulas, frustration can be a constant companion in the principalship. Yet the frustration can lead to success if one always searches for solutions and has faith in one's ability to face challenges with the help of others. In facing the challenges, a vision of the good school is essential. So what is our vision of the good school? What will one see on entering the doors of the school?

The Good School

When entering the school, a visitor quickly perceives that students and teachers are enjoying their time there. Here is where they want to teach and learn. The visitor notices that most students are actively interested and engaged in learning. Teachers are enthusiastic about their work. Student interest is shown through obvious excitement while working at a hands-on activity or through a look of serenity when quietly reading a book.

Some classroom teachers may, at first, be difficult to spot—they are sitting with students or with groups of students and examining student work. In another room, a teacher is talking to the class, his gestures indicating excitement about a student comment. In fact, the visitor notices that most teachers are enjoying their work and are patiently listening to and helping students. In various classes, students display looks of concentration and puzzlement, mixed with expressions of satisfaction and frequent smiles. The school visitor observes that some students seem less interested than others, yet the teachers are giving them equal time and showing patience when necessary. No students appear to be overlooked.

The visitor observes that the library and computer labs are busy throughout the day. In both areas, there are students working individually, in groups, or with teachers. Several students are gathered around computers. One group is sending an e-mail to a scientific team in Antarctica, while another group is analyzing a recent presidential speech. In other areas such as the music, art, physics, or foreign language rooms, students are all actively engaged, talking about their work, singing, writing, reading, drawing, experimenting, and showing interest in what they are doing. In the cafeteria the visitor notices that various racial and ethnic groups, and younger and older students, are sitting together and interacting during lunch. Also, several students are helping new Russian immigrant students with their English. Two elderly individuals, likely retired, are engaged in serious conversations with two older students.

Dropping into various classrooms with the principal, the visitor and principal notice a variety of teaching techniques. Some teachers are using overhead projectors while speaking with students, others are projecting computer images on a screen, still others are sitting with students, and a couple of teachers are walking around their rooms observing groups or watching students work individually. One teacher is lecturing, another is reading silently with his class, and another is writing in her journal with the class. Interestingly, the principal and visitor observe a lot of lively, engaged, and smiling faces in the various classrooms. The principal notices that students are unafraid to give "incorrect" answers and, at times, respectfully challenge a teacher's answer.

Our visitor notices that the teachers' lounge is frequented by colleagues who enjoy one another's company and share in the joys and frustrations of their classroom experiences. While in the lounge, teachers share a light experience, the humor of a classroom event. One teacher asks a colleague to read a poem written by a student the previous class period. It is clear that this group of teachers works and plays together. They share professional articles, problem solve, and encourage one another to pursue professional development opportunities. They team teach, co-plan, and peer coach.

On the playground, students are obviously enjoying themselves playing games or sitting and talking. In the middle and high schools, peer counselors are spending time with students who are new to the school or are having some difficulties. In the elementary school, a couple of kindergarten students run up to the principal proudly announcing that they picked up some litter from the sidewalk to keep the school clean.

The school buildings and grounds are inviting. The entrance doors to the school are murals, painted in bright colors by students. The halls of the school are lined with student work. The high school includes a permanent fine arts display that rotates the art, poetry, photographs, and ceramic work of various students. The restrooms and cafeteria are clean and graffiti free.

In general, the visitor perceives pride and a caring attitude regarding how adults feel about students and the school. The visitor's perception is based on the positive interaction observed between teachers and students, secretaries and teachers, maintenance personnel and the principal, and students and the cafeteria workers.

At the end of the day, the visitor notices that neither teachers nor administrators rush to leave the school. Many staff members remain in their classrooms either working quietly, helping individual students, or conferencing with parents. The principal is seen standing by the school buses saying good-bye to students and asking them how the school day went.

Take Time to Smell the Roses

A vision of the good school can help principals hold on to their convictions concerning what schooling should be all about. The vision and one's convictions can steer the school through rough seas and keep the school on course—a course guided by the needs of the students, needs that can be satisfied when exposed to a challenging school experience in a climate nurtured by caring adults.

As you reflect on your role in accomplishing this, take time to celebrate your deeds, learn from mistakes, "smell the roses" daily, make connections with others, and maintain a positive outlook for the future.

Reflections

This space provides for you a place to write in ideas that have been generated by this chapter, things you want to try, or adaptations of ideas presented herein.

1. Create two to three questions representing your own reflections on the principalship. Share these with a colleague.
2. What do you do to stay on course?
3. What actions will you take as a result of these readings?
4. What topics do you want to explore in greater depth?

Bibliography

References

Alvy, H. (1983). *The problems of new principals.* Doctoral dissertation, University of Montana.

Alvy, H. (1992, Fall). No secret formulas: One principal's view on leadership. *Near East/South Asia Notes*, pp. 24-26.

Alvy, H. (1993). Making the move to elementary school. *Independent School, 53* (1), 29-31.

Alvy, H. & Robbins, P. (1998). *If I only knew: Success strategies for navigating the principalship.* Thousand Oaks, CA: Corwin Press.

Armstrong, T. (1994). *Multiple intelligences in the classroom.* Alexandria, VA: ASCD.

Associated Press. (17 June 2002). Comments by Ann Duffett of Public Agenda in the *Great Falls Tribune Nation/World Section*, p. 2A.

Bagin, D., & Gallagher, D. (2001). *The school and community relations* (7th ed.). Boston: Allyn & Bacon.

Barnard, C. (1938). *The functions of the executive.* Cambridge, MA: Harvard University Press.

Barth, R. (1990). *Improving schools from within.* San Francisco: Jossey-Bass.

Barth, R. (2001, Feb.). Making happen what you believe in. *Phi Delta Kappan, 82* (2), 446.

Barth, R. (2001). Teachers at the helm. *Education Week, 20* (24), 33.

Bennis, W. (1991). *Why leaders can't lead.* San Francisco: Jossey-Bass.

Bennis, W. (1993). *An invented life.* Reading, MA: Addison-Wesley.

Bennis, W., & Nanus, B. (1985). *Leaders...The strategies for taking charge.* New York: Harper and Row.

Berkman, L., et al. (1992). Emotional support and survival after myocardial infarction. *Annals of Internal Medicine.*

Berman, P., & McLaughlin, M. (1978). *Federal programs supporting educational change: Vol. 8. Implementing and sustaining innovations.* Santa Monica, CA: RAND.

Bird, T., & Little, J. W. (1984). *Supervision and evaluation in the school context.* Paper presented at the annual meeting of the American Educational Research Association, New Orleans, April.

Blanchard, K., & Johnson, S. (1983). *The one minute manager.* New York: Berkley.

Brendtro, L., & Hinders, D. (1990). A saga of Janusz Korczak, the king of children. *Harvard Educational Review, 60,* 237-246.

Burns, J. (1978). *Leadership.* New York: Harper and Row.

Butler, K. (1992). *The bridging chart for learning styles.* Columbia, CT: Learner's Dimensions.

Caine, R., & Caine, G. (1991). *Making connections: Teaching and the human brain.* Alexandria, VA: ASCD.

Canter, L. (1989, September). Assertive discipline—More than names on the board and marbles in a jar. *Phi Delta Kappan, 71,* 57-61.

Caro, D. J., & Robbins, P. (1991). Talkwalking—Thinking on your feet. *The Developer,* pp. 3-4.

Champion, R. (2002). Good principals use informal and formal approaches to staff development. *White Paper for Principals.* Alexandria, VA: ASCD.

Costa, A., & Garmston, R. (1991, April). *Cognitive coaching action lab workshop.* Paper presented at the ASCD Annual Conference, San Francisco.

Costa, A., & Garmston, R. (1994). *Cognitive coaching—A foundation for renaissance schools.* Norwood, MA: Christopher-Gordon.

Covey, S. (1989). *The seven habits of highly effective people.* New York: Simon & Schuster.

Cunningham, W., & Gresso, D. (1993). *Cultural leadership: The culture of excellence in education.* Boston: Allyn & Bacon.

Curwin, R. (2002, March). Finding jewels in the rubble. *Educational Leadership, 59* (6), 80-83.

Curwin, R., & Mendler, A. (1988). *Discipline with dignity.* Alexandria, VA: ASCD.

Danielson, C. (1996). *Enhancing professional practice: A framework for teaching.* Alexandria, VA: ASCD.

Deal, T. (1985). Cultural change: Opportunity, silent killer, or metamorphosis. In R. Kilmann, M. Saxton, & R. Serpa (Eds.), *Gaining control of the corporate culture.* San Francisco: Jossey-Bass.

Deal, T., & Kennedy, A. (1982). *Corporate culture.* Reading, MA: Addison-Wesley.

Deal, T., & Peterson K. (1990). *Principal's role in shaping school culture.* Washington, DC: Department of Education.

Deal, T., & Peterson, K. (1993). Strategies for building school cultures: Principals as symbolic leaders. In M. Sashkin & H. J. Walberg (Eds.), *Educational leadership and school culture* (pp. 89-99). Berkeley, CA: McCutchan.

Deal, T., & Peterson, K. (1994). *The leadership paradox.* San Francisco: Jossey-Bass.

Deal, T., & Peterson, K. (1999). *Shaping school culture: The heart of leadership.* San Francisco: Jossey-Bass.

Drucker, P. (1992). *Managing for the future.* New York: Dutton.

DuFour, R. (2001, Winter). In the right context. *Journal of Staff Development, 22* (1), 14-17.

Dyer, K. (2001, February). The power of 360 degree feedback. *Educational Leadership, 58* (5), 35-38.

Dyer, K., Osher, D., & Warger, C. (1998). *Early warning, timely response: A guide to safe schools.* Washington DC: Department of Education. Retrieved April 28, 2002, from cecp.air.org/guide/guidetext.html.

Education Week's Staff. (2000). *Lessons of a century: A nation's schools come of age.* Bethesda, MD: Editorial Projects in Education.

Elias, M. (2002, March). *Building character education and social-emotional programs: A school leadership manual.* ASCD Annual Conference. San Antonio, TX.

English, F., & Hill, J. (1994). *Total quality education.* Thousand Oaks, CA: Corwin Press.

Fullan, M. (1997). *What's worth fighting for in the principalship.* New York: Teachers College Press.

Fullan, M., & Miles, M. (1992, June). Getting reform right: What works and what doesn't. *Phi Delta Kappan, 73,* 745-752.

Fullan, M., & Stiegelbauer, S. (1991). *The new meaning of educational change.* New York: Teachers College Press.

Gardner, H. (1985). *Frames of mind: The theory of multiple intelligences.* New York: Basic Books.

Gardner, H. (1995, November). Reflections on multiple intelligences: Myths and messages. *Phi Delta Kappan, 76 (3),* 200-203, 206-209.

Georgia Association of Educators. (1998-2001). *Teacher tips: Avoiding burnout and staying healthy.* Retrieved October 8, 2001 from http://www.gae.org/teacher/te_burnout.html.

Glickman, C. (1990). *Supervision of instruction.* (2nd ed.). Boston: Allyn and Bacon.

Glickman, C., Gordon, S., & Ross-Gordon, J. (2001). *Supervision and instructional leadership* (5th ed.). Boston: Allyn and Bacon.

Goldring, E., & Rallis, S. (1993). *Principals of dynamic schools.* Newbury Park, CA: Corwin Press.

Goleman, D. (1995). *Emotional intelligence.* New York: Bantam.

Goleman, D., Boyatzis, R., & McKee, A. (2002). *Primal leadership.* Boston: Harvard Business School Press.

Gorton, R. (1980). *School administration and supervision.* Dubuque, IA: William C. Brown.

Green, R. (2001). *Practicing the art of leadership: A problem-based approach to implementing the ISLLC standards.* Upper Saddle River, NJ: Merrill.

Gregorc, A. (1985). *Inside styles: Beyond the basics.* Maynard, MA: Gabriel Systems.

Grimmett, P., Rostad, O., & Ford, B. (1992). The transition of supervision. In C. Glickman (Ed.), *Supervision in transition* (pp. 185-202). *1992 ASCD Yearbook.* Alexandria, VA: ASCD.

Grove, K. (2002, May). The invisible role of the central office. *Educational Leadership, 59* (8), 45-47.

Hall, G. & Hord, S. (1987). *Change in schools: Facilitating the process.* Albany: State University of New York Press.

Hall, G. E., George, A. A., & Rutherford, W. L. (1979). *Measuring stages of concern about the innovation: A manual for the use of the SoC questionnaire.* Austin: Research and Development Center for Teacher Education, University of Texas.

Hall, G. & Loucks, S. (1978, April). *Innovation configurations analyzing the adaptation of innovations.* Paper presented at the American Educational Association Meeting, Toronto, Canada.

Hargreaves, A., & Dawe, R. (1989). *Coaching as unreflective practice.* Paper presented at the American Educational Research Association Meeting, San Francisco.

Harkavy, I. & Blank, M. (2002). Community schools: A vision of learning that goes beyond testing. *Education Week, 21* (31), 38, 52.

Harris, S., Petrie, G., & Willoughby, W. (2002, March). Bullying among ninth graders: An exploratory study. *NASSP Bulletin, 86* (630), 3-14.

Herman, J., Aschbacher, P., & Winter, L. (1992). *A practical guide to alternative assessment.* Alexandria, VA: ASCD.

Herzberg, F., Mausner, B., & Snyderman, B. (1959). *The motivation to work.* New York: John Wiley.

Hirsh, S. (1995, December–1996, January). Approaches to improving schools start with developing a shared vision. *School Team Innovator.* NSDC.

Hord, S., Rutherford, W., Huling-Austin, L., & Hall, G. (1987). *Taking charge of change.* Alexandria, VA: ASCD.

Houston, P. (2002, March). From tragedy emerge positive lessons for leaders. *The School Administrator, 3* (59), 46.

Hughes, L., & Hooper, D. (2000). *Public relations for school leaders.* Boston: Allyn & Bacon.

Hyman, R. T. (1974). *Ways of teaching.* Englewood Cliffs, NJ: Prentice.

Jentz, B., Cheever, D., & Fisher, S. (1980). How to survive your first year: A guide for new principals. *National Elementary Principal, 59* (3), 23-26.

Johnston, R. (2001). Central office is critical bridge to help schools. *Education Week, 20* (25), 18.

Joyce, B., & Showers, B. (1981, February). Improving inservice training: The message of research. *Educational Leadership, 37,* 379-385.

Joyce, B., & Weil, M. (1972). *Models of teaching.* Englewood Cliffs, NJ: Prentice Hall.

Kanter, Rosabeth Moss (1997). *On the frontiers of management.* Boston: Harvard Business School Press.

Kohn, A. (1996). *Beyond discipline: From compliance to community.* Alexandria, VA: ASCD.

Kriegel, R. (1991). *If it ain't broke—Break it!* New York: Warner.

Lawton, W. (April 2, 2002). Expert gives lesson in crisis communication. *The Oregonian* (Metro/Northwest Section), p. C5.

Lehmuller, P. & Switzer, A. (2002, March). September 11: An elementary school at ground zero. *Principal, 81* (4), 52-54.

Lewin, K. (1951). In D. Cartwright (Ed.), *Field theory in social science: Selected theoretical papers.* New York: Harper.

Lewis, C. (2002, Summer). Everywhere I looked—Levers and pendulums. *Journal of Staff Development, 23* (3), 59-65.

Lewis, T., Amini F., & Lannon, R. (2000) *A general theory of love.* New York: Random House.

Little, J. (1982, May). Keynote address to Napa mentor teachers. Napa, CA.

Maeroff, G. (1993). *Team building for school change.* New York: Teachers College Press.

Manobianco, M. (2002, Winter). Guiding practices for using data to improve student learning. *The Principal News: A Journal of the Association of Washington School Principals, 31* (1), 16-17.

Marzano, R., Pickering, D., Arredondo, D., Blackburn, G., Brandt, R., & Moffett, C. (1992). *Dimensions of learning.* Alexandria, VA: ASCD and Midcontinental Regional Educational Laboratory.

Marzano, R., Pickering, D., & Pollock, J. (2001). *Classroom instruction that works.* Alexandria, VA: ASCD.

Maslow, A. (1954). *Motivation and personality.* New York: Harper & Row.

Meek, A. (1999). *Communicating with the public: A guide for school leaders.* Alexandria, VA: ASCD.

Meier, D. (1995, January). How our schools could be. *Phi Delta Kappan, 76,* 369-373.

Merton, R. (1957). *Social theory and social structure* (Rev. ed.). Glencoe, IL: Free Press.

Miller, L., & Smith, A. (1997). *The road to burnout.* Retrieved October 8, 2001 from http://helping.apa.org/work/stress6.html.

Mintzberg, H. (1973). The nature of managerial work. New York: Harper Collins.

Mohlman-Sparks, G. (1983, November). Synthesis of research on staff development for effective training. *Educational Leadership,* p. 65.

Morrison, G. (2000). *Teaching in America* (2nd ed.). Boston: Allyn & Bacon.

Nair, K. (1997). *A higher standard of leadership; Lessons from the life of Gandhi.* San Francisco: Berrett-Koehler.

National Association of Elementary School Principals. (2001). *Leading learning communities: Standards for what principals should know and be able to do.* Alexandria, VA: Author.

National Association of Elementary School Principals and the Council for Exceptional Children. (2001). *Implementing IDEA: A guide for principals.* Arlington, VA: Author.

National Mental Health Association. (2001). *Coping with disaster: Tips for college students.* Retrieved from http://www.nmha.org/reassurance/collegetips.cfm.

National School Public Relations Association. (1996). The complete crisis communication management manual for schools. Excerpted in *Practical PR for principals: A handbook to help you build support for your school.* Arlington, VA: Author.

National Staff Development Council. (2001). *National standards for staff development.* Oxford, OH: Author.

Newell, C. (1978). *Human behavior in educational administration.* Englewood Cliffs, NJ: Prentice Hall.

Newmann, F., & Wehlage, G. (1995). *Successful school restructuring.* Madison: University of Wisconsin.

O'Neill, J., & Conzemius, A. (2002, Spring). Four keys to a smooth flight. *Journal of Staff Development, 23* (2), 14-18.

Ornstein, A., & Levine, D. (2003). *Foundations of education* (8th ed.). Boston: Houghton Mifflin.

Peters, T., & Austin, N. (1985). *A passion for excellence.* New York: Warner.

Peterson, K. (1982). Making sense of principals' work. *Australian Administrator, 3* (3), 1-4.

Puleo, P. (1993, April-May). Making supervision meaningful. *California ASCD Newsletter,* pp. 1-4.

Quinn, J. (2002). Must principals "go it alone." *Education Week, 21* (36), 40.

Robbins, P. (1991a). *The development of a collaborative workplace: A case study of Wells Junior High.* Doctoral dissertation, University of California, Berkeley.

Robbins, P. (1991b). *How to plan and implement a peer coaching program.* Alexandria, VA: ASCD.

Robbins, P., Gregory, G., & Herndon, L. (2000). *Thinking inside the block: Strategies for teaching in extended periods of time.* Thousand Oaks, CA: Corwin Press.

Rosenholtz, S. (1989). *Teachers' workplace.* New York: Longman.

Ross, A. (1981). *Child behavior therapy.* New York: John Wiley.

Sack, J. (2002). EPA pushing improved air quality for schools. *Education Week, 21* (33), pp. 1, 12.

Sarason, S. (1982). *The culture of the school and the problem of change* (2nd ed.). Boston: Allyn & Bacon.

Schein, E. (1985). *Organizational culture and leadership.* San Francisco: Jossey-Bass.

Scherer, M. (2001, September). How and why standards can improve student achievement: A conversation with Robert J. Marzano. *Educational Leadership, 59* (1), 14-18.

Schlechty, P. (2001). *Shaking up the schoolhouse: How to support and sustain educational innovation.* San Francisco: Jossey-Bass.

Senge, P. (1990). *The fifth discipline.* London: Century Business.

Soder, R. (2001). *The language of leadership.* San Francisco: Jossey-Bass.

Sparks, D. (1993). The professional development of principals: A conversation with Roland Barth. *Journal of Staff Development, 14* (1), 18-21.

Sparks, D. (1999, Summer). Try on strategies to get a good fit: An interview with Susan Loucks-Horsley, *Journal of Staff Development, 20* (3), 56-60.

Sylwester, R. (1995). *A celebration of neurons: An educator's guide to the brain.* Alexandria, VA: ASCD.

Teeter, A. (1995, January). Learning about teaching. *Phi Delta Kappan, 76,* 360-364.

Tierney, R., Carter, M., & Desai, L. (1991). *Portfolio assessment in the reading-writing classroom.* Norwood, MA: Christopher-Gordon.

Tucker, P. (2001, February). Helping struggling teachers. *Educational Leadership. 58* (5), 52-55.

Walton, M. (1986). *The Deming management method.* New York: Perigee.

Warner, C. (2000). *Promoting your school: Going beyond P. R.* (2nd ed.). Thousand Oaks, CA: Corwin Press.

Wayne, L., & Kaufman, L. (September 16, 2001). Leadership, put to a new test. *New York Times* (Money & Business Section 3), pp. 1, 4.

Wheatley, M. (1992). *Leadership and the new science.* San Francisco: Berrett-Kochler.

Wiggins, G., & McTighe, J. (1998). *Understanding by design.* Alexandria, VA: ASCD.

Wolfe, P. (2001). *Brain matters: Translating research into classroom practice.* Alexandria, VA: ASCD.

Wood, F., Thompson, S., & Russell, F. (1981). Designing effective staff development programs. In B. Dillon-Peterson (Ed.), *Staff development/organizational development* (pp. 59-91). Alexandria, VA: ASCD.

Additional Readings

Alvy, H., & Coladarci, T. (1985). Problems of the novice principal. *Research in Rural Education, 3*(1), 39-47.

Bolman, L. G., & Deal, T. E. (1993). *The path to school leadership: A portable mentor.* Newbury Park, CA: Corwin.

Doyle, M., & Strauss, D. (1986). *How to make meetings work.* New York: Jove.

Fullan, M. (1989). Staff development, innovation, and institutional development. In B. Joyce (Ed.), *Changing school culture through staff development* (pp. 3-25). 1990 ASCD yearbook. Alexandria, VA: ASCD.

Gardner, J. W. (1990). *On leadership.* New York: Free Press.

Gibbs, J. (1987). *TRIBES: A process for social development and cooperative learning.* Santa Rosa, CA: Center-Source.

Glickman, C. D. (1993). *Renewing America's schools: A guide for school-based action.* San Francisco: Jossey-Bass.

Hargreaves, A. (1990). Cultures of teaching. In I. Goodson & S. Ball (Eds.), *Teachers' lives.* Boston: Routledge & Kegan Paul.

Hoy, W. K., & Miskel, C. G. (1982). *Educational administration theory, research and practice* (2nd ed.). New York: Random House.

Hyman, R. T. (1974). *Ways of teaching.* Englewood Cliffs, NJ: Prentice Hall.

Little, J. W., & McLaughlin, M. W. (1993). *Teachers' work: Individuals, colleagues, and contexts.* New York: Columbia University, Teachers College.

Pajak, E. (1993). *Approaches to clinical supervision.* Norwood, MA: Christopher-Gordon.

Smith, S. C., & Piele, P. K. (1989). *School leadership: Handbook for excellence.* Eugene: University of Oregon, University Publications.

Sparks, D., & Loucks-Horsley, S. (1990). Models of staff development. In R. Houston (Ed.), *Handbook of research on teacher education.* New York: Macmillan and the Association of Teacher Educators.

Index

**CORWIN
PRESS**

The Corwin Press logo—a raven striding across an open book—represents the happy union of courage and learning. We are a professional-level publisher of books and journals for K–12 educators, and we are committed to creating and providing resources that embody these qualities. Corwin's motto is "Success for All Learners."